Heritage Tourism and Cities in China

China has surged into the 21st century as one of the most rapidly modernising countries in the world. Its burgeoning cities reflect this extraordinary growth with a dazzling array of new architectural forms and designs. In its transformation, the 5000-year-old heritage of its built civilization, embedded in its villages, towns and cities, has often been replaced. The Chinese Government, aware of the value of this heritage, has in recent years taken concrete steps to conserve and preserve not just national icons such as the Forbidden Palace in Beijing, the Great Wall of China and the Grey Goose Pagoda in Xian but also the more general historic fabric of its urban development over the centuries. The challenges are great, particularly as population growth and rural-urban drift have combined to place enormous pressure on city resources. The chapters in this book explore these challenges as well as analyse other institutional, cultural, social and economic issues related to urban heritage conservation and utilization, with a focus on the role of tourism in reinforcing conservation values by finding new uses for old buildings and districts. This book covers new areas of heritage tourism research in Chinese cities.

The chapters in this book were originally published in a special issue of the *Journal of Heritage Tourism*.

Honggang Xu is a Professor from Sun Yat-sen University, Guangzhou, China. Her interest is tourism geography. She is a Senior Editor for the journal *Tourism* Geographies, has published widely in leading international journals with her students and colleagues in China and abroad and is a frequent presenter at international tourism and geography conferences around the world.

Trevor H. B. Sofield is a Visiting Professor at the Center for Tourism Planning and Research, Sun Yat-sen University, Guangzhou, China and has been involved in more than 30 tourism planning and development projects and research in China for the past 25 years. Originally from Australia he has undertaken more than 100 tourism projects in more than 20 other countries in the Asia Pacific region and Africa, including with UNESCO.

Heritage Tourism and Cities in China

Edited by
Honggang Xu and Trevor H. B. Sofield

LONDON AND NEW YORK

First published 2018 by Routledge

2 Park Square, Milton Park, Abingdon, Oxfordshire OX14 4RN
52 Vanderbilt Avenue, New York, NY 10017

Routledge is an imprint of the Taylor & Francis Group, an informa business

First issued in paperback 2020

British Library Cataloguing-in-Publication Data
A catalogue record for this book is available from the British Library

ISBN13: 978-1-138-48102-2 (hbk)
ISBN13: 978-0-367-53110-2 (pbk)

Typeset in Minion Pro
by codeMantra

Publisher's Note
The publisher accepts responsibility for any inconsistencies that may have arisen during the conversion of this book from journal articles to book chapters, namely the possible inclusion of journal terminology.

Disclaimer
Every effort has been made to contact copyright holders for their permission to reprint material in this book. The publishers would be grateful to hear from any copyright holder who is not here acknowledged and will undertake to rectify any errors or omissions in future editions of this book.

Contents

Citation Information   vi
Notes on Contributors   viii

1   New interests of urban heritage and tourism research in Chinese cities   1
    Honggang Xu and Trevor H. B. Sofield

2   The heritage of Chinese cities as seen through the gaze of *zhonghua*
    wenhua – 'Chinese common knowledge': Guilin as an exemplar   9
    Trevor H. B. Sofield, Fung Mei Sarah Li, Grace H. Y. Wong
    and Jinsheng Jason Zhu

3   Suzhou's water grid as urban heritage and tourism resource: an urban
    morphology approach to a Chinese city   33
    Werner Breitung and Jing Lu

4   Industrial heritage tourism development and city image reconstruction in
    Chinese traditional industrial cities: a web content analysis   49
    Xueke (Stephanie) Yang

5   Spatial–temporal distribution characteristics of industrial heritage
    protection and the influencing factors in a Chinese city: a case study of the
    Tiexi old industrial district in Shenyang   63
    Xiaojun Fan and Shanshan Dai

6   Transnationalizing industrial heritage valorizations in Germany and
    China – and addressing inherent dark sides   78
    Leilei Li and Dietrich Soyez

7   Impacts of urban renewal on the place identity of local residents – a case
    study of Sunwenxilu traditional commercial street in Zhongshan City,
    Guangdong Province, China   93
    Ding Shaolian

Index   109

Citation Information

The chapters in this book were originally published in the *Journal of Heritage Tourism*, volume 12, issue 3 (July 2017). When citing this material, please use the original page numbering for each article, as follows:

Chapter 2

The heritage of Chinese cities as seen through the gaze of zhonghua wenhua – *'Chinese common knowledge': Guilin as an exemplar*
Trevor H. B. Sofield, Fung Mei Sarah Li, Grace H. Y. Wong and Jinsheng Jason Zhu
Journal of Heritage Tourism, volume 12, issue 3 (July 2017) pp. 227–250

Chapter 3

Suzhou's water grid as urban heritage and tourism resource: an urban morphology approach to a Chinese city
Werner Breitung and Jing Lu
Journal of Heritage Tourism, volume 12, issue 3 (July 2017) pp. 251–266

Chapter 4

Industrial heritage tourism development and city image reconstruction in Chinese traditional industrial cities: a web content analysis
Xueke (Stephanie) Yang
Journal of Heritage Tourism, volume 12, issue 3 (July 2017) pp. 267–280

Chapter 5

Spatial–temporal distribution characteristics of industrial heritage protection and the influencing factors in a Chinese city: a case study of the Tiexi old industrial district in Shenyang
Xiaojun Fan and Shanshan Dai
Journal of Heritage Tourism, volume 12, issue 3 (July 2017) pp. 281–295

Chapter 6

Transnationalizing industrial heritage valorizations in Germany and China – and addressing inherent dark sides
Leilei Li and Dietrich Soyez
Journal of Heritage Tourism, volume 12, issue 3 (July 2017) pp. 296–310

Chapter 7

Impacts of urban renewal on the place identity of local residents – a case study of Sunwenxilu traditional commercial street in Zhongshan City, Guangdong Province, China
Ding Shaolian
Journal of Heritage Tourism, volume 12, issue 3 (July 2017) pp. 311–326

For any permission-related enquiries please visit:
http://www.tandfonline.com/page/help/permissions

Notes on Contributors

Werner Breitung is an Urban Geographer with a PhD from the University of Basel (Switzerland), who has over the last 20 years taught and conducted research at universities in Hong Kong, Macau, Guangzhou and Suzhou. He was the principal investigator of seven research projects and has published widely on Chinese urban issues. He has also been involved in five tourism planning projects in China and is currently an appointed member of the Chinese Geographical Society's Tourism Geography Committee.

Shanshan Dai is a Lecturer in the School of Tourism, Sun Yat-sen University, Guangzhou, China with a doctoral degree in Management. Her study interest is resource and tourism management.

Xiaojun Fan is an Associate Professor in the School of Tourism and Hospitality Management, Shenyang Normal University, China. She received a doctorate from Sun Yat-sen University, and her research field is industrial heritage.

Fung Mei Sarah Li is an Independent Consultant in Tourism Education, Development and Planning based in Tasmania, Australia.

Leilei Li is based at the School of Mass Communication, Shenzhen University, China.

Jing Lu is an Urban Planner and Researcher with an MS from the University of Virginia, Charlottesville, USA and has over six years of experience in urban and environmental planning practice and research in the USA and China. She has participated in five research projects and published on Chinese urban and environmental issues. She has been involved in 13 planning projects in China, the USA and Ethiopia, four of which she led as the leading planner and project manager.

Ding Shaolian is based at the Department of Tourism Management, College of Forestry and Landscape Architecture, South China Agricultural University, Guangzhou, China.

Trevor H. B. Sofield is a Visiting Professor at the Center for Tourism Planning and Research, Sun Yat-sen University, Guangzhou, China and has been involved in more than 30 tourism planning and development projects and research in China for the past 25 years. Originally from Australia he has undertaken more than 100 tourism projects in more than 20 other countries in the Asia Pacific region and Africa, including with UNESCO.

Dietrich Soyez is based at the Institute of Geography, The University of Cologne, Germany.

Grace H. Y. Wong is based at the Center for Language Education, Hong Kong University of Science & Technology, China.

Honggang Xu is a Professor from Sun Yat-sen University, Guangzhou, China. Her interest is tourism geography. She is a Senior Editor for the journal *Tourism Geographies*, has published widely in leading international journals with her students and colleagues in China and abroad and is a frequent presenter at international tourism and geography conferences around the world.

Xueke (Stephanie) Yang is based at the Department of Geography, National University of Singapore.

Jinsheng Jason Zhu is based at the School of International Education and Exchange, Guilin Tourism University, China.

New interests of urban heritage and tourism research in Chinese cities

Honggang Xu and Trevor H. B. Sofield

Introduction

Towns and cities have been one of the key areas where Chinese civilization is embodied. China has a history of urban development reaching back over 5,000 years. Between 4,000 and 5,000, cities and towns with various functions were constructed before the existence of modern-day China (Dong, 2004). However, cities in China in the past century are also places which have experienced modernisation and rapid progress. As a result, the conservation and reuse of the built heritage in China's cities confronts great challenges. In addition to that, there are a number of other institutional, cultural, social and economic issues which influence urban heritage conservation and utilisation.

The heritage conservation system is new, both culturally and institutionally in China. The cultural heritage system was first adopted in the 1960s, while natural conservation was adopted earlier, in the 1950s. In 1961, the Chinese State Council issued the Temporal Regulation on Conservation of Cultural Relics. This regulation required that various culture-management administrations had to conduct regular investigations of cultural relics. In addition, cultural relics of significance should be identified and then registered as conservation units. In the same year, the first batch of protected cultural relics was announced by the State Council. From 1966 to 1976, however, the Cultural Revolution resulted in the destruction of many thousands of culturally significant buildings, artefacts, relics and sites. In 1982, a law for the preservation of antiquities was issued in order to protect and strengthen the conservation of cultural relics. As a result of promotion by the central government as well as scholars, Chinese cities began to implement strategies to conserve their historical districts or heritage sites in urban areas. In 1982, the first batch of historical cities was announced. In 2005, the regulation, 'Specification on the Historical Cities Conservation Plan', was issued. This legislation described the principles, strategies, contents and key areas for conservation. Furthermore, in 2006, the central government also issued a policy to strengthen intangible heritage conservation, and the first group of intangible heritage sites was announced. In 2008, the Regulation of Historical Famous City, Town and Village Conservation was adopted. The system was mainly pushed through from the top down, although identification and recommendations of conservation sites were made by local governments and bureaus. There is thus a sound legislative and policy framework for the conservation of built heritage, however, implementation can still be problematic.

Heritage conservation of built culture has no long-standing tradition in China (Qiu, 2003). For centuries it has been customary to destroy old structures and build new ones (see, for example, the analysis by Sofield *et al.* of the 2,200-year-old history of one of China's most famous monuments, the Yellow Crane pagoda in Wuhan, in Chapter 1). Especially in the last century, a key theme in China among ordinary people and reflected in government policies and activities has been an energetic and robust striving for modernisation and progress. In this context, constructing tall modern buildings has taken priority over any desire to preserve and conserve China's built heritage.

Since urbanisation has turned into the most important driving force for development over the past 30 years, cities are facing a dilemma over using limited resources either for economic growth or for conservation. Financial resources from cities' administrations are normally expended on new development rather than conservation. In addition, since land has turned into a major source of income for municipal governments, conservation is seen as increasingly expensive (for example, when an inner city heritage building of just two or three stories occupies a footprint where a multi-storey skyscraper could be built). Local governments therefore prefer to renovate their inner cities in a way that economic and financial benefits can be guaranteed, resulting in large-scale destruction of heritage areas (Qiu, 2003). The layout and features of the historical centres are completely changed, with only a few registered historical buildings remaining.

Beijing has been at the centre of this conflicting approach to heritage because of significant domestic and international debate about the future of its *hutongs* and *siheyuans* and their contribution to the conservation of its image. *Hutongs* are historic streets, lanes and alleyways, and *siheyuans* are the walled courtyard houses that line them. Combined, they represent the vanishing way of life of the common people and the urban identity of 'old' Beijing (Wu, 2000). According to Wu (2000, p. 76) a traditional *hutong* block had three characteristics. The first was accessibility to both main streets and to individual dwellings; the second was an integrated system of alleys and courtyard houses; and the third covered a variety of land uses with *siheyuans* functioning as residences for 'ordinary people', some much larger as mansions and others as temples, offices and shops, all co-located with no differentiated zoning. These characteristics allowed a *hutong* to offer its residents a dynamic living environment with a close-knit social network system, and this image remains in the public mind as "the primary tissue of the built and social fabrics of the imperial capital" (Wu, 2000, p. 76).

Beijing (Dado) was first established as the Yuan Dynasty capital of China in the 13th century by Mongol leader Kublai Khan, and over the next seven centuries it continued the historical pattern of urban development where *hutongs* and *siheyuans* dominated the architectural morphology. By the time the Ming Dynasty replaced the Yuan Dynasty in 1368 A.D. there were 384 *hutong* neighbourhoods with several thousand closely arranged courtyard houses constructed around the palace and military headquarters complex. The Ming Dynasty continued the *hutong*-based expansion of Beijing, with an Inner and Outer City of concentric circles within which the Forbidden Palace was constructed along the north-south axis in conformity with the age-old Daoist template to ensure harmony between Heaven and Earth and Earth and humans. Palace records of the time indicated that there were 1,236 *hutongs* in Beijing (Wang, 2007). The Qing Dynasty replaced the Ming Dynasty in 1644, and they continued the same pattern of urban development so that by 1912 when the imperial court was replaced with the Republic of China under Dr Sun Yat Sen, there were more than 2,800 *hutongs* and many more thousands of *siheyuans*. The growth of Beijing slowed over the next three decades, but in 1944, according to the Beijing Municipal Place Names Office (cited in Ma, 2014), there were 3,200 *hutongs*.

Beijing began to change dramatically following the 1949 founding of the People's Republic of China. The population of the capital expanded rapidly creating a major housing shortage; industrialization was also vigorously pursued, and under this duality of pressures the *hutong* and *siheyuan* began to disappear. When the second population increase under the Republic hit a new peak in the 1960s most of the remaining *siheyuan* were subdivided to provide housing for even more people, annexes were built haphazardly in ad hoc fashion with courtyard walls knocked down and *hutong* (street) space taken over for even more buildings. The neighbourhoods became chaotic, lost their original architectural integrity and their social fabric also broke down due to overcrowding. Without proper sanitation, electricity and piped water, many of them took on the form of slums. By the end of the 1970s, about two-thirds of Beijing's 8.5 million people resided in *hutong* neighbourhoods

(Guo & Klein, 2005), and in the early 1980s, a housing relocation plan called the *"weigai"* was implemented. This system gave property developers relatively unrestricted freedom for redevelopment without any regard to conservation. For the next 20 years more than one million people were relocated to *hutongs*, and their associated *siheyuans* were demolished on a massive scale, and many traditional *hutong* residential neighbourhoods were transformed into new high-density high-rise apartment blocks with modern utilities (Lo, 2010).

In 2002, then Vice Premier Wen Xibao drew attention to the urgency of the preservation of traditional *hutong* neighbourhoods in an address to the Third China Mayors' Association annual forum, when he said:

> At present, the pre-eminent problem existing in our country's urban construction is that some city leaders only see the economic values of natural and cultural relics but know little about the historical, scientific, cultural and artistic value of them. They seek only economic benefits and development while neglecting protection, so damage to natural and cultural relics is occurring frequently. Some city leaders simply deem the constructions of high-rise buildings as urban modernization while paying insufficient attention to protection of natural scenes and historical and cultural relics. Their large-scale dismantling and building during old city reconstruction have damaged many traditional districts and buildings with historical and culture values.

The need for conservation of *hutongs* and *siheyuans* became more widely acknowledged after the holding of the Olympic Games in Beijing in 2008 when further mass destruction of *hutong* neighbourhoods for modern Games facilities and venues occurred. While many of the new facilities such as the 'Bird's Nest' National Stadium and the 'Water Cube' National Aquatic Center won international plaudits for their daring architectural design and innovation, global attention was also drawn to the rich but diminishing heritage of the *hutongs* (Heath & Tang, 2010). Faced with increasing domestic and international concern about their future, the Beijing Municipal Institute of City Planning and Design formalised a development approach with three main types of *hutong* neighbourhoods based on location, history, function, management and planning context:

i A renovated *hutong* that is modernized: The emphasis is on upgrading, and traditional architectural form is not necessarily maintained as contemporary materials replace original features while all modern conveniences are incorporated into the building. Such buildings are rarely more than two storeys high. They are not integrated into their immediate neighbourhoods through courtyards or alleyways as traditionally occurred; they focus on facilitating mobility to workplaces outside the residential area, and so their social networks are more casual and dispersed.

ii A semi-renovated *hutong*: Both traditional and modern forms of architecture are evident, although often only the external façade is retained while the interior is fully modernised, with the shape, size and juxtaposition of rooms showing little resemblance to traditional spatial arrangements. They maintain some of the linkages with alleyways and central courtyards shared by a number of houses so that there are stronger elements of social interaction and neighbourhood integration than with Type 1 *hutong*.

iii A protected traditional *hutong*: This type has a significantly greater emphasis on retaining the original forms both externally and internally (although with modern conveniences brought into all households). As a neighbourhood they are more internally oriented, courtyards remain a central feature and they encourage social networks that are smaller and more intense than the other two types.

In September 2015, the Beijing Municipal Institute of City Planning and Design unveiled a general city plan for 2016–2035, which includes strengthening historic and cultural building conservation, although its priorities remain focused on modernisation and transport improvements (Beijing Municipal Institute of City Planning and Design, 2015). Part of this relatively stronger emphasis for conservation arose from a mix of top-down and bottom-up consultation where concerned groups of residences formally registered their associations with the Beijing Government (e.g. the Shijia Hutong Style Conservation Association, the Chaoyangmen ('Gate Facing the Sun') Hutong Committee, the Ju'er Hutong ('Chrysanthemum Lane') Conservation Project, etc.).

The tourism industry has been energetic in incorporating the centuries-old fabric of Beijing into historic tours of the *hutongs*, and there are now several small folk museums in renovated *siheyuan* (e.g. Shijia Hutong Museum) that interpret their history and culture for visitors. To a certain extent the tourism interest has resulted in the 'Disneyfication' of some parts of several hutongs modified by what Zhang Ke (Zhang, 2016) has described as "kitsch renovations that fake images of a nostalgic past." This is not an issue that is restricted to *hutongs* in Beijing but confounds many conservation and restoration projects in many cities not only in China but elsewhere. With reference to *hutongs*, the more subtle complexities associated with, for example, the exodus of original inhabitants and resultant breakdown of social networks and ethnic diversity are often overlooked by what architects term "tabula rasa" redevelopment (i.e. the place where a building has been entirely demolished and a new structure can be designed to replace it without reference to its historical origins or values). Defenders of historical restoration may also place more emphasis on 'bricks and mortar' than on the 'human face' of the *hutongs*, thus contributing along with modernising developers to the waning of the *hutongs'* traditional cultures.

Nevertheless Beijing has secured the future of several hundred *hutongs* and many *siheyuans* from destruction, some of their unique historic urban character has been retained and they have also achieved necessary revitalization (especially in terms of providing sewage, water and electricity). And at the micro level, an intervention to transform one 12-household courtyard into a contemporary living space with modern conveniences that retains the traditional architecture and enhances the social interaction of the residents at the same time in Cha-er *hutong* provides a model of how the various competing and conflicting forces can be harmonized. A "big messy courtyard" in Cha'er Hutong #8, Dashilar, was transformed by ZAO/standardarchitecture into the Micro Yuan'er children's library and art centre. The project has received international exposure for its sympathetic approach that captures both the 'hard' (built historical construction) and 'soft' (human) characteristics of hutong living (Zhang, 2016). The role of the Beijing Municipality in approving and supporting such projects for the conservation of its historical heritage is of national significance because it is known to serve as a model for China's urban planning policy (Ma, 2014).

Figure 1. Before intervention: 12 households all shared this common courtyard. While it was cluttered with unauthorized structures, face-to-face interrelationships were constant and close and required cooperation and tolerance among all families. Cha'er Hutong #8 Dashilar, Beijing.

Figures 2, 3. After: The 'big messy courtyard' that was developed by ZAO/standardarchitecture into the Micro Yuan'er children's library and art centre. The integrity of the space is maintained with retention of the original *siheyuan* buildings. The clever use of the rooftops of the new structures provides additional playground space for the children and therefore enhances social interaction.

Figure 4. *Images Courtesy of ZAO/standardarchitecture.*

The tourism industry, through the increased visibility that it has given to Beijing's *hutong* neighbourhoods both domestically and internationally, has played a role in realising the potential of saving parts of the old city as the authorities grapple with the need to harmonise the ever-expanding modern city with its ancient history.

Moving beyond Beijing to the broader landscape of conservation in China, in addition to the economic, political and cultural pressures that have constrained a more dynamic and sustained conservation ethic, the knowledge and understanding of heritage in Chinese cities are also not being sufficiently debated in the academic world with regard to how to interpret and identify Chinese heritage and the principles for conservation. For instance, the meaning of "authenticity", which is the central concept in Western conservation, does not have the same meaning in China. In Chinese culture, authenticity is often related with tradition rather than tangible materiality (Xu, Wan, & Fan, 2014; Sofield *et al.,* Chapter 1). Even when it does refer to materiality, the Nara Document on Authenticity in 1994 pointed out that since wood, which lasts less than stone, is the main material in architecture in Asia, the evaluation of authenticity should be different than in the West. Although these perspectives are important, other viewpoints and understandings should be discussed, debated, developed and disseminated.

Tourism plays an important role in the conservation of urban heritage. The potential reuse of many old buildings, especially through tourism, has helped local residents gain more support economically and culturally (Ruan, 2007). Especially since the year 2000, the visible effects of the rapid tourism development of world heritage sites in China has caused locals to desire and apply for world heritage status in the expectation that such status can help them generate income for conservation. However, due to the serious destruction of historical cities, only a few cities can still obtain the title of world heritage site. Most of the cities that attempt to rely on income from tourism for their conservation efforts cannot generate sufficient financial resources, and in addition, the reliance on tourism for urban heritage conservation also brings other negative consequences, such as the commodification of culture, gentrification, etc., and such is the case with the city of Zhongshan in this volume.

While there are many research topics in relation to urban heritage and also substantial research has been carried out on this topic, we feel that there are still some areas which have often been neglected in previous studies, such as transnational heritage, urban industrial heritage, modern commercial streets and the historical cities which are not politically significant but are nonetheless culturally significant. We hope that these studies will contribute to new knowledge of urban heritage in China.

In the conservation of Chinese heritage, the first important factor may be to recognise the features of that particular heritage in cities, and then conservation can be agreed on and actions taken. Conservation is not a historical part of Chinese culture, as in the long civilisation process of China, especially in the recent modernisation process, cities have been largely destroyed and then reconstructed again and again. The materiality of many Chinese historical cities keeps on changing, yet the essence of city buildings, which is the intangible heritage, has traditionally remained. By examining a tourist city, Guilin, Sofield *et al.* (2017) pointed out that millennia-old elements of urban traditions are still as visible as they were centuries ago, although the city has gone through major changes over time. However, this can be only understood through the Chinese gaze, particularly through the concept of feng shui. These authors challenge the Western hegemony over definitions of built heritage and authenticity espoused for example by UNESCO as 'universal values', since in Chinese culture quite different values determine the integrity of sites with indicators that do not necessarily 'fit' Western concepts.

Water systems are among the key features of Chinese cities, and monsoon rainfall patterns, for example, are believed to play a key role in Chinese culture. Chinese cities either suffer from flooding or from drought, and it is believed that the survival and prosperity of a place depend on whether it has a proper relationship with water. The traditional cities which have lasted for centuries usually have good artificial water systems, but from the late 19th century, the water systems have gradually disappeared due to the expansion of the cities and increasing sedimentation due to pollution. Still, Suzhou's water system managed to survive. Suzhou is a traditional commercial centre in the eastern part of China. The water grid, which was the main transportation system of the city, played an important role in commercial activities and social interactions in the city. In the modern times, while the transportation function is gone, tourism has instead had a focus on the key functions of the water system and has therefore contributed to maintaining the system. Breitung's chapter addresses this issue.

Although the industrial process in China has had a short history compared to the Western experience, Chinese cities are to a large extent heavily impacted by industrialisation. In 2012, China for the first time had a population more urban than rural, and industrialisation has been one of the driving forces. Yet, since Chinese people are in favour of looking forward and industrial cities are competing to move into the service industry, industrial heritage has not been seriously considered. By examination through web content analysis the industrial component in cities' images and city tourism, Yang (2017) pointed out that traditional Chinese industrial cities tend to change their image of industrial cities to match global trends. Fan and Dai's (2017) case study of the district of Tiexi further illustrates this argument. Tiexi, the old industrial district of Shengyang, which was the so-called heavy industry base of China, was undergoing changes from polluting factories to a business centre. Although a few heritage buildings were selected to be protected in the form of museums, the overall spatial and temporal pattern of the district was completed destroyed. In addition, the low attractiveness of the museums further discouraged any conservation efforts for its industrial heritage. The industrial process in China is also one of globalisation and colonisation in that the concepts of industry, technology, etc. are learned from Western countries, and some factories were directly created by foreign countries through military power. A transnational perspective should be adopted to study and evaluate these types of heritage (Li & Soyez, 2017); however, the identification and interpretation of these transnational heritage themes face great challenges because they often involve a dark history. Different countries often have different attitudes and interpretations, and the experiences of Germany, for example, can provide some lessons for China.

Over the past few centuries, the urban system in China has experienced tremendous changes. There is a general trend towards the importance of metropolitan cities, and the gap between these metropolitan cities and other cities is increasing. Most studies on these metropolitan cities have been due to their economic and political significance, and most of the so-called second-tier cities have not been well studied. Compared with metropolitan cities, whether second-tier cities can adopt similar conservation strategies is doubtful. Ding's (2017) work illustrates this dilemma. Zhongshan, one of the historically commercial cities in Guangdong province in China, has been reduced in economic significance due to the rise of Hong Kong and Shenzhen. The former inner business centre had lost its attraction, and a plan to change it into a pedestrian tourism shopping area was implemented in the hope that tourism could help to conserve its historical business heritage. However, the focus on emphasising the beauty of the landscape and attracting tourism has led to the loss of place attachment and place identity of the local residents.

Overall, we hope that the chapters presented in this volume raise further interest on heritage tourism in Chinese cities, especially in less researched areas such as industrial heritage in medium-sized cities and cities in peripheral areas.

References

Beijing Municipal Institute of City Planning and Design. (2015). *Beijing new master plan 2016 to 2035*. Beijing: Beijing Municipal Commission of Urban Planning.

Breitung, W. (2007). Suzhou's water grid as urban heritage and tourism resource: An urban morphology approach to a Chinese city. *Journal of Heritage Tourism*.

Chen, S. (2008). Typical analysis of Hutongs in old urban areas of Beijing. *Decoration*. 180(1): 82–84.

Ding, S.L. (2017). Impacts of urban renewal on the place identity of local residents—A case study of Sunwenxilu traditional commercial street in Zhongshan city, Guangdong province, China. *Journal of Heritage Tourism*. 12(3): 311–326

Dong, J.H. (ed.). (2004). *The history of urban construction in China*. Beijing: Chinese Architecture Press.

Fan, X.J., & Dai, S.S. (2017). Spatial-temporal distribution characteristics of industrial heritage protection and the influencing factors in Chinese city: A case study of Tiexi old industrial district in Shenyang. *Journal of Heritage Tourism*. 12(3): 281–295.

Guo, H., & Klein, B. (2005). Bargaining in the shadow of the community: Neighborly dispute resolution in Beijing hutongs. *Ohio State Journal on Dispute Resolution*. 20(3): 825–835.

Heath, T., & Tang, Y. (2010). Beijing's hutong and siheyuan: Conservation of an urban identity. *Municipal Engineer*. 163(3): 155–161.

Jiabao, W. (2002). *How to properly handle the relationship between the modernization of a city and the protection of historical relics*. Keynote address, China Mayors' Association 3rd Representative Conference, Beijing.

Li, L.L., & Soyez, D. (2017). Transnationalizing industrial heritage valorizations in Germany and China- and addressing inherent dark sides. *Journal of Heritage Tourism*. 12(3): 296–310.

Lo, Y.-N. (2010). Siheyuan and Hutongs: The mass destruction and preservation of Beijing's courtyard houses. *AIA Architects Newsletter*, 19 November, 2010. http://info.aia.org/aiarchitect/2010/1119/newsletter/, accessed 29 Nov 2017.

Ma, L. (2014). *An analysis of Beijing's Hutongs and Siheyuans: An urban tree approach*. Master Thesis, The Pennsylvania State University, College of Arts and Architecture. https://etda.libraries.psu.edu/catalog/22841, accessed 26 Nov 2017.

Qian, F. (2013). *Protecting the spirit of Hutong: A case study of Nanchizi Precinct, Beijing*. 16th Scientific Symposium of ICOMOS, Québec City, 29 September–4 October 2008.

Qiu, B.X. (2003). Development strategy of Chinese cities in the globalization. *City Planning Review*. 27(12): 5–12.

Ruan, Y.S. (2007). The conservation and utilization of Chinese historical town. *Chinese Relics Research*. 3: 12–18.

Sofield, H.B., Li, F.M.S., Wong, G.H.Y., & Zhu, J.J. (2017). The Heritage of Chinese Cities as seen through the gaze of zhonghua wenhua (中华文化–Chinese Common Knowledge): Guilin as an exemplar. *Journal of Heritage Tourism*. 12(3): 227–250.

Wang, Y. (2007). *The conservation and renovation of landscape of historic sites in old city- Qianmen East District, Beijing as an example*. Master Thesis. Beijing Forestry University. Beijing, 2007. Cited in Ma, Lan (2014).

Wu, L.-Y. (2000). *Rehabilitating the old city of Beijing: A project in the Ju'er. Hutong neighborhood (Urbanization in Asia)*. Vancouver: University of British Columbia Press.

Xu, H.G., Wan, X.J., & Fan, X.J. (2014). Rethinking authenticity in the implementation of China's heritage conservation: The case of Hongcun Village, *Tourism Geographies*. 16(5): 799–811.

Yan, H. (2004, October). Urban spatial patterns and infrastructure in Beijing. *Land Line Magazine*, Lincoln Institute of Land Policy. http://www.lincolninst.edu/publications/articles/urban-spatial-patterns-infrastructure-beijing, accessed 1 Dec 2017.

Yang, X.K. (2017). Industrial heritage tourism development and city image reconstruction in Chinese traditional industrial cities: A web content analysis. *Journal of Heritage Tourism*. 12(3): 267–280.

Zhang, Y. (2016). "Reporting from the Front" in China: A talk with Zhang Ke of ZAO/standardarchitecture. *Archdaily*, 9 May, 2016. https://www.archdaily.com/787041/reporting-from-the-front-in-china-a-talk-with-zhang-ke-of-zao-standardarchitecture, accessed 28 Nov 2017.

The heritage of Chinese cities as seen through the gaze of *zhonghua wenhua* – 'Chinese common knowledge': Guilin as an exemplar

Trevor H. B. Sofield, Fung Mei Sarah Li, Grace H. Y. Wong and Jinsheng Jason Zhu

ABSTRACT

The pursuit of modernization in cities all over China has at one level resulted in the disappearance of much built heritage; yet at another level, millennia-old elements of urban traditions are as visibly present in contemporary cities as they were centuries ago. This visibility, however, is not always apparent to non-Chinese observers. To reach an understanding of this phenomenon, it is suggested that the normative 'western' approach to heritage with its focus on physical materialities, an orientation that explores in great detail the built fabric of monuments, buildings and sites and which embeds a definition of authenticity in how close to the original the current, existing manifestations are, needs to be put to one side. In Chinese history, the fundamental importance of incorporating cosmology into the entire being of towns and cities to ensure harmony between Heaven and Earth, as defined in the selection of their location in the landscape, cardinal orientation, spatial layout and the disposition of principal buildings – has been recorded in a template known as the 'Zhou li' or *Rites of Zhou* (*circa* 1035 BC). It was compiled by the Duke of Zhou, who is credited with transforming an abstract concept, the doctrine of the Mandate of Heaven (through which emperors ruled as 'Sons of Heaven' by divine right), into physical city planning and design. However, he was preceded by the 'Three Sovereigns' and 'Five Sage Emperors', including Huang-di (the Yellow Emperor, eulogized as 'the Father of the Yellow Race') who in Chinese historico mythology received divine instructions that laid the basis for *feng shui* and Daoism and provided a context for the compilation of the *Zhou li*. While this template evolved over centuries, its four key tenets based around cosmology remained much the same and throughout imperial China it continued as the master guide for planning towns and cities. Despite attempts during the Cultural Revolution (1966–1976) to destroy the 'Four Olds' (Old Customs, Old Culture, Old Habits and Old Ideas), the essence of seeking harmony (integral to the belief system underpinning the *Zhou li*) remains a predominant ideal in contemporary China, and some elements of the ancient template continue to be actively applied to the present day. Thus even though many Chinese cities may have 'lost' their built heritage as defined by western 'authorities' such as ICOMOS (International Council on Monuments and Sites, the technical body that advises United Nations Educational, Scientific and Cultural Organization on applications for World Heritage

Site listing), their cosmological foundations remain and will often be as evident to Chinese observers today as when those cities were originally founded hundreds of years ago. The concept of 'Chinese common knowledge' is crucial to this comprehension. These varied historical and cultural traditions provide the setting to examine the origins of Guilin, a 2200-year-old city in Guangxi Province, which exhibits original aspects of its traditional heritage that are eminently visible in the twenty-first-century city to the Chinese gaze but are often out of sight from western observers who fail to recognize the Chinese tangibles and intangibles all around them.

Introduction

'Study the past, if you would divine the future'. So said Confucius, as recorded in *The analects* (论语 – 'Sayings') (Brooks & Brooks, 1998), one of the most famous Chinese classical texts of all times. In examining the heritage of China's cities in the twenty-first century, we wish to take the liberty of paraphrasing Confucius by suggesting that to understand the built heritage and physical design of many twenty-first-century cities in China, one needs to 'Study the past to understand the present'. This is because China has experienced a relative continuity in its culture for several thousand years that links its ancient history to contemporary development in a way that is matched by few other countries (Li, 1994). In the case of thousands of cities, towns and villages all over China, this ancient cultural heritage has provided the wellspring for their location in the landscape, their layout and key design features, enduring with significant consistency across the centuries. As Xu (2000, p. 2) states:

> The importance of Chinese urban history lies not only in its architectural distinctiveness from that of the West but in the fact that the range and variety of Chinese experiences in building, adjusting, governing and inhabiting cities as well as in relating cities to the rest of society is by far the largest block of such human urban experience. It therefore constitutes an indispensable parameter of comparison for urbanism in other cultural spheres.

Guilin with a continuous history dating back beyond the fifth century BC has been both an object of and a witness to the development of Chinese urban form and space as it transitioned through the socio-political upheavals of the Warring States period to the unified imperial structure of the Qin (221–206 BC) and Han (400 years to 220 AD), the mediaeval urban revolution initiated in the second half of the eighth century by the Tang Dynasty through to the Southern Song (1127–1279 AD), which then evolved into the market economy with a mature hierarchical system of cities and market towns in the Ming (1368–1644 AD) and Qing (1644–1911 AD) (Xu, 2000; Zhu & Wang, 1996). Within this 3000-year period, the unification of China by Qin in 221 BC, a defining moment in Chinese history, ushered in comprehensive social and political change that produced a transformation in the governance of China's city system. Under a single dominant government for the first time, all of the country's cities were subjected to a degree of central control and subordinated to the needs of the state.

In this context, Braunfels (1988), surveying a thousand years of urban architectural heritage in western Europe, presents a view of those pre-industrial cities as commonly possessing separate legal and political status as organized entities which set them apart from the countryside, often exercising a degree of independence from an over-arching central government, whereas Xu (2000, p. 3) asserts that:

> No Chinese city in the imperial era was ever a corporate entity of its own, nor did any of them have the organizational features that set European cities apart in legal and political ways. The Chinese city was an instrument of the imperial government and thus an integral part of its 'one world'; its area of existence was more than interwoven with the state to which it was subordinated and with the rural areas that surrounded it

The Chinese city thus served not only as a form of urban planning that encompassed the built heritage of architecture and engineering, but also as the centrepiece of social order, religious belief and political control, and thereby governed the structure and operation of the Chinese state as a whole. And it is the transformation of these intangibles that is manifested in the physicality of cities, towns and villages throughout China as much as the tangible 'bricks and mortar' of their many buildings. According to Nelson (1988, p. 217):

> … this traditional system of urban civilization was so closely tied to social control and the application of political power that conquerors of China, such as the Mongols and Manchus, were compelled to become Chinese in order to secure the fruits of their conquests.

China's urban heritage throughout the 2500-year imperial era was characterized by both its remarkable continuity and its great complexity (Xu, 2000), and Guilin is simply one urban expression among many of both of these factors.

China is currently in the embrace of perhaps the greatest twenty-first-century explosion of modernization of any country in developing and redeveloping its urban areas; yet manifestations of its past are as evident in its cities, towns and villages today as they were centuries ago. To be able to perceive this rich heritage requires an exploration of some of the ancient values and philosophies that have driven its culture and remain extant in the landscapes and urban-scapes of contemporary China (Han, 1992), even if the 'bricks and mortar' evidence of built heritage desired by western or Eurocentric values is sometimes absent. It is generally accepted that urban planning in China originated during the settlement of the Yellow River valley in the Neolithic Age by the Yangshao and Longshan tribal cultures (Bai, 2003). Although several cultures formed competing states, many commentators accept that the direct ancestor of the Chinese state was Longshan culture that generated a synthesis of traditional cosmology, geomancy and astrology. (The Duke of Zhou is credited with adding numerology 1000 years later: Montgomery, 2014.) This synthesis was stylized through a chart of the cosmos, which placed man, state, nature and heaven in harmony. Settlements were planned in the context of this cosmic diagram to maintain harmony and balance, and thus Longshan culture is credited with developing the prototype of urban planning for Chinese cities that was followed down the centuries (Bai, 2003). A key element in this phenomenon is the text entitled *Zhou Li* compiled about 1000 years after the demise of Longshan society and its replacement by first the Xia, then the Shang and subsequently the Zhou dynasties. The *Rites* embodies many aspects of Daoist philosophy and tenets because of its detailed exposition of principles of *feng shui* (风水) – even though it was written several hundred years before Daoism began its formalization through such writings as the *Daode jing* (*Scripture of the way and its power*) circa fourth century BC (Ames & Hall, 2003). The *Zhou li* is considered the classical text on city theory, especially its last section entitled 'Kao Gong Ji' (*Book of diverse crafts*, 考工记). This is a blend of the science and technology of ancient China and *inter alia* provides prescriptive components of city planning, a template for designing a city. However, its set of instructions cannot be understood without going even further back in time to explore its antecedents, and this approach may be likened to exploring the world of the *xiàng-yá-qiú* 象牙球 (sometimes called a Chinese puzzle ball), which is a sequence of intricately carved concentric ivory balls, one carved inside the other in increasingly smaller sizes, often 14–15 layers deep, a complex, highly structured world in miniature. As one set of features and characteristics is explored, another is revealed deeper within, and then another, and another; and so we journey back in time to set the context and uncover some of the elements of ancient cosmology and associated beliefs hundreds of years before the *Zhou li* was written.

Methodology

In more orthodox terminology, the above approach is called 'historical methodology', and we have coupled this research tool with annual field trips of two weeks each to Guilin over the past six years

(2011–2016) involving discussions each year with the city's mayoral office, its urban planning and public works authorities, its heritage officials, the Guilin Tourism Department and planning staff from the Guilin Institute of Tourism (upgraded to the Guilin Tourism University, April 2015), and field inspections of a range of sites around the city. We thus add a six-year contemporary time-line of understanding to our historical analysis of Guilin.

'History' as Towner and Wall (1991, p. 72) observed, 'is concerned with the dimension of time and attempts to understand social processes and institutions within this context.' This comment echoes Barraclough's (1979, p. 3) emphasis that time 'provides the depth which comes from study-ing society not as a static but as a dynamic constellation of forces manifesting itself in continuous and constant change.' There have been numerous research approaches adopted by historians, ran-ging across positivism, structuralism, generalization, its opposite, particularization and Marxist interpretation, to name a few. A French school of historical research, 'Annales', stressed the need for integration of the findings and methods of other disciplines into studies of the whole of human activity, and the interplay between long-term continuities and short-term cycles of econ-omic, political, demographic and social change (Braudel, 1958, cited in Towner & Wall, 1991). In the context of this paper, we suggest that such an approach is not simply useful but essential in order to unravel the underlying forces shaping the way in which Guilin has evolved (Sofield & Li, 1998b).

Historiography (the study of writings of history) reveals that contemporary values and circum-stances always influence the interpretation of historical fact. Interpretation may change to suit or satisfy particular needs because heritage, its ownership and its presentation will involve consider-ations of changing values, power structures and politics. In examining China's historical records, the first point is that Chinese bureaucrats have been meticulous in recording past events mainly of concern to monarchy and officialdom. According to Jenner (1992, p. 7):

> The main historiographical tradition has been one of impersonally written history compiled by officials (edu-cated in the Confucian tradition) through processes that were essentially bureaucratic. The most influential his-tories were those compiled by central governments ... in order to give both the present and the future a standardized, a 'correct', view of the rise and fall of past regimes. Thus ... we have a remarkably well-organized published record, covering systematically the last two millennia.

In this instance, we consider it necessary to use historiography to draw a distinction between a Chinese perception of city heritage and a western view that sees built heritage firmly anchored in materialities (bricks and mortar). This does not mean that Chinese cities are immune from change despite their constancy, but rather that there remains a consistency in their structure with long-held values of society manifested in their being, even as those values have changed, been rein-vented to meet contemporary needs or reinstated to enhance continuity with the past. Unlike Boorstin's (1964) newly created 'pseudo' this-and-that's, the modern Chinese city is a manifes-tation drawn from 'real' history by a society cognizant of its deep roots and philosophical heritage, and it may therefore claim a degree of cultural authenticity denied to more fanciful and recent trends in urban development. The use of methodology derived from the discipline of history and historiography to unravel the processes of development provides a hermeneutic approach to permit a deeper understanding of the durability of the city and its concomitant linkages into the social, political, cultural, economic and power structures of China over centuries. This com-plexity requires the researchers to delve into the historico-mythical record of Chinese civilization over the past 6000–7000 years, including a short introduction to the culture heroes known var-iously as the 'Three Sovereigns and Five Emperors', a brief mention of two great philosophical/ religious systems of China, Confucianism and Daoism, and the *common* thread of *feng shui* which weaves its way through the ages, prefaced by a brief outline of *zhonghua wenhua* 中华文化 – 'Chinese common knowledge' (Ang, 1994; Li, 2006; Ogden, 1992; Schwartz, 1985). Utiliz-ing this exceptionally rich sociocultural fabric, we are able to interpret both the tangible and intan-gible urban heritage of Guilin through Chinese eyes and suggest that it is 'Chinese common knowledge' which allows millions of Chinese to 'read' and experience the heritage of a city in a way that is outside the scope of a non-Chinese gaze.

Chinese 'common knowledge' – *zhonghua wenhua* 中华文化

This concept refers to those Chinese possessing the capacity to access *zhonghua wenhua* 中华文化, which is generally translated as 'Chinese common knowledge' (Ang, 1994; Li, 2006). *Zhonghua wenhua* relates to a broad range of information shared by millions of Chinese about its culture heroes, Chinese philosophies, history, religions, literary heritage, art, calligraphy, famous people and so forth that has been transmitted in a continuous fashion over millennia through the use of common templates used to learn to read and write classical Chinese script. These templates date back hundreds of years and are derived from imperial collections of leading calligraphers of the time whose writings were engraved on stone tablets. Each individual character (there are more than 54,000, a university graduate masters about 8–10,000) is embedded in a context (an ancient poem, an extract from a famous essay, an incident in history, etc.), and thus in learning how to form each character, the context of each one is also absorbed. Chinese common knowledge is thus a 're-anchoring' by each succeeding generation of educated individuals to the origins of Chinese civilization (Li, 2006). This also means that the Chinese tourist gaze moves beyond the purely visual and captures invisibles as well, resting on a platform of Chinese common knowledge that encompasses historicism, Confucianism and Daoism as foundational building blocks. Out of these paradigms, philosophies and religions have come some of the great classical *shan shui* ('mountain-water', 山水) literary works and poetry that are also part of Chinese common knowledge. The influence of this body of knowledge, while less for the current younger generation in China, continues to provide shape for much of the social, cultural and physical structure of what China is today (Li, 2006), especially as there has been a revival in learning to read and write traditional Chinese characters. This is partly because of the perception that mastery of it signifies a 'civilized person' (as per Confucian values) and its close association with the intellectual superiority ascribed to the imperial mandarin class. In fact all modern rulers in China, including Mao Zedong despite his introduction of a simplified version of the Chinese characters, have displayed their prowess in classical calligraphy and there are numerous schools in calligraphy flourishing all over contemporary China. And with exposure to classical Chinese automatically comes a continuation of the thousands of threads that constitute *zhonghua wenhua*.

Ancient history, myths and legends

To understand the history of city heritage in China, we need to start with a brief outline of the 'Three Sovereigns and Five Sage Emperors', 'a group of mythological rulers or deities in ancient northern China who in later history have been assigned dates in a period from circa 2852 BC to 2070 BC' (Hucker, 1995, p. 22). The Three Sovereigns (also called the 'Three August Ones')

> were said to be god-kings or demigods who used their abilities to improve the lives of their people and impart to them essential skills and knowledge. The Five Emperors are portrayed as exemplary sages who possessed great moral character and lived to a great age and ruled over a period of great peace. (Morton & Lewis, 2005, p. 14)

For some Chinese they are historical figures, acknowledged in Chinese common knowledge as 'culture heroes' (Bai, 2003). While all of them are credited with adding some elements to the mainstreams of Chinese cosmology, religious beliefs and philosophy, and are all evident in the compendium of Chinese common knowledge, four in particular are more prominent in terms of attribution of factors that may be deemed relevant to understanding the ancient origins of urban heritage in China. They are the first two of the Three Sovereigns, Fu Xi (伏羲) and Nu-wa

(女媧), and two of the Five Sage Emperors, Huang-di (黃帝), the Yellow Emperor (whose title as 'Father of the Chinese Race' attests to his importance in the overall scheme of things), and Yu the Great (大禹), the 8th-generation descendent of Huang-di and the founding emperor of the Xia dynasty. All of these figures and many of their stories have been passed down through the generations, recorded in famous books and classics, and are an accepted part of Chinese common knowledge (Windridge & Fong, 1999).

In the context of the *Rites of Zhou*, the traditional view is that the magico-religious-philosophical belief system, upon which 'laws' and principles for constructing towns and cities are based, is an amalgamation of many different threads attributed in the first instance to the Three Sovereigns and the Five Sage Emperors. Their different contributions had matured into a complex coherent religious, philosophical and political system by the time the Duke of Zhou applied them to the planning of cities, towns and villages. It is not possible to ascertain a strict chronological order for the cumulative process of elements being added to the base structure, although a number of the ancient texts all record that some aspects are attributable to a specific culture hero, while others, not surprisingly, are at variance. Where there is such an agreement, the mutual reinforcement of their stories/achievements has lent weight to those interpretations, and they have tended to find their way in Chinese common knowledge. At this juncture, we therefore need to set out details of this cosmology, and then relate that to the archaeological record of the construction of the ancient Neolithic settlements of the Yangshao and Longshan cultures to allow an understanding of the prescriptive injunctions of the *Zhou Li* as the ideal for cities all over China from the ninth century BC to 1911, and with some variations, into the twenty-first century.

Legendary/mythical beginnings

Chinese legend has ordered society beginning with the Two Sovereigns, Fu Xi and Nu-wa, who were half-human brother and sister. They later married, had a family and thus established the laws of marriage and the extended family (Ji, 2007). Symbolically, Nu-wa is represented by the compass and Fu Xi by the carpenter's square – both instruments that are foundational in the design and construction of settlements in China. The compass is derived from the legend of Nu-wa separating the Heaven and Earth after the former had tilted disastrously to the north. To accomplish this, she had to re-establish the four cardinal points, hence the compass. Fu Xi invented the carpenter's square to restore equilibrium on Earth. Both instruments have been essential in China's construction industry ever since. As Li (2006) notes, socio-linguistics take our understanding of this relationship further: the word for compass, *gui*, and for square, *ju*, when combined as *gui ju* 規矩 denotes 'rules and regulations', or 'order', and Fu Xi's ascription as 'the first emperor' implies the advent of government, law and order. The compass/square dichotomy also symbolizes female and male, Heaven and Earth, and *yin* (陰) and *yang* (陽).

As the centuries passed and the Three Sovereigns gave way to the Five Sage Emperors, the set of beliefs were refined and elaborated. Heaven and Earth were believed to be ruled by the Jade Emperor from his palace in Polaris (the North star). From there, he directed the cosmic energy force of *qi* (literal translation: 'heavenly breath') down to Earth into and through the divine emperor, out of his palace city and out of the gates into his dominion where it converged in *shan* (mountains) and *shui* (waters). This in turn led to the concept of the need for man in the role of emperor to maintain harmony between Heaven and Earth.

The fusion of astrology, cosmology, geomancy and numerology was continued by the Yangshao culture during the Neolothic Age whose tribes settled along the middle reaches of the Yellow River around 6000 BC. Further refinements were made by its successor, the Longshan culture which moved into the region from the east around 2500 BC under the leadership of Huang-di. This advent is mythologized in the chronicles about Huang-di, the pre-eminent Sage Emperor, and Longshan culture is regarded by many as the beginning of Daoism (Chang, 1983; Cohen, 2012;

Jan, 1981). Huang-di is attributed with another development concerning the physical and spatial concepts related to cosmic forces and their first application to urban planning – that of the Earth as a square divided into nine-squares-in-one-square with a round Heaven revolving around it (later known as the 'well-field' system or 'Holy Field', in Chinese *jingtianzhi* (井田制): Allan, 1991). But other sources such as Sima Qian's (1961) 'Record of the Grand Historian' (famous through Chinese common knowledge: Hardy, 1999) credit Yu the Great (who divided China into nine provinces as a national extension of the grid system) with this honour. Nevertheless, all sources agree that the origin of this concept came from divine intervention through the instrument of a sacred tortoise sent from the Jade Emperor, on whose carapace was inscribed the shape and relationship of Heaven to Earth with the nine squares oriented north–south. This system became the essential factor in divining the 'Holy Field' through *feng shui* principles for the siting of capital cities and imperial palaces in the central (fifth) square. The Duke of Zhou systematized the nine-squares-in-one-square through numerology (Montgomery, 2014). According to He (2007a), the importance of this system cannot be underestimated as it formed the geometric basis of ancient Chinese architecture, urban planning and geography, and was subsequently adopted by imperial China throughout its 2000-year development as the ideal form for cities, towns and villages.

As another manifestation of the symbolism of the figure nine and its association with the Mandate of Heaven, Yu the Great cast nine bronze cauldrons standing on three legs to be used in sacrificial rites to the ancestors from Heaven and Earth. Only the emperor as the 'Son of Heaven' could use all nine ritual cauldrons (*jiu ding,* 九鼎), with a strict hierarchical order regulating their use by vassal lords (seven), ministers of state (five) and the mandarin class (one to three cauldrons according to their rank and seniority). From the time of the Shang Dynasty until 1911, the *jiu ding* symbolized the power and authority of the ruling dynasty (Watson, 1961), and to this day Daoist temples all around contemporary China feature bronze three-legged cauldrons, their significance immediately apparent to locals because of Chinese common knowledge.

Feng Shui

The Yangshao/Longshan fusion of beliefs evolved into the cohesive ideology of *feng shui* (geomancy), which weaves its way through 2500 years of imperial China and into the twenty-first century. Yan (1965, p. 24) described *feng shui* as 'a combination of Chinese philosophical, religious, astrological, cosmological, mathematical and geographical concepts'. Some of the rules for *feng shui* were recorded in the *I Ching* (*The book of changes*), attributed to the Duke of Zhou by several ancient scholars, and to Confucius by others. Since the endeavours of humans are subjected to the twin influences of Heaven and Earth, *feng shui* was designed to provide a mechanism by which the *yin* and the *yang* of *qi* could identify where the forces of Heaven and Earth would be in harmony. Below ground, the forces of *qi* flow through dragon's veins; above, they manifest chiefly as wind (*feng*) and water (*shui*) (the term *feng shui* literally means 'wind' and 'water'). Thus, crucial to *feng shui* are features in the landscape (Kong, 1988). For example, mountains (*shan*) are *yin*, meaning passive, with ascribed characteristics of the dragon, tiger, turtle or phoenix, and could be balanced by water which is *yang*, meaning active, able to attract and hold wealth; and their juxtaposition would determine the flow of forces or energy between them and whether a site was to be avoided or developed for a particular purpose (traditionally a town, a shrine, a grave – now extended to include the premises of a business) (Sofield & Li, 1998a). Through the application of geomancy, auspicious sites could be identified where a building or town or city could benefit from the energized spot called the *xue* 穴, literally translated as 'the dragon's lair', where the *qi* collects/focuses and is the best possible site for human ingress into a landscape, marking the centre of the Holy Field inside the 'Magic Square' (Fan, 1992; He, 2007a; Schinz, 1996). Identifying the *xue* was essential for this purpose and the expert (geomancer) utilized a *luopan* wheel (罗盘), one of the world's first compasses (Plate 1). The application of *feng shui* reflects the notion that

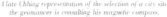

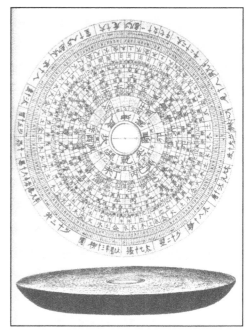

A late Chhing representation of the selection of a city site. the geomancer is consulting his magnetic compass.

The geomancer utilized a form of compass called a *luopan*.

Plate 1. Feng shui assessment of a site was carried out by an expert called a geomancer (Eitel, 1984).

'Human alterations of the landscape do not simply occupy empty space. Rather, sites are viewed as manifesting certain properties which influence, even control, the fortunes of those who intrude upon the site' (Knapp, 1992, pp. 108–109).

The last section of the *Zhou Li*, the 'Kao Gong Ji' (*Book of diverse crafts*), encapsulates those elements of *feng shui* that ideally should be applied in man-made constructions of all kinds right down the scale from cities to individual buildings. Thus, a city, town, village, temple or house should be built on a south-facing slope flanked by the arms of encircling hills – the dragon behind, the tiger on the left and the white horse in front. Such a location would ensure warming sun, shelter from the cold northerly winds and protection from floods. A *feng shui* grove of trees should be maintained on the uphill slope behind the village, which will provide further protection from the winds, lessen the risk of landslides, prevent soil erosion and regulate water flows. There should be a meandering river in front of the village to provide a steady water supply and ensure that wealth, at least rich silt, accumulates in contrast to a swiftly flowing river which is characterized as carrying wealth away in floods. On flat land, the *feng shui* wood takes the place of the protecting hill to the rear of the village. Other *feng shui* groves away from the village may be retained and/or planted where they act as screens against malevolent spirits (*shaqi*, 殺氣). The Purple Cloud Temple in Wudangshan, constructed between 1119 and 1125 AD, is an exemplar of *feng shui*-determined placement in the landscape (Box 1). In viewing this temple and other landscapes, Chinese will be able to 'read' the evidence of 'feng shui' application in the juxtaposition of cities among hills, rivers and remnant forests, understanding for example that a particular feature that appears natural is actually human-made to harmonize elements or block harmful *shaqi* influences. That is to say, the invisible will meld with the visible in a distinctive Chinese gaze (Li & Sofield, 2008).

BOX 1: The Daoist Purple Cloud Temple *(Zi Xiao)* in the famous Daoist *kung fu* mountains of Wudangshan, Hubei Province, is considered one of the best *feng shui* sites of any temple in China.

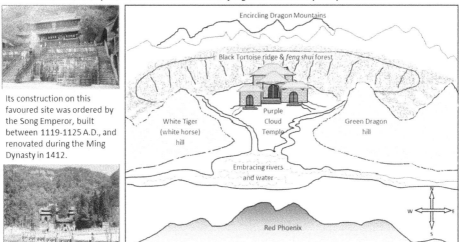

Its construction on this favoured site was ordered by the Song Emperor, built between 1119-1125 A.D., and renovated during the Ming Dynasty in 1412.

The Purple Cloud Temple demonstrates a classical *feng shui* arrangement of mountains and water .
* The Temple is located facing south with the Dragon Mountains and the Black Tortoise ridge encircling it and protecting it from the chill north winds
* A *feng shui* forest covers the slope of the Black Tortoise ridge
* The White Tiger Hill on the west blocks the malignant glare of the western sun
* The Green Dragon Hill on the east guards the site if the White Tiger gets out of hand
* The Red Phoenix range in front (south) is low enough to allow a vista but high enough to protect the site from *shaqi* influences
* The temple is located on a slope above the streams, pool and river so it will thrive because its foundations will not be undermined
* The temple faces the water, is embraced by the streams, and so will enjoy prosperity. (A site in the bend of a body of flowing water will accumulate riches as the river slows down and deposits its wealth, whereas one which is located on the banks of a straight flowing river will have its wealth swept away).

In terms of a Chinese gaze, it is of interest that while the official guide books and pamphlets issued in both Chinese and English mention that Purple Cloud Temple is excellent *feng shui*, none of them provide any details as per this diagram and explanatory notes above. Through their 'common knowledge' Chinese visitors can see and read the site without the need for such interpretation.
[Diagram and explanatory text courtesy of Li, 2006]

The practices of *feng shui*, stripped of Daoist beliefs and superstition, are in fact consistent with principles of conservation and good land management (Williams & Webb, 1994). They predate by two millennia some of the elements of the contemporary notion of ecologically sustainable development (ESD), especially in terms of site placement for passive energy (warming and cooling), protection from the elements, minimization of the effects of human construction in terms of erosion and ecological degradation, and environmental risk avoidance. *Feng shui* shares with ESD the fundamental tenet of the need for humans to harmonize with, not disrupt or destroy, nature, although it also seeks to provide a measure of control by humans over natural forces. While the goal of *feng shui* is to tap the Earth's *qi* in ways which will achieve the desired harmony and its consequential sustainable prosperity, it would be naive to expect that the ideals were always rigorously implemented. However, they have been applied in thousands of cases, they have represented 'best practice', and as such have a demonstrated sensitivity towards sustainable development (Anderson & Anderson, 1973; Fan, 1992; Hammond, Adriaanse, Rodenburg, Bryant, & Woodward, 1995; Sofield & Li, 1998a). Even in contemporary China, striving for harmony between man and nature constitutes a major theme in much physical planning, although its parameters are often difficult to define (Xu, Cui, Sofield, & Li, 2014).

The archaeological record

The archaeological record substantiates the legendary origins of the theosophical system attributed to the Three Sovereigns and the Five Sage Emperors and provides details about the application of these astrological, cosmological, geomantic and numerological phenomena to the actual construction of settlements and urban planning (Li & Chen, 2012). The first archaeological excavation of a Yangshao site called Banpo in 1953 contained the remains of several well-organized villages, each of which consisted of about 200 round pit-houses surrounded by a ditch with rammed Earth walls enclosing as much as 35 acres. Carbon-dated to 3600–4700 BC (Chang, Xu, Allan, & Lu, 2005), a common feature of these villages was their rectilinear shape, north–south alignment with all doors facing south, position of gates at the cardinal points of the compass and a centrally positioned much larger rectangular building called the Great Hall which was used for religious and cultural ceremonies. This hall is believed to be one of the very first examples of specialized architecture (i.e. of something other than a house). Archaeological evidence from several sites suggests that these simple villages may be considered emerging forms of urbanization since their common orderly orientation and division of space unambiguously presage the configuration of early Chinese cities (Chang, 1987; Nelson, 1988; Schinz, 1996).

One thousand years later, the Longshan culture and Huang-di arrived, settled in the same region of the Yellow River and coexisted with the Yangshao tribes (Dai & Gong, 2003, p. 32). Huang-di and the Longshan tribes established a higher level of governance over Yangshao culture and the ideological and social fusion evolved into components of a new state and modified civilization, with Longshan emperors supported by Yangshao advisers in a two-tiered elite. One outcome of this credo was its application in the first systematic approach to urban planning in China through the Neolithic settlements of the Yellow River, an approach designed to maintain harmony and balance (Bai, 2003). There were three levels of settlements in this schemata, carefully regulated and defined by size: the village or *Jū* (up to 1 hectare); the town or *Yi* (1–5 hectares) and the capital city, called *Dū* (greater than five hectares). According to Wang (1997, p. 13):

> The original Yangshao Jū villages formed a matrix of production that channeled goods upward to larger Longshan Yi and ultimately to the Dū. Political power was therefore defined as the amount of the highly productive matrix of agriculture and villages under control. The greater the area, the more wealth passed upwards to the capital.

Another aspect of Longshan culture attributed to Huang-di is that he established a complex system of religious ceremonies and rituals as part of government organization, and this required the erection of alters and the construction of temples in the villages, towns and capital city, with the Ancestral Hall of the Yangshao evolving into the palace of the Longshan leaders, as much a centre of religion as of governance and power. The altars and temples had to be sited according to strict application of *feng shui* principles to ensure harmony between Heaven and Earth. The combination of a ruling class, an adviser class, religious constructions and a palace resulted in increasing the differentiation of the spatial arrangements of urban areas.

The archaeological record of excavations of the Xia, Shang and Zhou dynasties indicates that after the founding of the Xia dynasty by Yu the Great, the position of the overlord became hereditary, and thereby arose the need for a permanent and more complex residence near the ancestral altars of the overlord. This was the beginning of the first real city. The three dynasties maintained a similar Longshan structure of village, town and city, with governance of a supreme ruler guided by a set of advisers, which in imperial China was formalized in due course as the Mandarin class (Chang, 1983). The design and location of the Xia and Shang palaces were in essence miniature diagrams of the nine-squares-in-one-square system. When the Shang dynasty was toppled by one of their vassal tribes, the Zhou, in 1046 BC the Shang were quick to claim that the Zhou had violated the will of Heaven and upset the natural and harmonious order of the universe because the Shang had ruled by divine right. The Duke of Zhou as the acting Regent immediately carried out two main measures to counteract the allegations of illegality. First, he authored a treatise asserting that the Shang had become so corrupt that it was the will of Heaven that the Zhou had been able to defeat them. And second, he placated the Shang by resettling their aristocracy, scholars and craftsmen in a holy city, Zhengzhou, that he built especially for them in about 1038 BC. He also installed King Yu's nine-tripod cauldrons in Zheng's palace. Through such actions he became acclaimed as a paragon of virtue (Confucius extolled him as a role model), promoting a philosophy of a just and honourable ruler in harmony with Heaven; and hence the highly complimentary phrase used in all Chinese-speaking societies: 'Your words have the weight of nine tripod cauldrons' (一言九鼎), meaning that the individual's comments carry authority and sincerity and he/she would never break his/her promise. The *jiu ding* thus became ensconced in Chinese common knowledge (Li, 2006). The site of Zhengzhou was discovered by the archaeologist Han Weizhou in 1950 and excavations began in 1951. Laid out according to exact geomantic principles, it was a radical synthesis although it drew on hundreds of years of design precedent, and according to Li (2004) is regarded as the first truly planned city in China. In essence, the Duke of Zhou established the ideal standard of urban planning through Zhengzhou, and most new cities were modelled after its design (Li, 2004; Nelson, 1988; Schinz, 1996).

To conclude, in terms of historical ecology, we can perceive that the ancient practice of *feng shui* represents a response to the environment which resulted in a major modification of that environment. Furthermore, it has been a primary determinant in the pattern of human settlement in China over centuries, and in visiting a city such as Guilin, many Chinese see – through the medium of Chinese common knowledge – a landscape that holds a profound heritage largely hidden from non-Chinese eyes without carefully constructed interpretation to reveal it to them.

The unification of China and continuation of the Duke of Zhou's urban planning schemata

Confucius and his contemporary, the philosopher Laozi, accredited author of the *Daode Jing* (*The way*), and accepted in Chinese common knowledge as the founder of Daoism (Ames & Hall, 2003), lived about 400 years after the Duke of Zhou during the tumultuous times known as the Spring and Autumn period (ca. 770–475 BC) and the Warring States period (ca. 475–221 BC). The centuries were characterized by constant rivalry between competing warlords whose territories covered modern China. By the end of the wars in 221 BC, the Qin state and its ruler, Ying Zheng, had unified most of the states, occupied some lands south of the Yangtze River (including Guilin) and proclaimed himself 'Qin Shi Huang' (秦始皇; literally 'First Emperor of Qin'), thus establishing the Qin dynasty (秦朝). Qin was ruthless in his unification of China. A very firm believer in the *Zhou Li* as it embraced the Mandate of Heaven and the sacred task of the emperor to ensure that his city was designed to focus *qi* and establish harmony between Heaven and Earth, Qin destroyed all the great capitals of ancient China that he conquered to prevent their *qi* being used against him. He transferred to Xian all the religious and secular artefacts and surviving archives of his enemies to concentrate their *qi* in his capital, seeking to strengthen his rule according to the Mandate of Heaven. 'Thus, he united China spiritually and sanctified his own bold actions' (Nelson, 1988, p. 218). As he then set about re-establishing his own cities, he applied the Duke of Zhou's template very closely, and ancient Guilin (known then as Shi An) was developed according to the geomancer's prescriptions (Fan 1175 AD).

Qin's reign was relatively short-lived (he died in 210 BC) and his son, Hu Hai, was deposed in 206 BC and replaced by the Han Dynasty (206 BC–220 AD). At its inception, the Han Dynasty was immediately faced with the task of rebuilding the urban infrastructure which had been destroyed by Qin Dynasty purges and the war of succession after its downfall (Nelson, 1988, p. 218). That civil war had resulted in the destruction of much of the great library of archival material housed in Xian by Qin, and the Han were therefore without written rules for city planning and government administration. They launched a systematic nation-wide search for any surviving archival data, which *inter alia* recovered much of the book of the *Rites of Zhou*. Drawing on this and supporting documents that had not been destroyed, Han scholars utilized Zhou's numerology as the structural and organizational ideal, and collated the information into an additional chapter, which they appended to the *Zhou li* called the *Kao Gong ji*. Box 2 provides details of Zhou's numerological system expounding on the nine-squares-in-one Holy Field and the Magic Square. This codified synthesis of urban planning was used by the Han to extend Zhou's city plan to a national master plan with uniform standards that divided China into provinces based on the nine regions of Zhou, thus maintaining integrity with the concept of China as a square Holy Field.

The Han national master plan created a hierarchy of political and economic cities within the provinces that extended imperial authority more or less uniformly throughout the empire, with the imperial capital as its apex in a replication of the societal urban hierarchical system that originally existed within the Longshan and Yangshao systems of settlements. The imperial capital was laid out in the nine-squares-in-one formation as a microcosm of the national master plan (Nelson, 1988, p. 19). Under the patronage of the emperors, *feng shui* became an official state practice and the Han approach to urban development and governance persisted as the foundation of national planning, administered as part of the responsibilities of the Board of Rites in Beijing, until the overthrow of the imperial system and the advent of the Republic of China in 1911.

Box 2: The Numerology of the Duke of Zhou's 'Holy Field'

The 'Holy Field' according to the *"Kao Gong Ji"* in the *"Rites of Zhou"* (After He, Cong Rong, 2007b)

The Duke of Zhou is credited with advancing the theory of emblematic numbers in which three, nine and twelve were of particular importance. Three denotes the components of the universe – heaven, earth and mankind. Nine is the square root of three and symbolizes the ancient world of China based on the establishment of the nine original provinces by Yu the Great. Twelve represents the calendar months of the year and is 9+3. There are four seasons, and 12 divided by 4 thus returns to 3. In the same way, time is divided into quarters and the 12 hours yields 3. Thus, all calculations revert back to the square root of all fundamental numbers (Nelson 1988). Not only were these numbers considered essential for urban planning they were also reflected in the structure of imperial governments which had an inner cabinet of three ministers for defence, finance and public works, and an outer ministry of nine lower ranked ministers covering other portfolios necessary for the functioning of the state (Nelson 1988).

Zhou's numerology specified the organizational and structural model for a city as a perfect square with each side nine li in length, thus echoing the shape of the earth which was considered to be a square. This perfect square was aligned along the polar meridian and intersected by the north-south/east west axis. Each square was given a number so that all columns, whether horizontal,

vertical or diagonal, always add up to 15 as per the diagram – forming the so-called Magic Square (Schinz 1996).

The central square was numbered 5, and the four squares at the corners were the even integers (2,4,6,8), while the five axial squares were the odd integers (1,3,5,7,9). The five axial squares are *yang* (powerful, male) and the four even integer squares are *yin*. Combined, they are believed to produce the right balance to create a positive current of *Qi* to generate harmony for the whole.

Square 5, the Holy Place as the centre of the square, was the site for locating the Palace. It was surrounded by a complex of administrative facilities and temples, which in turn was surrounded by the outer city. This spatial arrangement reflected the three dimensions of the universe as well as signifying the threefold structure of Chinese society into the sacred as embodied in the emperor, the scholar-administrator elite, & commoners.

The north-south/east-west axis was used to divide the outer city into quarters of equal dimensions. Each quarter was then subdivided into four wards with enclosing walls and gates, and each ward was again divided into quarters. Nelson (1988,p.19) noted that in the ideal plan: *"There were twelve city gates, three in each of the walls, representing the twelve months of the year. These gates defined a grid work of major thoroughfares of which the north/south were of primary importance in defining the use of space and movement within the city. This was in keeping with the orientation of the city to heaven's pole, with its principle gate where the meridianal axis bisected the south wall. Secondary avenues were distributed among the major thoroughfares to produce a grid of nine north/south and nine east/west streets."*

Other facilities such as parks, cemeteries and so on were located in designated spaces around the city and associated activities were similarly assigned to specific places according to their political and religious functions, all in conformity with the transformation of cosmological beliefs into principles for urban planning as codified by the Duke of Zhou and subsequently elaborated upon by the Han Dynasty.

With the cessation of national guidance of *feng shui*, and the accompanying attenuation of religious values and their influence on patterns of behaviour, the application of *feng shui* turned from the public good to private benefit. Its current use has tended to be focused on individual buildings, houses, businesses and grave sites, rather than geographical areas. While *feng shui* was officially banned by Mao Zedong as contrary to the scientific atheism of Marxism, it was such an integral part of the Chinese landscape that it simply could not be banished or destroyed. Although individual manifestations such as *feng shui* shrines were destroyed during the Cultural Revolution (1966–1976), *feng shui* was never fully suppressed and continues to flourish today in communities throughout China and among overseas Chinese, whether they are residents in Hong Kong, Singapore or San Francisco. Even to date, many tourism developments are based on *feng shui* analysis of the site, which determines the location of specific buildings and their orientation, placement of embankments or artificial hills, introduction of a body of water, tree-planting and so forth. It moves well beyond the aesthetics which western architects and landscape specialists would apply.

Guilin history and design

Guilin's vibrant historical record is overshadowed by its beautiful natural scenery and it is known throughout China not as a strategic frontier city (its role for centuries), but by a 1600-year-old poem engraved in a cave at the foot of a 200-m-high karst pinnacle in the heart of the city, Solitary Beauty Peak (*Duxiu Feng*, 独秀峰), which was – and is – the axis for the city's north–south orientation. Composed by the eminent Southern Song dynasty poet, Yan Yanzhi (顏延之, 420–479 AD), Guilin's natural scenery has become so famous that it has entered Chinese common knowledge and is the signature image of the city: 'Guilin's water and mountains are the best under the Heaven' ('桂林山水甲天下') (Fan, 2010). The pinnacle itself has also achieved similar fame. Another example of calligraphy was inscribed in the same cave by Yan Yanzhi who described it as 'The sky-supporting pillar in the south – none can surpass this solitary peak in beauty'. The selection of the site for Guilin, set among mountains, rivers and lakes, is immediately recognized as 'good *feng shui*' by millions of Chinese visitors who flock to Guilin each year (27.8 million in 2014: Guilin Tourist Administration), more than one million of whom visit Solitary Beauty Peak and the Princes' Palace in the very centre of the city as it dominates its Holy Field (see Plate 2).

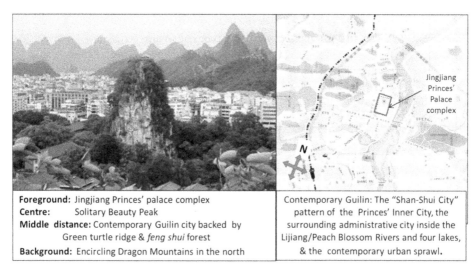

Foreground: Jingjiang Princes' palace complex	Contemporary Guilin: The "Shan-Shui City"
Centre: Solitary Beauty Peak	pattern of the Princes' Inner City, the
Middle distance: Contemporary Guilin city backed by	surrounding administrative city inside the
Green turtle ridge & *feng shui* forest	Lijiang/Peach Blossom Rivers and four lakes,
Background: Encircling Dragon Mountains in the north	& the contemporary urban sprawl.

Plate 2. The location of the Jingjiang Palace complex within Guilin, as determined by the Duke of Zhou's template for urban planning

Guilin actually existed as a minor tribal settlement dating as far back as 2000 BC before it was upgraded and designated as the administrative centre of an official prefecture in 214 BC by the Emperor Qin. In the same year, he authorized the construction of the 36-km-long Xing'an Lingqu Canal (灵渠) to join Guilin's Lijiang River and the Xiang River which, as tributaries of the Pearl and Yangtze Rivers, therefore linked two of the largest river systems in China (the canal was the first such construction to be awarded UNESCO World Heritage status, in 2013). This connection facilitated trade and travel over a vast area, with obvious strategic interests that unified north and south and allowed the Emperor to consolidate his power. Guilin thus became one of the gateways between the Central Plains and the region covering Guangdong, Guangxi and Hunan.

One of the earliest descriptions of Guilin is found in Fan Chengda's *Treatises* (Fan, 2010) when he was appointed 'Supervisor and Guardian' of Jingjiang Municipality (Guilin's second most ancient name) by the Southern Song Emperor Qiandao. Fan Chengda is known in literary history as an outstanding poet and writer, with his *shi* (poetry) commanding the most attention. Fan Chengda reached Guilin on 23 April 1173 in the ninth year of the reign of Qiandao. He describes how Guilin's first city wall was built in 621 AD by Tang general, Li Jing, in a perfect square 3 li in length, and how the city and its wall were enlarged in the ninth century and again in the eleventh century, each time its design and disposition of key buildings based on the Holy Field as prescribed in the *Kao Gong ji*. Fan commended its perfect north–south orientation, noting how the Li River curved around the north-eastern to south-eastern side of the city to form a natural moat behind which its city wall was built. In the north-west and west, the series of four lakes also formed a natural moat in front of the western wall, and the Peach Blossom River (*Tao-hua-jiang* 桃花江) flowed down from the north-west to the south where it joined the Li River to form part of the natural barrier along those meridians. To the west, the peaks of 'The Old Man' mountain constituted the white tiger hill, and to the east the Seven Stars Peak formed the green dragon hill. The placement of the city amidst the two rivers and four lakes, ringed by a circle of karst peaks in the north, east and west, affirmed its 'good' *feng shui*. As is common with descriptions of other cities at the time, more attention was paid by Fan to the location and layout of Guilin than to its individual buildings, an ancillary acknowledgement of the supreme importance of the relationship of Heaven and Earth and man, and the indivisibility of man and nature. It is Chinese common knowledge that allows Chinese visitors to Guilin to see these relationships in the city's physical and material existence among the *shan-shui* landscape, despite the urban sprawl and high-rise buildings of the modern city that extend far beyond the ancient city's feng *shui*-determined boundaries.

However, Guilin also has tangible built heritage as well as the intangibles that determined its existence in this specific place. It has two built heritage sites of national significance that in part meet orthodox (western) understanding of this term. Both sites are also perfect examples of the Duke of Zhou's numerological, *feng shui*-based, urban planning. The first is the Jingjiang Princes' Palace which served as the abode of 12 generations of imperial princes, and the second is the site of 11 of their mausoleums. In order to strengthen the centralization of state power, the first Ming emperor, Zhu Yuan Zhang (1328–1398)

> revived the feudalistic institution of 'enfeoffed princedoms' (the deed by which a person was given land in exchange for a pledge of service). This system invested his sons and other relatives with substantial power and responsibilities within a familial and dynastic framework. Zhu Yuanzhang anticipated that these princedoms would serve as a bulwark against outside enemies, the Mongols, and various internal dynastic rebels. (Chan, 2007, p. 48)

By Imperial Decree of May 1370, the emperor announced the first 10 such appointments – 9 for his elder children and 1 for Zhu Shou-qian (1364–1392), his grand-nephew, who was invested with the title of Prince of Jingjiang and granted Guilin as his enfeoffed region (Chan, 2007). (Over the next 30 years, the number of princedoms subsequently rose to 23.) Zhu Shouqian sited his palace in Guilin in the heart of the Holy Field (19.8 hectares), which centuries earlier had been identified by *feng shui* as the *xue* (dragon's lair, holy place) of Guilin where the *qi* concentrates. The Holy Field, as Fan

(1175 AD) noted, is located within a much larger area that is surrounded by the Lijiang and Peach Blosson Rivers and the four conjoined lakes, with the Solitary Beauty Peak rising above its northern perimeter. Zhu spent the next 20 years (1372–1392 AD) constructing his complex and placing the various components (4 halls, 4 pavilions, 6 temples and 40 other buildings surrounding the main buildings) along the north–south axis in strict accordance with the Duke of Zhou's nine-squares-in-one numerological template: Zhu & Wang, 1996). He also restored the moat formed on the west by the four lakes and enlarged the 1.5-km-long wall around his Inner City (Plate 2).

Of particular interest is that while the layout of the palace and its ancillary buildings followed the template devised by the Duke of Zhou, with Solitary Beauty Peak acting as the attractor for the *qi* from the North Polar Star and the palace complex thus oriented southwards from it, the entire complex is actually aligned 30° to the east of the centre of the peak. This was designed deliberately to ensure that the princes could not attract superior forces of *qi* to the emperor in Beijing and thus become a rival to overthrow him, a completely logical application of the tenets of Daoism (Figure 1).

The Jingjiang princes continued to rule Guilin for 257 years until the overthrow of the Ming by the Qing Dynasty in 1644. The site now has a history of more than 640 years and is older than the Forbidden City in Beijing. The palace was burned down twice in the Qing Dynasty and during the Japanese invasion in the 1930s; however, it remains as the best preserved of all former Princes' City in China. The only original remains are foundations of many buildings and the marble stairs and carved balustrades of the current Chengyun Hall (the Prince's Audience Hall from where the official governance of the region was conducted) which was rebuilt in 1947 according to its traditional Ming dynasty design, but using modern materials, by Chiang Kai Shek, leader of the Kuomintang Republican Government. A firm believer in Daoism, he purportedly rebuilt the Audience Hall and Chengyun Gate to capture the site's *qi* as he fought Mao Zedong for supremacy over China, in much the same way as the ancient Han dynasty rebuilt the cities destroyed by Emperor Qin more than 2200 years before to ensure the prosperity of their regime. The residential palace, other buildings, gates, walls, etc., are more recent with the site developed as a major tourist attraction in the late 1980s. In 2006 it was awarded 5A status as a heritage site of the most important order by the central Government and in 2014, it attracted almost one million (995,000) mainly Chinese tourists.

The second built heritage site of merit is the imperial mausoleum of the Jingjiang royal family, located in an eastern suburb of Guilin at the foot of Yao Mountain, 7 km from the palace complex. The 4-hectare site was carefully selected according to the principles of *feng shui*, with an inner and outer area linked by a north–south Sacred Way. More than 300 tombs that follow the north–south orientation are spread around the site, 11 of them for Jingjiang princes. Only one has been excavated to date (Zhuangjian, the third Jingjiang prince), and nationally important mortuary objects including

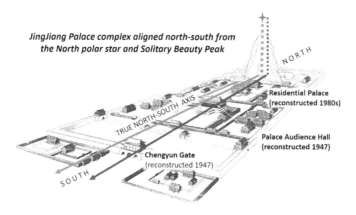

Figure 1. The Jingjiang Palace complex is sited 30° off-centre from Solitary Beauty Peak.

over 300 pieces of porcelain, gold, silverware, jade articles, swords and 50 stone tablets (inscribed with authenticated historical details of the Ming Dynasty) are now housed in the Jingjiang Mausoleum Museum constructed on site in 1987 (Zhu & Wang, 1996) directly in front of the mound holding the burial tomb of the first prince, Zhu Shou-qian. Many of the stone carvings of the princes, senior officials and various animals (lions, dragons, turtles and elephants) that lined the Sacred Way were destroyed during the Cultural Revolution and have been replaced in the last 30 years with new sculptures; but about one quarter are surviving originals dating back 1000 years. In recent years, the site has witnessed the revival of the annual Ching Ming Festival (April tomb cleaning ceremony by family members), with descendants of Zhu gathering *en masse* to clean the site. For example, in April 2015 more than 1000 descendants of Zhu, including one of these authors, participated in the ceremony. This ritual is fundamental to *yang* in establishing the fortunes of the living through tracing their male ancestors back in time to an illustrious past. In 2014 the royal tombs attracted more than 70,000 visitors and it would be interesting to ascertain numbers who were descendants of the princely families, and thus engaged in a form of 'ancestral tourism'.

The road to the royal tombs is now lined for several kilometres on either side by several thousand tombs of contemporary Chinese as current generations seek to benefit from the *qi* of the royal family. *Feng shui* masters hold office outside the extended burial area to assist current Chinese find an auspicious location for their own burial site. Thus, both tangible and intangible heritage, both ancient and contemporary practices, are incorporated in the mausoleums of the Jingjiang princes.

From a western perspective, using the UNESCO/ICOMOS guidelines (2015) for restoration as the benchmark (wherein about 90% of a restoration must adhere to the original materials, architectural form and construction methods), the set of buildings now occupying the Jingjiang Princes' site, and the new statues erected around the Mausoleum, fail to meet the criteria related to authenticity (specifically UNESCO, 2015, Article 86): they have minimal significance. For many Chinese, the significance of the buildings *as buildings* is not so significant either: whether they are new or ancient, whether they are 'authentic' or not in a western sense, is almost immaterial. What is fundamental is the *context* of their existence in a *shan-shui* landscape, based on their continuity and conformity with the history of urban settlement founded on a deep and rich cultural heritage that stretches back for several thousand years, so that the landscape is as much a social and cultural landscape as it is geophysical (Kong, 1988). And through *zhonghua wenhua*, many Chinese can 'read' this multi-themed-scape. The lack of 'hard' ancient edifices, as demanded for example by UNESCO's (2015) series of guidelines on historic cities or precincts or a group of monumental buildings, has not deterred the Chinese Government from approaching the matter from its own cultural perspective, granting the Jiingjiang site national heritage protection status in 1993 and designating its remnants as 'Key cultural relics of national level importance' in 1996.

The Yellow Crane Pagoda (黄鹤楼; Huáng hè lóu) in Wuhan, Hubei Province, is an example of the importance accorded by Chinese to contextual, holistic place and its hermeneutics over the antiquity of a building. The tower is famous in Chinese common knowledge through two Tang Dynasty eighth-century poems by two of China's most famous poets: Cui Hao who wrote 'Yellow Crane Tower' and Li Bai who wrote 'Farewell to Yellow Crane Pagoda' (Yu & Xu, 2016). When we first undertook a study of Hubei Province in 2001 and were taken by the Province Tourism Authority to see the pagoda, in response to our query as to how old it was we were told '2200 years'. However, on close examination, the building was revealed as constructed of reinforced concrete and steel with glass windows and an elevator, among other modern features. Puzzled by the obvious discrepancy in the answer to our question, we again asked how old it was and again received the same answer: 2200 years old. After some discussion during which we learned about the tower's history as a strategic military structure that had seen many battles over two millennia, we finally asked the correct question: How old is this current 'reincarnation'? And we were informed that it was built over five years from 1981 to 1985. Externally it looks ancient, its architectural form is traditional, but it bears no resemblance to its most immediate predecessor which was constructed during the Qing Dynasty in 1868 and destroyed in 1884. Yet its age is affirmed in brochures and other tourism material as dating back to 237 BC when the first tower was constructed on the banks of the Yangtze (e.g. Wen, 2005). It is the intangibles of the tower and site that are important, and in semiotic terms (after Mac-Cannell, 1976), it may be seen as a 'marker' signifying and representing the history of its many structures and architectural forms, the battles fought and lost around it, the generals and poets and other famous people associated with it, and additional aspects of the site itself such as the Yellow Crane wharf below the bluff which was, for hundreds of years, the main point of embarkation for journeys up and down the Yangzte River from Wuhan. In short, its place in Chinese common knowledge asserts its antiquity. It is not the age of the monument nor whether its reconstruction is faithful to its predecessors that concerns Chinese, but the associated history of 2200 years, and its literary/artistic record (poems, essays and paintings) that create its authenticity for the Chinese gaze. Three million Chinese visit the Yellow Crane pagoda each year, reinforcing their links to a past which is present. The tower *per se* – now designed for twentieth-and twenty-first-century tourism with its elevator and two separate circular staircases for up and down tourist flows, not as a military tower – is largely symbolic. And while it is one of the two or three most famous towers in all of China (Grey Goose pagoda in Xian is equally as well known), it fails all Eurocentric criteria for being listed as a heritage building. For example, UNESCO (2015, Article 86) states that: 'In relation to authenticity, the reconstruction of archaeological remains or historic buildings or districts is justifiable only in exceptional circumstances. Reconstruction is acceptable only on the basis of complete and detailed documentation and to no extent on conjecture'. The Yellow Crane Pagoda like many heritage sites in China defies easy classification into the 'normal' categories of whether it is objective, constructive or existential authenticity, or whether it is simulation or dissimulation, or in fact 'real'.

We have observed the same phenomenon in many cities and towns all over China, and the 'faux' reconstruction of 'ancient' towns and villages in many provinces throughout China as tourism sites (and most recently as film sets) with which we are familiar (Yunnan, Sichuan, Henan, Shanxi, Guangdong, etc.) bears witness to the lack of concern about 'authenticity' of built heritage as defined by western criteria and included in legislation by many western countries for their own built heritage (Britain, Europe, Australia, Canada, New Zealand, the USA, etc.). Often such reconstruction and repairs do not necessarily retain or maintain the fabric of their ancient origins. In reproducing and replicating ancient buildings, in many cases with which we are familiar (including in World Heritage listed sites such as Lijiang), the exterior form is often only a façade covering modern materials and modern construction methods.

Simply making buildings look old has no impact on their authenticity from a western perspective. For example, when a new interpretation centre and restaurant were built at Wolong (World Heritage site reserve for the giant panda in Sichuan Province) in 2006, an ancient Zhang traditional water wheel-driven flour grinding mill located over a mountain stream was included. This mill took just four weeks to construct, and to make it look as if it had been on site for hundreds of years, the workers gathered only moss-covered rocks to completely cover the reinforced concrete frame. Again, as with the Yellow Crane Pagoda, it looked ancient, its design was authentically Zhang traditional, but it was in fact brand new, had not used traditional stone-masonry and timber and had not been constructed using traditional methods. In western and Chinese eyes, it certainly looked nice, but it could never receive heritage listing in western countries. In effect it was paying 'lip service' to the prevailing western notion of what built heritage should look like, whereas in other than tourism sites in China the new will almost always replace the old without disguise.

This is not to say that within China there are not western forms of conservation, and a simultaneous growth in understanding by many Chinese of the western sense of antiquity/authenticity. The World Heritage listed ancient towns of Hongcun and Xi-di in Anhui Province which are visited and appreciated by several million Chinese visitors each year are examples. It is acknowledged that the two approaches (i.e. western and Chinese) to built heritage can and do exist in parallel: but we suggest that the 'Chinese-ness' (Ang, 1994; Ogden, 1992) of China's urban planning that is evident in cities, towns and villages, embedded in the *Zhou Li*, provides a significantly different foundation for a Chinese gaze that does not accord with western practice.

Guilin and a re-emergence of *Feng shui/Shan-shui* planning principles

Feng shui has made a resurgence in China to a certain extent as evidenced by the authors when undertaking planning for development projects in China over the past 20 years. The extraordinary expansion of grave sites around the Jingjiang princes' tombs with their attendant *feng shui* masters lining the road for several kilometres is further testimony to this fact. In addition, in the early 1990s, the study of *feng shui* was offered as an elective course in architecture open to all students at Beijing University. An architectural centre associated with Nanjing University in September 2005 started a course in *feng shui* and physical planners were one of the targeted recruitment areas. Discussions by the authors over a period of years with Chinese planners suggest that these *ad hoc* observations are indicative of a trend which has brought *feng shui* back into consideration in some physical and conceptual planning projects for tourism development. In the case of Guilin, it was raised to a national level with the publication in 1987 of Wu Lian-yong's paper on 'Guilin, *Shan Shui* City' (cited in Chen, 2010). Wu (1996c) reinforced this first work with two subsequent texts in which he analysed the cities of Sanya and Wuxi according to their *shan shui* patterns. He followed these with a third book on the sciences of human settlements (Wu, 2001) where he expounded on the topic at length. Chen (2010) suggests Wu's (1987) paper constituted the beginning of a formal revival of *feng shui* concepts in contemporary research in Chinese urban planning, the theoretical concepts of 'Shan-Shui-City' firmly located within the human settlement sciences, with numerous papers and books written about the topic by a number of other authors since that date.

In introducing the concept of Guilin as a 'Shan-Shui-City', Wu (1996a, 1996b) noted that the integration of the city and natural environment arose from a rich and deep historic background of thousands of years. He argued that the renowned beauty of Guilin lay not only in the scenic quality of the mountains and water, but in the integration of the two with 'urban interactions' that filled the space in and around them and was itself encircled by them. Chen (2010, p. 6) suggested that the essence of the 'Shan-Shui-City' could be understood in terms of

> functional mutual dependence. First, the natural environment offers cities with natural resources and defense. Second, it is about aesthetics bringing out the best in each other. People living in the human settlement can be cultivated by 'Shan-Shui' via building traditional gardens, exploring beauty spots and 'Shan-Shui' related art work creation. Third, it is about cultural integration. Both the 'Shan' and the 'Shui' have special cultural meaning in China, and people have been shaping local culture when creating the city together with the natural environment system for thousands of years. … This integration takes place under the guidance of Chinese traditional human settlement ideas.

Again, the emphasis is on man in harmony with nature, a mix of the intangible with the tangible and a lack of focus on 'built heritage' as commonly understood from a western standpoint. The allusion to *shan* and *shui* having special cultural meaning in China is a further reference to 'Chinese common knowledge' and the shared heritage that it entails. Thus in Daoism, mountains are *yin*, feminine, and rivers and lakes are *yang*, masculine; and in the teachings of Confucius, mountains are benevolent (bringing rain that flows down to irrigate fields and meadows), while rivers signify wisdom (*Analects of Confucius*, Brooks & Brooks, 1998).

The words of Wu inspired the then Mayor of Guilin, Li Jinzao, to announce a new Master Plan for the regeneration of central Guilin in a speech delivered on 28 November 1998, entitled 'Shaping a Water Vision', 'which greatly stirred the population of the city at that time' (Wang, Zhang, & Zhang, 2010, p. 4). Guilin's mountains and rivers may have been 'the best under Heaven' 1600 years ago, but in 1998, three of the lakes were small, shallow, stagnant malodorous ponds of raw sewage, grey water and solid waste; the fourth was completely filled with wastes. They were no longer joined but separate; all were surrounded by crumbling and decrepit buildings and their original capacity to serve as a continuous body of water for a moat had disappeared many years ago. The nearby rivers were also dumping sites for all kinds of waste, and water pollution levels were among the highest in China. A Ten-Year Plan was initiated, beginning with the relocation of about 10,000 people and slum clearance to create open space around the lakes. A channel was

Figure 2. Guilin and renewal of its 'shan-shui' heritage in the twenty-first century.

excavated to rejoin the lakes and part of the Li River diverted to flow through them, so that the water in the lakes is replaced every 2–7 days. This included upgrading an ancient irrigation channel (8 km) and constructing 4 km of closed pipeline from the river to the lakes. Mulong Lake was completely re-excavated. The other lakes were enlarged and deepened, with 1.5 m of toxic sludge removed from their beds as a key factor in their healthy rehabilitation. More than 22,000 cu.m of daily sewage effluent was diverted to treatment plants 8 km from the lakes. Locks were installed on the lower Peach River to create sufficient depth to increase oxygenation and regeneration of aquatic flora and fauna; and all pollutants and storm water were diverted away from the lakes and rivers (Figure 2). As engineering works progressed, the area around the lakes was beautified with extensive landscaping and open spaces, with about 15 km of parks and paths (no vehicles allowed), and many sites were designed for public use and recreation. Every evening, thousands of residents and tourists alike throng the lakesides. Roads were reconfigured, new roads were built and new bridges were constructed across the lakes. To conserve the ambience of the surrounding karst pinnacles, the mayor introduced a height restriction of eight storeys for central Guilin; no skyscrapers are allowed (all technical details derived from Pei, Zuo, Luan, & Gao, 2013; Wu, 1996c). The lakes were no longer needed as a moat, so they were given a new function befitting of the twenty-first century. a '4-lakes cruise' was established in 2004, and a Peach Blossom River cruise in 2013, and they now cater to 6.5 million tourists per year (3 companies, 225 registered boats). In 2005, Guilin was awarded the 'Most livable City in China' by the National Ministry of Construction, and in 2008 it received the National China Habitat Environment Prize. The Jingjiang Palace complex and the Jingjiang Mausoleums in their restored states are also now tourist destinations visited by several million tourists each year. *Shan* and *shui* have returned to once again capture the *tezhi* (essence) of Guilin city's *Zhou li* urban characteristics, albeit in a modern form.

Conclusions

In this paper, it has been argued that the built heritage of cities in China needs to take into account a city's entirety, and its richness as built heritage cannot be measured in how few or how many ancient buildings actually survive in original, physical form. We suggest that a lack of western-authenticated ancient buildings is not a valid reason to say that China's built heritage has been 'lost', because the entire settlement, whether a city, town or village, will often preserve its ancient heritage to a consistent pattern that has been followed for centuries. European/western observers need the 'markers' (in semiotic terms) of ancient bricks and mortar to 'see' built heritage: without these markers as solid evidence of the fabric of ancient times, there is no built heritage. But we contend that because of culturally determined values in China, the presence or absence of bricks and mortar is not fundamental in the way it is in a western world view, and that Chinese can see this heritage in intangibles because of *Zhonghua wenhua*. Xu (2000, p. 4) makes this point succinctly:

> Consequently how the city in all its varied specific aspects is perceived by the Chinese in history is taken as no less important than what the city physically looks like – the conceptual realm is the important focus. Common features of China's urban heritage are therefore found mainly in areas of attitudes, principles and symbolic functions.

The synthesis of astrology, cosmology, geomancy and numerology accumulated over centuries into a cohesive body of lore, practices and ideas about city building so that around 1000 BC, the Duke of Zhou was able to compile them into the *Zhou Li*, the classical source of city theory that continued as a template for more than 2500 years of Chinese built history. So pervasive has been its influence and application over the centuries that its major principles remain visible in thousands of cities, towns and villages throughout contemporary China, its many manifestations able to be 'read' by millions of Chinese through the vehicle of Chinese common knowledge.

The application of the Duke of Zhou's template for cities produced another characteristic that makes many Chinese cities, towns and villages distinctive from their European counterparts. The principles of *feng shui* tend to dictate the placement of settlements *within* the landscape at the foot of hills or mountains. While rivers and lakes (and moats) were used for defensive purposes, and surrounding hills could form a protective surround, defence was not necessarily the primary determinant of a location. In pre-industrial Europe, the opposite was often the case: because of the paramount need for defence, thousands of cities, towns and villages were placed on top of peaks, preferably those with steep slopes or cliffs so that the landscape contributed to their security from attack – a hilltop site which left them completely exposed to the elements – and from a Chinese perspective not at all in harmony with nature. Under China's unified imperial system, there was far less need for impregnable locations: defensive needs were commonly fulfilled by a perimeter wall with towers that were in many ways a symbol of authority over the population within (as per Foucault's (1982) panoptic power) rather than of enemies without, and relatively rarely was the landscape used for defence as perceived by European city overlords. In this context, Xu (2000, p. 7) notes 'the conceptual and institutional inseparability of the walled city from its status as the regional or administrative centre of the imperial government'. Their positioning on top of steep hills, exposed to all the elements, constitutes bad feng shui and 'harmony' from the Chinese perspective thus played no role in European selection of these sites.

Yet 'harmony' is the paramount objective guiding the panoply of built heritage in China: harmony between Heaven and Earth, harmony between man and Heaven and harmony between man and nature. China's belief system as it evolved over millennia was transformed into a unique building code by the Duke of Zhou and manifested in four major criteria: the selection of sites for cities, towns and villages; their cardinal north–south orientation; their spatial layout and the juxtaposition of key structures within the Holy Field. And it is Chinese common knowledge that provides Chinese with a looking glass, the capacity to interpret and understand this profound heritage inherent in their cities today.

In considering the built heritage of cities and towns, the western emphasis is on the architectural form, the actual solid fabric of individual buildings and monuments and the 'romance of ruins' as Macaulay (1984, p. 2) described it. But generally, for Chinese there is no particular romance in ruins and China has not followed the quixotic practice of European cultures actually building artificial ruins, described by Macaulay (1984, p. 24) thus:

> Producing new Tivolis (amusement gardens), ruined temples and all, proved an immensely charming occupation for estate-owners, and ruins came into their own as objects in a landscape. So began the fashion of building artificial ruins, which raged over Europe through the eighteenth century and well into the nineteenth ...

New ruins, classical Greek, Italian and Gothic, and even Chinese, sprang up in every fashionable gentleman's grounds, in Great Britain, France, Germany, Austria and the Netherlands.

In China the dominant philosophy is that the old is to be replaced – and that has been the pattern for not just hundreds, but several thousands of years. This is consistent with the prevailing Daoist philosophy in which nothing is constant, all things change: Spring replaces winter with new birth, some things changing so slowly that within a lifetime, the human eye cannot perceive the change, for example, a boulder that takes millennia to weather (Lau & Ames, 1998). Buddhism, which arrived in China in the seventh century when the Tang Dynasty was open to philosophies from across the world, has its reincarnations, the old replaced by the new. In general terms, therefore, it is not the 'oldness' of a building that gives it significance, in contrast to the west where something that is 50 or 100 years old is given a special status and described as 'vintage' or 'antique', respectively (although commercially China's elite is now exploiting this western idiosyncrasy as these descriptors increase their value commensurately). In China the old is there to be replaced in due course. A building or monument is viewed in contextual and relational terms, not perceived in isolation, and if it outlives its usefulness, then it is most often replaced, not conserved and preserved and museumized. Thus, perhaps the most famous tower in all China, the Yellow Crane Pagoda in Wuhan, cannot be divorced from the embrace of its historical/social/cultural milieu, its original key military and strategic purpose replaced by a building designed for tourists. This change has not devalued its status: it is seen as a whole in relation to its entire history.

In this context, the restoration of the Jingjiang palace complex buildings in the 1980s underscores the importance attached to the perceived good *feng shui* of the site and is symbolic of endeavours to capture for modern Guilin all factors that could contribute to its prosperity. This does not mean that the Communist Party Government of China adheres to any belief in Daoism as evidenced by Chiang Kai Shek's 1947 restoration of the Chengyun Audience Hall. Nevertheless, many Chinese perceive its reconstruction in terms of the millennia-old tenets of *feng shui* in the same way that twenty-first-century inhabitants of Guilin seek to ensure prosperity for their descendants by co-locating their graves with the ancient royal tombs. In other words, it is the *act* of restoration on the site, not the adherence to any strict notion of western authenticity as determined by UNESCO and ICOMOS, that is significant in the Chinese gaze. And they point to the status of the site as a nationally significant heritage site and its success in generating millions of yuan through tourism as evidence of this process.

In emphasizing this aspect of Chinese-ness, we are not overlooking the fact that the western concept of built heritage also has a strong focus on 'the story' of that place or monument: UNESCO makes interpretation mandatory for its world heritage sites. Ruins (e.g. archaeological sites such as China's Banpo Neolithic villages) may be sufficient in themselves without any restoration or reconstruction to qualify as built heritage in the western sense, but if the built fabric fails the western test of authenticity, then the site would fail to attain heritage status according to UNESCO and ICOMOS guidelines. Ancient battlefield sites or other places that have some claim to fame even where there are no monuments or ruins may attain an iconic heritage status with very detailed interpretation, but they do not represent built heritage. (For a detailed list of ICOMOS-compiled definitions by one of its French conservation architects, LeBlanc, 2011, see www.icomos.org/~fleblanc/documents/terminology/doc_terminology_e.html).

In adopting a position that challenges western hegemony over definitions of built heritage and its authenticity, it is acknowledged that western forms of conservation are increasing in China, and that many Chinese are developing an understanding of the western sense of antiquity/authenticity as they visit such sites. The World Heritage listed ancient towns of Hongcun and Xi-di in Anhui Province are examples. It is thus clear that the two approaches (i.e. western and Chinese) to built heritage can and do exist in parallel: but as noted above (p. 23), it is our contention that the 'Chinese-ness' (Ogden, 1992) of China's urban planning that is evident in cities, towns and villages, embedded in the *Zhou li,* provides a significantly different foundation for a Chinese gaze that does not accord with western practice.

It is axiomatic that perceptions will often be determined by cultural values. Thus our stance is that the Chinese values bound up in *zhonghua wenhua* allow a Chinese gaze to interpret the built heritage of China as 'place-making extending over centuries' that owes little to western definitions of 'built heritage'. In other words, the connotations associated with the term as it relates to cities in China differ markedly between Chinese society and western perspectives, as expressed in such august documents as UNESCO's so-called universal principles of assessment for World Heritage site listing. We therefore suggest that the common western definitions of built heritage need to be put to one side when seeking an understanding of just how profound the built heritage of cities in China is.

In terms of further research, we suggest that ancestral heritage tourism and the practical implications of and management issues for built heritage conservation in China arising from the different western and Chinese paradigms concerning built heritage could constitute topics for other papers.

Disclosure statement

No potential conflict of interest was reported by the authors.

References

Allan, S. (1991). *The shape of the turtle: Myth, art, and cosmos in early China*. Albany: SUNY Press.
Ames, R., & Hall, D. (2003). *Daodejing: 'Making this life significant' a philosophical translation*. New York, NY: Ballantine Books.
Anderson, E., & Anderson, M. (1973). *Mountains and water: Essays on the cultural ecology of South Coastal China*. Taipei: The Chinese Association for Folklore.
Ang, I. (1994). The differential politics of Chineseness. *Southeast Asian Journal of Social Science, 22*(1), 72–79.
Bai, Y. (2003). 'On the early city and the beginning of the state in ancient China.' Bureau of International Cooperation, Hongkong, Macao and Taiwan Academic Affairs Office. *Chinese Academy of Social Sciences*. Retrieved November 10, 2015, from http://www.worldlibrary.org/Articles/AncientChineseurbanplanning=Bai,Yunxiang
Barraclough, G. (1979). *Main trends in history*. New York, NY: Holmes and Meier.
Boorstin, D. J. (1964). *The image: A guide to pseudo-events in America*. New York, NY: Atheneum.
Braudel, F. (1958). L'histoire et les sciences sociales: La longue duree. *Annales: Economies, Societes, Civilisations, 4*, 725–753.
Braunfels, W. (1988). *Urban design in Western Europe: Regime and architecture, 900–1900*. (K. J. Northcott, Trans.). Chicago, IL: University of Chicago Press.
Brooks, E., & Brooks, A. (1998). *The original analects*. New York, NY: Columbia University Press.
Chan, H. (2007). Ming Taizu's problem with his sons: Prince Qin's criminality and early-Ming politics. *Asia Major, 20* (1), 45–103.
Chang, K. (1987). *The archaeology of ancient China*. New Haven, CT: Yale University Press.
Chang, K.-c. [張光直] (1983). *Art, myth, and ritual: The path to political authority in ancient China*. Cambridge, MA: Harvard University Press.
Chang, K.-c., Xu, P., Allan, S., & Lu, L. (Eds.). (2005). *The formation of Chinese civilization: An archaeological perspective, culture & civilization of China*. New Haven, CT: Yale University Press.
Chen, Y. (2010, September 19–23). *Shan-Shui-City: A Chinese spatial planning tradition*. 46th ISOCARP Congress, International Society of City and Regional Planners, Nairobi, Kenya.
Cohen, A. (2012). Brief note: The origin of the yellow emperor era chronology. *Asia Major, 25*(pt. 2), 1–13.
Dai, Y. 戴逸, & Gong, S. 龔書鐸. (Eds.). (2003). *Zhongguo tongshi: xuesheng caitu ban* 中國通史--學生彩圖版 [General history of China] (in Chinese), *1. Shiqian, Xia, Shang, Xizhou* 史前 夏 商 西周 [Prehistory, Xia, Shang, and Western Zhou]. Hong Kong: Zhineng jiaoyu chubanshe 智能教育出版社 [Intelligence Press].
Eitel, E. (1984). *Feng Shui*. Singapore: Graham Brash.
Fan, C. (1175 AD, translated 2010). *Treatises of the supervisor and guardian of the Cinnamon Sea. Completed on the road to Chengdu, 1175*. (J. M. Hargett, Trans.). New York, NY: University of Washington Press.
Fan, W. (1992). Village Feng Shui Principles. In R. Knapp (Ed.), *Chinese landscapes: The village as place* (chap. 2, pp. 35–62). Honolulu: University of Hawaii Press.
Foucault, M. (1982). *The subject and power*. Chicago, IL: University of Chicago Press.
Hammond, A., Adriaanse, A., Rodenburg, E., Bryant, D., & Woodward, R. (1995). *Environmental indicators: A systematic approach to measuring and reporting on environmental policy performance in the context of sustainable development*. Washington, DC: World Resources Institute.

Han, P.-T. (1992). *External forms and internal visions – The story of Chinese landscape design*. (Carl Shen, English Trans.). Taipei: Youth Cultural Enterprise Co.

Hardy, G. (1999). *Worlds of bronze and bamboo: Sima Qian's conquest of history*. New York, NY: Columbia University Press.

He, C. R. (2007a). *Architecture of Xia, Shang, Zhou Dynasties and Spring and Autumn period*. CORE OCW. Retrieved November 2, 2015, from http://www.essential-architecture.com/STYLE/STY-119.htm

He, C. R. (2007b). Comparison of the Gridiron from the pattern in book of diverse crafts and the pattern in Hippodamus. *Architectural Journal, 2*, 65–69.

Hucker, C. (1995). *China's imperial past: An introduction to Chinese history and culture*. Bloomington: Stanford University Press.

Jan, Y. (1981). The change of images: The yellow emperor in Ancient Chinese literature. *Journal of Oriental Studies, 19* (2), 117–137.

Jenner, W. J. F. (1992). *The Tyranny of history. The roots of China's crisis*. London: Penguin.

Ji, X. (2007). *Worshiping the three sage kings and five virtuous emperors – The imperial temple of emperors of successive dynasties in Beijing*. Beijing: Foreign Language Press.

Knapp, R. (Ed.). (1992). *Chinese landscapes: The village as place*. Honolulu: University of Hawaii Press.

Kong, X. (1988). Landscape scenic environment design. In W. H. Ding, Y. M. Xu, & Y. X. Lin (Eds.), *The study of natural scenery and heritage sites* (pp. 451–474). Shanghai: Tongji University Press.

Lau, D. C., & Ames, R. (1998). *Yuan Dao: Tracing Dao to its source*. New York, NY: The Ballantine Publishing Group.

LeBlanc, F. (2011). *ICOMOS: Heritage conservation terminology: Definition of terms*. Retrieved September 1, 2015, from www.icomos.org/~fleblanc/documents/terminology/doc_terminology_e.html

Li, F. M. S. (2006). *Chinese common knowledge, tourism and natural landscapes*. Gazing on 別有天地, 'Bie you tian di', 'An Altogether Different World'. PhD thesis, Murdoch University, Western Australia.

Li, F. M. S., & Sofield, T. (2008). Huangshan – Cultural gazes. In C. Ryan & H. Gu (Eds.), *Tourism in China, chapter nine* (pp. 168–180). London: Elsevier.

Li, L. (2004). *The Chinese neolithic: Trajectories to early states*. London: Cambridge University Press.

Li, L., & Chen, X. (2012). *The archaeology of China: From the Late Paleolithic to the early Bronze Age (Cambridge World Archaeology Series)*. Cambridge: Cambridge University Press.

Li, Z. (1994). *An overview of Chinese culture*. Beijing: Hua Wen Press.

Macaulay, R. (1984). *Pleasure of ruins*. London: Thames and Hudson.

MacCannell, D. (1976). *The tourist: A new theory of the leisure class*. New York, NY: Schocken Books.

Montgomery, L. (2014, July 28). The Duke of Zhou – The China History Podcast, presented by Laszlo Montgomery.

Morton, W. S., & Lewis, C. M. (2005). *China: Its history and culture*. New York, NY: McGraw-Hill.

Nelson, C. M. (1988). Urban planning in pre-industrial China. *US-China Review, XII*(2), 17–21.

Ogden, S. (1992). *China's unresolved issues. Politics, development and culture*. Englewood Cliffs, NJ: Prentice Hall.

Pei, Y., Zuo, H., Luan, Z., & Gao, S. (2013). Rehabilitation and improvement of Guilin urban water environment: Function-oriented management. *Journal of Environmental Sciences, 25*(7), 1477–1482.

Schinz, A. (1996). *The magic square: Cities in ancient China*. Berlin & Frankfurt: Edition Axel Menges.

Schwartz, B. (1985). *The world of thought in ancient China*. Cambridge, MA: Harvard University Press.

Sima, Qian (1961). Records of the Grand Historian (Shiji 史記, c. 100 BC), Chapter 1, 'Wudi benji' 五帝本紀 ['Basic Annals of the Five Emperors']. (B. Watson, Trans.). New York, NY: Columbia University Press.

Sofield, T. H. B., & Li, F. M. S. (1998a). China. Tourism development and cultural policies. *Annals of Tourism Research, 25*(2), 323–353.

Sofield, T. H. B., & Li, F. M. S. (1998b). Historical methodology and sustainability: An 800-year-old festival from China. *Journal of Sustainable Tourism, 6*(4), 267–292.

Towner, J., & Wall, G. (1991). History and tourism. *Annals of Tourism Research, 18* (1), 71–84.

UNESCO. (2015). *Operational guidelines for the implementation of the world heritage convention*. Paris: UNESCO World Heritage Centre.

Wang, J., Zhang, G., & Zhang, Z. (2010, September 19–23). *The water vision for a water city: A case study on the 'two rivers and four lakes' spatial planning project in Guilin, China*. 46th ISOCARP Congress, International Society of City and Regional Planners, Nairobi, Kenya.

Wang, Z. (1997). *Zhongguo wenhua shi* 中國文化史 ['Chinese cultural history'] (in Chinese). Wunan: Wunan tushu chuban gufen youxian gongsi 五南圖書出版股份有限公司 [Tushu Publishing House].

Watson, B. (1961). *Records of the grand historian of China*. (English Transl.). New York, NY: Columbia University Press.

Wen, Y. (2005). *Into the new three Gorges: Tourism guidebook to the three gorges and surrounding areas*. Beijing: Sinomaps Press.

Williams, M., & Webb, R. (1994). Rural landscapes. In M. Williams (Ed.), *The Green Dragon: Hong Kong's living environment* (pp. 113–127). Hong Kong: Green Dragon.

Windridge, C., & Fong, C. K. (1999). *Tong Sing: The Chinese book of wisdom based on the ancient Chinese Almanac*. London: Greenwich Editions.

Wu, L. (1987). *Guilin, shan shui city*. Guilin: GLCPB [Guilin City Planning Bureau].

Wu, L. (1996a). Architecture culture, city pattern and protection measures of Guilin city. In Wu (Ed.), *Urban research papers of Wu Liangyong (1986–1995): Meeting the new era* (pp. 238–336). Beijing: China Architecture & Building Press.

Wu, L. (1996b). Reasoning on Shan-Shui City. In Wu (Ed.), *Urban research papers of Wu Liangyong (1986–1995): Meeting the new era* (pp. 337–334). Beijing: China Architecture & Building Press.

Wu, L. (1996c). *Urban research papers of Wu Liangyong (1986–1995): Meeting the new era*. Beijing: China Architecture & Building Press.

Wu, L. (2001). *Introduction to sciences of human settlements*. Beijing: China Architecture & Building Press.

Xu, H., Cui, Q., Sofield, T. H. B., & Li, F. M. S. (2014). Attaining harmony: Understanding the relationship between ecotourism and protected areas in China. *Journal of Sustainable Tourism, 22*(8), 1131–1150.

Xu, Y. (2000). *The Chinese city in space and time: The development of urban form in Suzhou*. Tahiti: University of Hawaii Press.

Yan, L. (Ed.). (1965). *Wuqiubeizhai Laozi jicheng, xubian* [A Laozi compendium from the studio of not seeking completeness]. Taipei: Yiwen yinshuguan [Yiwen Publishing House].

Yu, X., & Xu, H. (2016). Ancient poetry in contemporary Chinese tourism. *Journal of Tourism Management, 54*, 393–403.

Zhu, Y., & Wang, H. (Eds.). (1996). *Places of historical and cultural interest in China*. (L. Sun & Y. Wu, Trans.). Shanghai: Shanghai Foreign Language Education Press.

Suzhou's water grid as urban heritage and tourism resource: an urban morphology approach to a Chinese city

Werner Breitung and Jing Lu

ABSTRACT

Historically, many cities were served by water transport as an important mode of circulation. Suzhou in China is a case in point. Its orthogonally designed water-based grid was connected to the Grand Canal and the Tai Lake. Merchants and travellers entering into Suzhou would go through city gates serving both waterborne and road traffic. The water grid once played an important role for commercial activities and social interactions in the city, but over time, more and more canals were filled to pave roads and build houses. The transport system has by now almost entirely switched to the street grid. Drawing on historical maps, chronicles, artwork and existing studies, this paper employs urban morphology as a method to understand the significance of waterways for the identity of Suzhou. The authors argue that the waterways have a high heritage value, but lack practical functions. Tourism development is then presented as a chance to reactivate the water grid for heritage conservation, transport and the enhancement of tourist experiences. The paper supports this argument based on concrete findings, and it critically reflects on the meaning of heritage and discusses the appropriateness of the urban morphology approach for heritage research.

Introduction

Suzhou, located near the historical Grand Canal in Jiangsu Province, is one of the Chinese cities with a relatively well-preserved old town. Dubbed as the 'Venice of the East' by Marco Polo, it is famous for its dual grid of streets and canals. Historically, water transport was as important in this city as roadside transport. However, the canals have been deteriorating and lost most of their functions. They are not even extensively used for tourism purposes.

This paper now argues that the water grid should be reactivated as a prime tourism resource to achieve several goals: enhance the attractiveness of Suzhou as a tourist destination, relieve some of the road-level traffic congestion by extending the circulation of tourists to the water level, and infuse new functions into the canal system in order to revive this outstanding urban heritage. However, if this revival is to serve the conservation and enhancement of heritage, a deep understanding of the water grid as an inseparable part of the whole urban landscape is first needed, including

- Its development path and the emotional value of the water grid for local people.
- The multi-scalar character of the urban landscape as a system.
- The morphological diversity of landscape elements and spatial patterns.
- The connections of the waterways to other components of the urban landscape.

An urban morphology analysis helps to identify the development principles of Suzhou's historical urban landscape, to reveal the role of the water grid for this landscape and to discuss implications for heritage protection and tourism development. This is valuable beyond the individual case, because waterways are important features in the historical development and urban landscape of many cities. Suzhou stands for a larger group of water towns, and even has relevance beyond this specific urban type.

Furthermore, we need to test the methodology. Whitehand and Gu (2010) recommend the urban morphology approach when urban landscapes as a whole, as opposed to individual buildings or monuments, shall become objects of heritage conservation, and because the historical time dimension is crucial for the concept of heritage. Both is the case here, but we still question whether the urban morphology-based methodology relies on a too formal, too physical concept of heritage.

Conceptual framework and methodology

Urban morphology

Urban morphology as an interdisciplinary field of study has expanded beyond geography, into the domains of architecture, planning, sociology, archaeology and so on. Given the different perspectives of these disciplines, the term is applied to different types of investigation (Whitehand, 2001), all focusing on the physical form of urban areas. The International Seminar on Urban Form (ISUF) defines urban morphology as 'the study of the city as human habitat which analyses a city's evolution from its formative years to its subsequent transformations, identifying and dissecting its various components' (Moudon, 1997).

There are three major schools of urban morphology: M.R.G. Conzen of German–British origin, Muratori of Italian origin and Versailles of French origin (Moudon, 1997; Whitehand, 2001). Each school has its own distinct purpose of urban morphological analysis that yields different kinds of theories. The Conzenian School studies urban form for descriptive and explanatory purposes, to develop theories of how cities are built and why. As they primarily study the dynamic state of the city and the pervasive relationship between its elements, many urban morphologists also distinguish this approach as 'urban morphogenesis' (Whitehand, Gu, Whitehand & Zhang, 2011). The Muratorian School in contrast is more prescriptive, pursuing theories of how cities should be built, and the design-oriented French School critiques differences and similarities between normative theories and actual urban form (Moudon, 1997).

The morphological research across schools is based on three fundamental components: form, scale and time (Moudon, 1997). Urban form is defined by buildings and open spaces, by plots or lots, and the grid of streets. It can be analysed at different geographical scales; and it can only be understood historically, since the elements of which it is composed undergo continuous transformation and replacement. Although the focus of Conzen's theory is clearly on the urban form, he also considered its utilisation and functions, and he interpreted urban landscapes as an 'objectivation of the spirit' of the societies that created them (Whitehand et al., 2011, p. 172). His interest thus went beyond the purely physical fabric.

Also across different schools, urban morphology identifies what Conzen called plan units (Moudon, 1997). They are groups of buildings, open spaces, lots and streets, which form a cohesive whole, either because they were built at the same time or within the same constraints, or because they underwent a common process of transformation (Moudon, 1997; Whitehand, 2001, 2009; Whitehand & Gu, 2007; Whitehand et al., 2011). Surprisingly, urban waterways are not explicitly mentioned, and although of key importance for urban development as routes of transport, sources of water, and arenas for trade, social interaction and cultural articulation, they are not prominently covered in traditional urban morphology analyses. They have typically been regarded as merely the background on which urban patterns unfolded, and only in recent decades have urban morphologists begun to pay attention to waterways themselves (Hohensinner et al., 2013; Mauch & Zeller,

2008; Smith, 1998). In China, Kelly and Chen (2013) studied the historical roles of urban rivers, which they termed as 'hydraulic civilisation', and related them to the principles of *fengshui*.

Application in Chinese cities

The main application of urban morphology research is the identification of conservation priorities and strategies, especially for larger urban conservation areas (Whitehand & Gu, 2010). This appears suitable, because it links the physical environment with historical meanings and an understanding of scale. Authors have also established connections between urban morphology and tourism, as tourism increasingly depends on the distinctiveness of places and the attraction of different urban environments (Gospodini, 2001).

In China, urban planning research and practice tend to emphasise physical planning and therefore have a great interest in urban form (Ji & Zhuang, 2014; Liu, Yang & Feng, 2012), but the existing theoretical research on how Chinese cities are built (Chen, 2002, 2003, 2006; Xu, 2000) is only weakly connected to urban conservation practice, which mainly focuses on individual monuments rather than urban landscapes. This leads to vague criteria for conservation priorities and jeopardises the credibility of conservation planning. There have already been attempts to narrow this gap with morphogenetic analyses in Beijing and Guangzhou (Whitehand & Gu, 2007; Whitehand et al., 2011). We now add the category of water cities and especially Suzhou to the debate.

Suzhou is known as a heritage-rich city. Mote (1973) studied its urban evolution and was amazed at the continuity of its urban form. Xu (2000) and Chen (2002, 2003) both have also carefully examined the morphological evolution of Suzhou in the pre-industrial era, Chen (2006) even to the end of the twentieth century. Both touch upon the development of the water grid as one of the many components of Suzhou's urban form, but their work remains at a descriptive stage. Gu (2006, 2008) crafted the term 'Suzhou historical water block' as the 'urban unit' in her analysis but she does not provide thorough investigations on the relationship between the canals and other components of urban form. She especially does not go beyond the two-dimensional view of the ground plan. In short, some urban morphological research foundations have been laid, but a thorough investigation of its water grid as one of the most important aspects of Suzhou's historical identity is still missing, especially across different spatial scales and stretching from its formative years to today.

Concepts of heritage

At this point, we need to reflect a bit on the notion of heritage itself. Graham (2002) defines heritage as a form of knowledge. According to him, heritage is more about meanings than physical artefacts; and the meanings are created in the present, not in the past. Furthermore, the meanings give value to the artefacts, not the other way round (Graham, 2002). Cultural heritage may be worth conserving because of its artistic value, symbolic value or significance for the collective memory of some people. Ashworth (1998) adopts a similar view when he describes the conserved city as a 'text' that can be interpreted. He portrays conservation as a purposeful act to convey symbolic messages, for example, to commemorate certain events, legitimise the nation state or local identities, or uphold the values of a certain time period. Among the questions he asks, two are particularly important for decisions on conservation. One is what message shall be conveyed, and the other to whom this message is addressed. To the latter, there are two obvious answers: tourists and local people. However, these two groups attach different meanings to heritage and base their understanding of it on different sets of experiences. Given that it is the meaning that matters, the same urban landscape is not necessarily the same for different people.

The answers to the question what should be conserved depend on values, purposes, functions and also existing conditions. As the meanings are ascribed in the present, the heritage value depends on the choices heritage conservation makes. Three such choices concern time, ownership and scale. Which period is most worthy for conservation? Whose heritage shall be conserved? And do we talk about national, regional or local heritage? These questions need to be answered later in this paper. Especially when we chose the morphological approach, we need to remind ourselves that it is not the physical form as such that creates a certain heritage value, but the human perception of the built environment and collective memories.

Since perceptions and memories change as well as the physical form, we need to apply a dynamic view to the concept of heritage. The meanings attached to pieces of urban fabric develop over time in close connection to their functions. A key point we want to make is that it is important to consider functions together with the objects of conservation and view heritage as 'living' or 'lived-in' space. The heritage value for both residents and visitors emerges through interaction with space and people, through the perspectives from which we perceive urban landscape and from its usage (be it washing clothes at the canal or enjoying a ride in a sightseeing boat).

Methods and approach of this paper

The main part of the paper (Sections 3 and 4) is a morphological analysis of the layout and evolution of the Suzhou water grid. It focuses on the core principles of time, form and scale that are shared by all urban morphology schools. Given that the waterways are the morphological elements most resistant to change, Conzen's 'ground plan' analysis is particularly suitable in this case. The primary components usually analysed in the 'ground plan' are street system, plot pattern, building form and function (Whitehand et al., 2011). We add urban waterways next to streets as an additional linear component.

To trace the historical development of the urban landscape, all the available historical maps were analysed regarding both road and water grid. We overlaid maps of different periods to capture the time dynamics of the ground plan and of landscape elements such as bridges and street profiles. Additionally, historical written records and well-known artistic and literary material, including historical novels, poems and paintings, have been consulted. This mix of sources helps to understand the functions of urban features and portray both the urban landscape at the time and its representation nowadays in people's minds. Both are relevant for the assessment of heritage value.

Our analysis is multi-scalar. We first analyse the overall grid structure (macro scale). This is presented in a chronological and morphogenetic way. After that, the 'historical water block' as the most suitable 'plan unit' (meso scale) is established and described, and finally details are studied at micro scale. These are the profiles of streets and canals and especially elements linking land and waterways with each other (piers, bridges, riverbanks).

Finally, possible implications for heritage conservation and tourism development are presented in Sections 5 and 6. These two sections are more prescriptive.

Growth and decline of the Suzhou water grid

The formation of the double grid

Suzhou located in the lower Yangzi River Plain, an alluvial land with an average elevation of about 3–4 m above sea level, which is characterised by waters, fertile soils and rich natural resources. Even to date, there are over 10,000 watercourses within the administrative boundary of Suzhou (Zhai, 2007). The first inner-urban canals were excavated by the founders of the Wu Kingdom in 514 BC for purposes of fortification, agriculture, transport and water supply (Zhai, 2007). At that time, the city was called *Helu Dacheng*. It had eight gates in its outer wall and at least two in its inner enclosure, each of them serving road and water traffic (Wu, 1985; Zhao, 1999). The same sources also imply the existence at that time of multiple rivers within the city walls, although only one is specified as 40 m wide, and stretching from Ping Gate in the north to She Gate in the south.

Four north–south and five east–west canals were dredged in Suzhou after Lord Chunshen of the Chu Kingdom made it the capital of his fiefdom in 248 BC (Zhang, 1985), and at least from the third century onwards, the city's current water and road systems have begun to take shape,[1] The completion of the Grand Canal connecting the political centre in Beijing and the economic centre at the Yangzi River in 610 AD (Dong, 1993) made Suzhou the hub of water transport in eastern China and laid the economic foundation for a population boom in Tang Dynasty (Xu, 2000). The overall form of Suzhou became a slightly irregular rectangle of around 15 km². It was divided into 60 residential wards, which were very probably enclosed by walls and each divided internally by about five alleys. A well-developed network of street and canals with over 300 bridges (Lu, 1986) has been formed between the early Tang and late Northern Song Dynasties, in coordination with residential wards, walled market quarters, government offices and other institutions. Its basic structure was determined by three east–west and four north–south arteries.

The canals multiplied to an extent that they became a constant theme in poems depicting the city. In his famous Song Dynasty poem *Songren You Wu*, Du Xunhe described the scenery of the city in the ninth century:[2]

Reaching Gusu [i.e. Suzhou] you will see
People's houses pillowed on the rivers,
Within the old palatial area little land is vacant,
Over the rivers small bridges are many.
Water chestnut fruits and lotus roots are sold in late evening markets,
And spring boats are loaded with luxurious silken fabrics.
In the distance I know that wakeful under the moon,
Fishermen's songs will accompany homesickness.

This poem is so popular that even nowadays people are imprinted with its image of Suzhou being composed of canals, bridges and houses 'pillowed on the water'.

Substantial change came during the Northern Song period (960–1126) with the disappearance of the enclosed marketplace and walled ward system and the emergence of a much freer street plan in which trade and commerce could be conducted anywhere in the city and its suburbs.

The earliest known map of Suzhou, the carved-in-stone *Pingjiang Tu* from 1229 (Qian, 1959), shows watercourses running through the dual gates of Suzhou to connect the landscape outside to the walled city. Though mostly man-made, the inner-urban waterways of Suzhou were adapted to the natural landscape of waters and rivers. They brought the dominant form of circulation of the villages and towns, fields and waters of this landscape into the urban context and thereby supported a close economic and cultural connection between the city and the countryside.

Pingjiang Tu indicated an equal circulation importance of water and road grid. The city had two circles of moats inside and outside the city wall. The inner walled enclosure and moat protected the palace of the Wu kings. The water and road double grid was most elaborated in the densely populated city centre to the north of it, but in the northern and southern parts, the walled city still contained farms and waterways flowing in more natural patterns. Back then, the inner waterways and moats served not only for circulation, fortification and water supply, but also for agricultural irrigation.

Stable and densifying period (1229–1639)

It is recorded that almost every 200 years, Suzhou has completely burnt down due to wars or invasions, and each time, the city was reconstructed at the exact location (Zhai, 2007). While most architectural structures were made of wood, the water grid was a very important factor perpetuating the urban form of Suzhou over time. For example, during the invasion by the northern Kingdom of Jin in 1130, all buildings except for a few temples within the city walls burned down (Fan, 1999; Xu, 2000). However, according to *Wudiji* (Lu, 1986), the existing canal network largely survived.

In the early Yuan Dynasty (thirteenth century), Marco Polo referred to the same urban elements as Du Xunhe 400 years earlier, when he called Suzhou the 'Oriental Venice' and described the many canals and bridges (Mote, 1973). His was perhaps the earliest image of Suzhou that has reached Europe and the rest of the outside world.

N

0   200   600   1200m

Legend

——— Canals presented on 1229 Map   ·········· Canals emerged on 1639 Map

░ Streets   ▭ Bridges

Map 1. Water and street grids of Suzhou in 1229 and canals added until 1639. Sources: Adapted from Qian (1959) for Pingjiang map of 1229 and Xu (2000) for Wuzhong Shuili Quanshu map of 1639.

The layout of the city canals in the late Ming Dynasty was almost identical to the one in 1229, except that some canals, especially in the northeast and, to a lesser degree, in the southwest quarters, have been linked up (Map 1). In the 1639 map shown in Zhang (1987), based on an official survey conducted from 1567 to 1619, the total length of the canals was between 87 and 92 km – longer than the total length of the street grid in Suzhou at that time (Chen, 2002), and longer than documented on any other map of Suzhou throughout history. The total canal length in the *Pingjiang Tu* of 1229 was about 82 km, equal to 78% of the total length of the streets at that time (Yu, 1980).

Map 2. Water and street grids of Suzhou in 2015 and canals lost since 1748. Sources: Adapted from Xu (2000) for Suzhou Fu Zhi map of 1748 and from Google Maps (2015).

Decline of branch waterways (1639–1745)

Suzhou rose to prominence as a regional metropolis from the early sixteenth century and became one of the most populated cities worldwide between the seventeenth century and eighteenth century when its population peaked at 1.3 million (Zhai, 2007). The physical impact of the economic growth on the watercourses may not have been felt until the second half of the seventeenth century, when encroachment by houses and other structures on the canals became a serious problem. Urban growth in the first half of the eighteenth century also led to the deterioration of canal quality. Five instances of full-scale canal dredging were recorded mostly within a period of 38 years in the early eighteenth century (Xu, 2000).

A map published in the official government records of Qing Dynasty (*Suzhou Fu Zhi*) in 1748 (Xu, 2000) showed a dramatic loss of over a quarter of the inner-urban canals after this period, as can be seen when comparing the 1639 grid in Map 1 with the 1748 grid in Map 2. The damage to certain sections must have been gradual from the mid-seventeenth century or somewhat later. It concerned mostly small branch canals, not yet the major arterial waterways. Apart from a few canals in the northeast corner, it was the business area close to Chang Gate in the northwest, and the adjacent western area with family-based textile industries that experienced a significant loss of canals. These areas had been densely populated from the Tang Dynasty onwards, and pressures on them must have increased dramatically since the mid-seventeenth century. While the steady decay of the branch canals continued into the second half of the eighteenth century, the arterial canals still played a role to complement roadside circulation.

Decline of arterial waterways (1745–1986, and after)

Starting from the Opium War in 1840, Shanghai rose as the main trading port, and Suzhou gradually lost its status (Chen, 2003). In 1860, the Taiping Rebellion brought war fire to Suzhou and the once prosperous area around the Grand Canal. In the 1920s, roads and railways had assumed the role of connecting Suzhou to the surrounding county cities and to Shanghai. Ring roads were built, a new gate opened and others expanded to accommodate the car traffic into the inner city (Xu, 1986). In the 1960s, several hundred thousand workers were involved in levelling 12 canals, which were not connected well to the remaining water grid (Suzhou Chronicles Committee, 1995). After 1969, some of the canals were turned into air defence fortifications and parts of a wastewater system. A total of 23 rivers or canals of together 16 km were lost since 1949 (Suzhou Chronicles Committee, 1995), leaving a network of only 35–36 km (Map 2). With the advancement of road circulation, the canals were increasingly viewed as useless (Chen, 2003). The 1927 urban plan of Suzhou considered only the moat as a useful part of the water system, while the inner waterways became dumping sites. The plan suggested levelling up branches of the water grid to gain room for roads and ensure a cleaner urban environment (Lu, 1989). By then, even the arterial canals lost their significance, and the inner moat and north–south arterial canals in the most densely populated northwest of the city disappeared. The double grid was almost gone. A total of 110 bridges were removed since 1949, and many of the remaining 179 bridges were converted to level bridges for road traffic (Zhai, 2007).

During this process, the functions of the canals were reduced to a minimum. With the establishment of heavy industries after the 1950s, the environmental quality of the canals continued to degrade. Today, neither the inner-urban waterways nor water from wells can be used as source of drinking water anymore. But, some daily uses of the canals can still be seen from historical photos and records. Until the 1970s, boats from Xu River and Tai Lake sailed into the city to supply the urban dwellers with drinking water, the canals were used for laundry, and waterborne tours for locals and tourists operated on the moat and some canals. At the moat, piers for long-distance ships were established. People could distinguish water-trading boats from grocery boats, passenger boats and tourist boats (Zhai, 2007). They used to chat, play chess and cool down under the trees along the canals or at bridges. The canals were still a good part of their life.

In the early 1980s, heritage preservation and environmental upgrading started to be considered in the historical downtown (Whitehand et al., 2011). The pattern of three north–south and three east–west canals was restored (Huang, 1986), and no further decrease in canal numbers occurred afterwards. However, increased industrial pollution, especially from upstream areas in the northwest of Suzhou, further degraded the inner-urban canals, and many road expansions and urban renewal projects have fundamentally transformed the image and lifestyle of Suzhou. This change was less about the network as such, but the demolition of individual blocks and the alteration of small-scale settings and proportions of the urban space defined by canals, streets and buildings. These changes were by no means less severe in their impact on the morphological identity of Suzhou than previously the filling of the canals.

Detailed urban morphology

To understand the morphological characteristics of Suzhou, we need to analyse the city's plan units and the spatial relationships between their components. The main components in this case are the streets, the canals and the buildings (in addition to open spaces, trees, etc.). We have analysed the relative constellation patterns of these three main elements. Particular attention needs then to be paid to those smaller elements that link streets and watercourses spatially to each other – the piers, banks and bridges.

The 'historical water block' and its main components

When we take a closer look at the 1229 map (Map 1), we find many rectangular-shaped, east–west-oriented blocks. Their shape matches the rectangular residential wards in the Tang Dynasty, and reflects the preference for north–south-oriented houses for better sunlight and *fengshui*. The rows of houses preferably extend from east to west, and most branch canals follow their direction. Much less canals are north–south oriented. They are mostly larger arterial canals built to ensure connectivity. It is ultimately the traditional orientation of the houses that determines the layout of the branch canals and by extension of the whole grid.

The Chinese term for 'block' is *jie xiang*. In this term, *jie* means streets and *xiang* stands for waterways (Gu, 2006). This means, the concept of 'block' inherently contains both. Despite their similar and sometimes competing functions, the canals and streets both evolved along each other. Therefore, we refer to the urban waterways when we examine the 'plan unit' of Suzhou, which is what Gu (2006) calls the 'historical water block'. A historical water block is bounded by streets in the north and south, and by arterial waterways at the east and west ends (Whitehand et al., 2011). Within the block, land is mostly used residentially and sub-divided by parallel alleys and canals.

When we zoom further into Map 1 and analyse the relative constellations of the three main components, we find four different patterns of canals, streets and houses. In general, there are front-facing and rear-facing canal–alley patterns (Figure 1(a) (c)). In front-facing patterns, an alley runs between a canal and the front of the houses, either on one side or on both sides of the canal. In rear-facing patterns, the row of houses lies between the canal and the alley, normally with entrances from both sides. This, again, can be on one side or both sides of the canal. In the latter case, there is no street access to the canal (Ji & Zhuang, 2014; Whitehand & Gu, 2007). Houses facing to the front were mostly home to officials and scholars. The front door oriented to the alley and the back door to the canal, and the house took up the entire land in between. Rear-facing houses with the canal as primary access were mostly home to ordinary people and occupied smaller lots. A particular form of a rear-facing house lies across the canal with a covered bridge connecting the two parts of it (Zhai, 2007). We can find that the canal–alley patterns at the arterial canals in both north–south and east–west directions are mostly front facing, while those at the branch canals are mostly rear facing.

All the different patterns of streets, canals and houses demonstrate a central role of the canals in the urban form of historical Suzhou. At least in the pre-industrial era, they served as an alternative circulation system and as public social space (Ji & Zhuang, 2014). The poem *Songren You Wu* implies that waterborne transport was a major way of circulation and also served the exchange of goods. Given the fact that at least during Tang Dynasty ordinary citizens were only allowed to

a. Historical front-facing canal-alley pattern - both sides

b. Historical front-facing canal-alley pattern - one side

c. Historical rear-facing canal-alley pattern

d. Expanding the streets by levelling the canals

e. Expanding the streets by setting back the buildings

f. Expanding the streets by setting back the buildings

Figure 1. Historical and recent canal–alley patterns. Source: Adapted from Ji and Zhuang (2014).

build their entrances towards the canals, not to the streets, a lot of commercial activities took place on the boats. Already in the 820s, Bai Juyi had written in another famous poem *Deng Changmen Xian-wang* that 'by the door of every house are moored sailing boats'.[3] Paintings such as *Gusu Fanhua Tu* (1751) show many merchant boats travelling or anchoring on the rivers and canals, and houses and shops orienting to the canals with commercial activities taking place at both canals (on the boats) and streets.

The linking elements: piers, banks and bridges

It has become clear that streets, canals and houses form a closely interwoven spatial system. For both the functioning of the system and the emotional attachment of the people, the interconnectivity within the system is crucial. While the canals have lost most of their functions, they are also increasingly disconnected from circulation and daily life. This has severed the links between the streets, canals and buildings and affected the canals' emotional value for the residents and the heritage value for the city. Any heritage conservation strategy should therefore concentrate on reconnecting the waterways with the rest of the system. Functionally, tourism can play a role in this, as it can make good use of the waterways. Morphologically, special attention must be paid to the elements forming the links between the two grids – in particular, the stone stepped piers reaching from the houses and streets to the water and the numerous bridges.

The stone stepped piers were central points for people to collect water, wash laundry, board boats, purchase goods and socialise with neighbours and merchants. As small but vital elements, they gave physical and visual access to the canals. Three different styles of piers stretching from houses adjacent to canals can still be seen. Some are hidden between the houses without reaching into the profile of the canal; some are attached alongside the façades parallel to the canal and some stretch out orthogonally into the canal. The obvious difference in privacy and visibility between the three styles affects their possible roles for locals and tourists. A hidden pier can protect residents from the tourist gaze, whereas a pier stretching into the canal provides excellent photo opportunities. However, the number and quality of piers have been declining. Especially, the full access to in-house water supply and the ban on wastewater dumping led to the abandoning of piers. When river banks were transformed from natural to hard banks for flood prevention (Zhai, 2007), this has further separated the canals from citizens or tourists. Heritage and tourism planning need to pay attention to the linking elements and recognise their role as inviting gestures for the appreciation and usage of the water grid.

Bridges can be viewed as separating canals and alleys, but they are actually also connecting elements. By providing visual connection, they unify urban space and serve as landmarks and meeting points. Trade has previously been conducted on them or from boats to bridges, and after the gradual collapse of the residential ward system in the Song Dynasty, people even referred to bridge names as their home address (Xu, 2000). According to *Wujun Zhi* (Fan, 1999), there were 395 bridges in the Northern Song period. The *Pingjiang Tu* of 1229 (Qian, 1959) shows 314 bridges, most of which were still shown on the 1639 map of *Gusu Cheng Tu* (Zhang, 2012). For the convenience of waterborne traffic, the majority of these bridges were shaped as high arches. All the poems describe them in very positive tones, and consider them as distinguished landmarks and appreciated features of Suzhou. From the above-mentioned painting of *Gusu Fanhua Tu* (1751), a few varieties of bridges could be recognised: with one arch, multiple arches and rectangular hollows. Bridges built since the seventeenth century are mostly level bridges for the smooth flow of road traffic. This illustrates that the street grid had by then already trumped the water grid in terms of transport function. Today, especially the remaining arched bridges have mainly a symbolic value, serving to the tourist gaze as landmarks and backdrops for photographs. Due to the considerable height difference between the water level, the bridge top and the street level, they also provide enhanced options for urban landscape appreciation and photography.

Proportions

For the subjective perception of the urban landscape, scale and proportions of the built environment are crucial factors. Yu (1980) speculated in his work on the *Pingjiang Tu* that the canals were probably no less than 10 m wide and 3–5 m deep. Today, the typical width of an arterial canal in Suzhou's old town is 6–12 m (Zhai, 2007), and 3–6 m for a branch canal. A typical street is 6 m wide and an alley 3–4 m (Whitehand & Gu, 2007). The streets and canals are not straight lines. They have slight turns and tend to narrow down or open up somewhat unexpectedly (Xiang & Gu, 2000). This is related to a varying enclosure rate, the proportion of building heights to street widths. If the width equals to the height, it causes a comfortable feeling of enclosure. If the width is smaller than the height (enclosure rate >1), it may make people feel uncomfortable. If the width is much more than one and a half times the height (enclosure rate <0.6), the feeling of enclosure will fade away. Due to the canals, the enclosure rates in Suzhou range from 0.5 to 2.5 (Ji & Zhuang, 2014; Whitehand & Gu, 2007). The constant variation of the enclosure rate within the comfort limits creates a pleasant rhythm, which makes the streets, alleys and canals functional and interesting. Along with the differentiation of styles of building façades along the canals, the traditional scale and enclosure rate patterns help to ensure a varied sense of place.

However, due to expanding streets, the pleasant human scale and enclosure rate of canals and streets are no longer sustained (Figure 1(d)–(f)). The change can be illustrated by comparing Pingjiang River and Ganjiang River. The preserved Pingjiang River is still at the original enclosure rate. Nearby Ganjiang River, although of about the same width, lies now sandwiched between the lanes of a wide road. The enclosure rate has changed to about one-fourth of the original, to a degree that people will no longer experience any sense of enclosure. Pedestrians or drivers hardly notice the Ganjiang River. It now looks only like a planted medial strip of a dual carriageway. Such changes happened so fast that only within a generation, a great sense of loss was experienced by locals and visitors (Suzhou Chronicles Committee, 1997, 2001). A group of experts mentioned in the mid-1990s that even then, they could not recognise Suzhou compared to when they visited in the early 1980s (Suzhou Chronicles Committee, 2001).

From the relation between canals and other urban morphological components, we can better understand the diversity of urban form. For example, the different patterns of alignment of canals, streets and buildings indicate a diverse range of historical layers. Those canals with a pleasant human scale and enclosure rate have existed since the formative year of Suzhou, while those providing little sense of enclosure are mostly transformed within the last generation. And among the historical canal patterns, whether the pattern of enclosure or human scale is made up of arterial canals or branch canals or whether the pattern is front facing or rear facing also makes a difference. The historical backgrounds are different, and the diverse styles of bridges, piers and banks are collage pieces that reveal the transformation of urban form over time, the different functions and the varying significance of the canals. The combinations of these elements paint a fascinating and highly varied image. The preservation of historically authentic diversity should therefore be one of the imperatives of heritage conservation.

Implications for heritage conservation

Referring back to Ashworth (1998), we first have to state that tourists and local residents form their views on urban space in different ways. The tourists' view of the city is influenced by pre-conceptions from literature, guidebooks, media and art. These may not be accurate, but they have a great impact on the place image. As imprinted by notions such as 'houses pillowed on the river' or 'Oriental Venice', tourists tend to have a vague image of the Suzhou several hundred years ago. They interpret the actual touristic experience through the lens of this artistic imaginary, and when their experience contradicts the pre-existing image, a 'lack of local identity' is conceived. Local residents, however, form their perception of place identity from daily encounters with the city through their lifetime. The significant changes experienced within one generation lead to a feeling of loss, affecting their sense of history and sense of place in Suzhou. It may be small features such as colours, smells or building materials, which evoke memories of many people and symbolise place identities, community or certain periods of their lives to them. In Suzhou, many such memories are related to water, and the fading away of the water grid has affected the collective memory of the city.

This leads to Ashworth's next question: Which time period should be emphasised? The Suzhou water grid has evolved over time and served different functions in different periods. Tourists may overemphasise accounts of the place's 'Golden Age', possibly referring to the seventeenth century, or images derived from Song Dynasty poems, whereas locals may overemphasise the last few decades. Given that conservation should serve multiple audiences and offer diverse options for interpretation, the ideal conservation strategy captures traces of all different periods. This means the inclusion of industrial heritage, different styles of arched and level bridges, and also traces of recent transformation. It would also imply openness to future developments of and around the water ways.

The question whose heritage is to be preserved includes another aspect. As different patterns were applied to the houses of nobility, traders and simple people, conservation should reflect the whole range of living conditions. This presents an opportunity to introduce more variety of distinctive urban streets and quarters. Local people will appreciate the authenticity coming with it, and tourists will appreciate the variety of different sightseeing choices. It would be boring for them to find the same type of heritage everywhere in the city, regardless of whether it is all huts or all palaces.

Heritage conservation in Suzhou needs to pay utmost attention to the unique water grid and the 'historical water block', and it needs to strive for diversity in the forms and meanings ingrained in them. The integrity of the grid and the visibility of the waterways in the whole city need to be preserved, and if necessary, restored. Currently, conservation mainly concentrates on a few conservation zones, for example, Pingjiang Road and Shantang Street, which are developed as tourist attractions. The water grid as a whole is so far not the primary target of restoration efforts. Based on our analysis, the variations in morphological patterns indicate the usage patterns at different periods of time and by different social groups. Conservation should retain the full spectrum of canal–alley patterns, canal–building patterns, and types of bridges, piers and banks. It should pay attention to the widths of canals and alleys and to the variation of enclosure rates.

The most famous case of conservation in Suzhou, Pingjiang Road, has rightly received much praise for its authentic style and for the beauty of the resulting ensemble of canal, street and buildings, but it would be a mistake to replicate it throughout the city. The development paths, and as a result also the typical morphology, differ between the quarters of traders, aristocrats and manufacturers; they vary between central and peripheral parts of the old town, and according to the functions they have served. These differences should become visible to tourists and residents alike.

Last but not least, conservation also needs to be concerned with functions. The canals were once a very essential part of the local people's lives, but many of the functions they have performed are now obsolete. They do not and should not serve the discarding of rubbish and washing of laundry anymore. The transport function they have once performed will not be restored, nor their role in urban freshwater supply. Instead, new functions need to be found in order to sustain the liveliness of the canals and to continue their co-evolution with the city. This puts the spotlight on tourism, but the canals can also continue to be essential parts of local people's lives. Provided the water is clean and pleasant, it increases the value of adjacent residential properties. People like to sit, walk and play by the water. Floating restaurants and teahouses and floating stages for performances could serve local people and tourists.

Related prospects of tourism development

To reactivate Suzhou's largely abandoned water grid as a resource for tourism development offers three most promising prospects: new tourism products, new perspectives of the city and an alternative mode of transport.

First, there are potentials for developing the canals into more attractive tourism products. The interconnected canals are tourist attractions in themselves, and they provide contextual linkages among heritage sites and other tourist spots. Inner-urban boat tours are very popular tourism products in cities such as Paris, Amsterdam, Berlin and Venice. Compared to these places, Suzhou does not yet fully utilise its potential as a water city. Canal tours can take different forms, by individual boats or by tour boats of different sizes, with fixed or negotiable routes. Hop-on hop-off stops at many piers can help to integrate the two circulation networks of streets and waterways and give tourists additional flexibility to combine sightseeing and consumption activities. As proposed in the most recent Historical City Conservation Plan of Suzhou (2013–2025) (Ji & Zhuang, 2014), the north–south canals in the central area of Suzhou shall be re-opened and re-connected for tourism purposes.

Second, waterways also open new perspectives for the tourist gaze. The view of the urban landscape differs between the water, the street and the bridge levels. The water-based perspective to buildings, bridges, piers and city walls will offer alternative views and revive a Suzhou-specific sense of place and sense of history. When tourism emerged in Suzhou over 1000 years ago, waterborne traffic was the primary way of circulation. Boat tours offer the opportunity to follow the paths of these early visitors, to experience the urban form and building details along the canals, and to open the eyes to local lifestyles performed on and beside the water. The bridges and piers also provide excellent opportunities to capture different scenes photographically.

Third, the revitalisation of the water grid can in a practical sense separate parts of the tourist flows from roadside circulation and thereby ease existing issues of congestion. The high numbers of visitors in Suzhou's old town cause frequent conflicts, especially with local residents on bicycles and motorcycles, who share the same ally space. This is annoying for both sides. Tourists prefer the alleys to be pedestrianised, whereas locals insist on their customary right of way. An increased use of waterways for tourist circulation would not completely resolve this problem, but it could bring some relief. It would facilitate a better distribution of visitors within the city and allow for moments of quietness on the boat.

Conclusions

By using the urban morphology approach to identify the development principles over time of Suzhou's old town, this paper has uncovered distinctive structures and elements and shown that it can inform conservation planning. The value of the morphological approach lies in its spatial, evolutionary, holistic and systematic characteristics. Our analysis has revealed the distinctive role of the water grid and of diversity in Suzhou, including geographical variations and variations over time due to changing functions, changing lifestyles and changing conservation priorities. Traces of different periods can be found to be coexisting throughout the city. Heritage conservation and tourism planning need to take account of this and offer a varied and colourful image with a multiplicity of meanings for the people's interpretation and enjoyment. It is critical for conservation to take functions into consideration to justify costs and create a 'living' or 'lived-in' heritage. Tourism and leisure have been portrayed as the best opportunity to turn specific physical features to new uses without compromising their historical meaning.

Theoretically, this paper has addressed the potential mismatch between a modern heritage concept that emphasises on meaning rather than physical form and the urban morphology approach, which is clearly grounded in a physical understanding of landscape. To do justice to Conzen, we need to remember that he viewed urban form as a manifestation of a 'spirit' that he aimed to capture in his analysis. We should develop this aspect of his concept further and look at urban landscapes not only in a formal way, but include meanings and symbolic landscapes. Graham writes that meanings give value to artefacts – but meanings are also embodied and transmitted through artefacts such as physical landscapes. The relationship between the ideological and material dimensions of heritage is mutual and close, and urban morphology is not obsolete as long as both dimensions are considered together.

To expand the practical value for tourism planning, the methodology would need to be expanded. Apart from evaluating artistic sources and interpreting the traces in the built environment, it would be necessary to conduct interviews and focus groups to capture the needs and expectations of different users such as tourists and residents. These would be questions where morphological analysis alone gets to its limits.

Notes

1. Based on the 'Poem of City Wu' (*Wudu Fu*) composed by Zuo Si in the third century AD (retrieved from www.zwbk.org/MyLemmaShow.aspx?lid=108548).
2. Retrieved from www.shicimingju.com/chaxun/list/3208.html.
3. Retrieved from www.shicimingju.com/chaxun/list/79103.html.

References

Ashworth, G. J. (1998). The conserved European city as cultural symbols: The meaning of the text. In G. J. Ashworth & P. J. Larkham (Eds.), *Building a new heritage: Tourism, culture and identity in the new Europe* (pp. 13–30). London: Routledge.

Chen, Y. (2002). Gu Dai Suzhou Cheng Shi Yan Hua Yan Jiu [Study on the morphological evolution of ancient Suzhou]. *Cheng Shi Gui Hua Xue Kan* [City Planning Review], *141*(5), 55–60.

Chen, Y. (2003). Jin Dai Suzhou Cheng Shi Yan Hua Yan Jiu [Study on the morphological evolution of modern Suzhou]. *Cheng Shi Gui Hua Xue Kan* [City Planning Review], *148*(6), 62–71.

Chen, Y. (2006). Dang Dai Suzhou Cheng Shi Yan Hua Yan Jiu [Study on the morphological evolution of contemporary Suzhou]. *Cheng Shi Gui Hua Lun Tan* [Urban Planning Forum], *163*(3), 36–44.

Dong, G. (1993, originally in early 19th Century). *Quan Tang Shu* [The history of Tang Dynasty]. Beijing: Zhonghua Press.

Fan, C. (1999, originally 1191). *Wu Jun Zhi* [Local chronicles of Wu]. Nanjing: Jiangsu Chronicle Press.

Gospodini, A. (2001). Urban design, urban space morphology, urban tourism: An emerging new paradigm concerning their relationship. *European Planning Studies, 9*(7), 925–934.

Graham, B. (2002). Heritage as knowledge: Capital or culture? *Urban Studies, 39*(5–6), 1003–1017.

Gu, Y. (2006). Suzhou Li Shi Shui Jie Qu Yan Jiu [Study on Suzhou's historical water block]. *Guangxi Youjiang Ming Zu Shi Zhuan Xue Bao* [Journal of Youjiang Teachers College for Nationalities Guangxi], *19*(1), 86–89.

Gu, Y. (2008). Suzhou Li Shi Shui Jie Qu Lu You Xing Xiang She Ji [Research on tourism image design of Suzhou historical water block]. *Jing Ji Yu She Hui Fa Zhan* [Economic and Social Development], *6*(5), 30–33.

Hohensinner, S., Lager, B., Sonnlechner, C., Haidvogl, G., Gierlinger, S., Schmid, M., Krausmann, F., & Winiwarter, V. (2013). Changes in water and land: The reconstructed Viennese riverscape from 1500 to the present. *Water History, 5*(2), 145–172.

Huang, M. (1986). Geng Hao De Jian She Suzhou Gu Cheng Qu [Constructing the historical downtown Suzhou to a better place]. *Gui Hua* [Urban Planning], *5*, 36–39.

Ji, X., & Zhuang, J. (2014). Ti Shen Jie Xiang Te Se, Zhang Xian Shui Cheng Nei Han – Suzhou Gu Cheng Chuan Tong Jie Xiang Yu Di Fang Wen Hua De Rong He [Upgrading the characteristics of streets and revealing the connotation of water city: the integration of traditional streets and local culture in Suzhou ancient city]. *Cheng Shi Gui Hua* [City Planning Review], *38*(5), 46–49.

Kelly, S., & Chen, Y. (2013). China's urban rivers as public space. *Delft Architectural Theory Journal, 2013*(12), 27–44.

Liu, B., Yang, Z., & Feng, Z. (2012). Suzhou Gu Cheng Ping Jiang Li Shi Jie Qu 'Jiexiang – Heliu' Kong Jian Fu He Yan Jiu [Space composite study on the 'street-river' of the Suzhou Pingjiang historic district]. *Suzhou Ke Ji Da Xue Xue Kan* [Journal of Suzhou University of Science and Technology], *25*(3), 26–28.

Lu, G. (1986, originally compiled in late Tang Dynasty). *Wudi Ji* [Ancient local chronicles of Wu]. Nanjing: Jiangsu Ancient Works Press.

Lu, W. (1989). *Suzhou Wu Xian Zhi* [Wuxian county of Suzhou Chronicles]. Suzhou: Suzhou Archives Bureau.

Mauch, C., & Zeller, T. (2008). *Rivers in history: Perspectives on waterways in Europe and North America*. Pittsburgh, PA: University of Pittsburgh Press.

Mote, F. W. (1973). A millenium of Chinese urban history: Form, time, and space concepts in Soochow. *Rice University Studies*, 59(4), 35–65.

Moudon, A. V. (1997). Urban morphology as an emerging interdisciplinary field. *Urban Morphology*, 1(1), 3–10.

Qian, Y. (1959). Pingjiang Tu Bei [The stone monument of Ping Jiang map]. *Wen Wu* [Cultural Relics], 2(2), 16–17.

Smith, D. (1998). British urban mapping of waterways, canals and docks. *The Cartographic Journal*, 35(1), 17–26.

Suzhou Chronicles Committee. (1995). *Suzhou Di Fang Zhi* [Suzhou chronicles]. Nanjing: Jiangsu Science Press.

Suzhou Chronicles Committee. (1997). Suzhou De Bo An [The piers of Suzhou]. *Suzhou Di Fang Xin Xi* [Local information of Suzhou]. Retrieved from www.dfzb.suzhou.gov.cn/zsbl/226227.htm

Suzhou Chronicles Committee. (2001). Suzhou Gu Cheng Bao Hu De Kun Nan He Tiao Zhan [Difficulties and challenges in conservation practices in the historical town of Suzhou]. *Suzhou Di Fang Xin Xi* [Local information of Suzhou]. Retrieved from www.dfzb.suzhou.gov.cn/zsbl/233827.htm

Whitehand, J. W. R. (2001). British urban morphology: The Conzenian tradition. *Urban Morphology*, 5(2), 103–109.

Whitehand, J. W. R. (2009). The structure of urban landscape: Strengthening research and practice. *Urban Morphology*, 13(1), 5–27.

Whitehand, J. W. R., & Gu, K. (2007). Urban conservation in China: Historical development, current practice and morphological approach. *Town Planning Review*, 78, 643–670.

Whitehand, J. W. R., & Gu, K. (2010). Conserving urban landscape heritage: A geographical approach. *Procedia Social and Behavioural Sciences*, 2, 6948–6953.

Whitehand, J. W. R., Gu, K., Whitehand, S., & Zhang, J. (2011). Urban morphology and conservation in China. *Cities*, 28, 171–185.

Wu, P. (1985, based on ancient chronicles by Yuan Kang). *Yue Jue Shu* [The ancient local chronicles of Yue]. Shanghai: Shanghai Press of Ancient Works.

Xiang, B., & Gu, W. (2000). Suzhou Gu Cheng Chuan Tong Jie Xiang Ji Cheng Shi Kong Jian Xing Tai Fen Xi [The analysis on the historic lanes and the whole spatial morphology in ancient Suzhou City]. *Cheng Shi Yan Jiu* [Urban Research], 82(3), 26–27.

Xu, Y. (1986). *Shang Shi Ji Er Shi Nian Dai Suzhou Cheng De Jian She* [The establishment of Soochow in the 1920s]. Suzhou: Suzhou Archives Bureau.

Xu, Y. (2000). *The Chinese city in space and time: The development of urban form in Suzhou*. Honolulu: University of Hawaii Press.

Yu, S. (1980). Zhongguo Gu Dai De Zao Cheng Jie Zuo – Song Pingjiang (Suzhou) Tu [Masterpiece of ancient Chinese city planning – the city map of Song Pingjiang (Suzhou)]. *Jianzhu xuebao* [Architectural Journal], (1), 16–19.

Zhai, W. (2007). *Suzhou Shui Li Zhi* [Suzhou chronicles of rivers and canals]. Beijing: Jinlin People's Press.

Zhang, G. (1987, originally in 1638). *Wuzhong Shuili Quanshu* [The drainage chronicles of Wuzhong]. Shanghai: Shanghai Ancient Works Press.

Zhang, Q. (2012). Gusu Cheng Tu [Gusu city map]. *Suzhou Za Zhi* [Suzhou Magazine], 4(4), 22–25.

Zhang, S. (1985, originally in 736 AD). *Shiji Zhengyi* [The explanations of historical records of China]. Beijing: Peking University Press.

Zhao, Y. (1999, originally in Donghan Dynasty). *Wu Yue Chunqiu* [Historical records of spring and autumn period of China]. Nanjing: Jiangsu Local Chronicle's Press.

Industrial heritage tourism development and city image reconstruction in Chinese traditional industrial cities: a web content analysis

Xueke (Stephanie) Yang

ABSTRACT

Studies on industrial heritage and industrial tourism development at the city level in China are limited. Through a web content analysis of the industrial components in cities' images and tourism, this paper attempts to explore whether old industrial cities are promoting industrial heritage tourism and rebuilding postindustrial images. A total of 20 traditionally industrial cities were selected as samples for data collection based on the content of their official websites, and this study finds that industrial heritage and industrial tourism are rarely promoted or even mentioned on those websites, indicating that industrial culture is gradually being eroded in China. Traditional Chinese industrial cities tend to look for opportunities to participate in global competition rather than reflecting and preserving their past through the process of urban development. More attention should be paid in the future to integrating industrial culture into Chinese urban development, both in academic research and in practice.

Introduction

With the spread of the concept of industrial heritage, important industrial remains in cities that were faced with deindustrialization are gradually being viewed as industrial heritage sites in many countries, and are being conserved and transformed into valuable assets for regeneration (Firth, 2011). Industrial heritage sites have been called landscapes of nostalgic memory, since these sites provided jobs for thousands of people and contributed to economic growth during the industrial era (Oevermann, Degenkolb, Dießler, Karge, & Peltz, 2016). Industrial heritage is increasingly becoming a resource to construct new social identities and develop industrial heritage tourism (Caffyn & Lutz, 1999). Industrial heritage tourism is a subset of cultural tourism, and refers to 'the development of touristic activities and industries on man-made sites, buildings and landscapes that originated with industrial processes of earlier periods' (Edwards & Coit, 1996, p. 342). Turning such sites into tourist attractions can help promote the value of the industrial past and may enhance the identities of the residents who shaped the character of former industrial cities (Xie, 2015). The significance of industrial heritage and the function of industrial heritage tourism have gained attention at all levels, from grassroots organizations to governments, and hence, industrial heritage tourism is now becoming a significant socioeconomic phenomenon (Xie, 2006).

Industrial heritage sites are usually geographically concentrated in industrial cities, and so studies on industrial heritage are often discussed in the context of industrial cities in decline, and the increase in popularity of industrial heritage tourism may be attributed to the growing numbers of this type of city (Xie, 2006). These cities are usually former centers of industry that encountered problems due to the decline of traditional manufacturing. Even though there are many ways to redevelop urban economies, industrial heritage tourism is regarded as an interesting 'new combination' (Hospers, 2002, p. 401) to improve a city's image and to play a role as a tool to counteract public biases toward former industrial cities (Xie, 2006). Like industrial heritage tourism, city marketing is also regarded as a helpful tool to rebuild and redefine a city's image for urban rejuvenation, especially for industrial cities in decline (Xie, 2015). For example, in the UK, the cities of Bradford and Glasgow shook off their old industrial images and marketed their new postindustrial images through industrial heritage tourism and other city-marketing strategies (Bramwell & Rawding, 1996; Garcia, 2005).

Although the concept of industrial heritage began in the 1990s and attracted attention in China from grassroots organizations to scholars, industrial heritage sites are still faced with the risk of being destroyed or moved, especially in traditional industrial cities. In China, the term 'traditional industrial cities' refers to the industrial cities that emerged from the 1950s to the 1960s through huge national investment in large-scale manufacturing. These industrial cities made important contributions to the growth of urban economies and changed the unbalanced distribution of manufacturing industries in China (Chen & Song, 2004). With the influences of the global economic environment, however, since the 1990s Chinese traditional industrial cities have had to face the problem of declining industrial manufacturing and so have had to look for potential strategies to attain industrial upgrades and urban regeneration. Currently, these cities are going through a transition process, shifting from the secondary sector of the economy to the tertiary sector. Since competition among traditional industrial cities has become more intense in this transition period, some of them are reconstructing and promoting new distinctive city images through city marketing in order to attract investment and tourists for urban regeneration (Dong & Zhang, 2008). Unfortunately, it seems that not all traditional Chinese industrial cities understand the significance and function of industrial heritage tourism for image reconstruction and urban rejuvenation, since many industrial heritage sites have been destroyed rather than being adaptively reused as tourist attractions (Fan, Soyez, & Dai, 2012).

After reviewing the literature, it is noted that city-level research on industrial heritage and industrial heritage tourism in traditional industrial cities in China is limited. Hence, at the city level, little is known about which kinds of traditional industrial cities are reconstructing new city images instead of keeping their original industrialized images, and whether and to what extent they are making use of their industrial heritage to develop tourism. This paper will fill this gap through web content analysis of 20 traditional industrial cities' official websites, since the analysis of written information can offer a great deal of insight into the tourist attractions and image projected by a tourist destination (O'Leary & Deegan, 2005). In sum, this study sheds light on the features of industrial heritage tourism development and city image reconstruction in Chinese traditional cities, and provides possible explanations for this situation.

Study background

The concept of industrial heritage was first brought to China in the 1990s, but did not attract much attention in either the academic or practical fields. The conservation and reuse of industrial heritage sites have only been paid more attention in the twenty-first century, especially after 2006 when the first official document on industrial heritage was published. The acceptance of industrial heritage has involved a tortuous process, from first being ignored, to being regarded as a trendy resource, and finally to the development of industrial heritage tourism. Basically, the process can be divided into two stages: the exploratory stage (1990s–2005) and the development stage (2006– now). The division point between these two stages was the first official document on industrial heritage, issued in 2006, which changed the attitude toward industrial heritage research and practices. The period from the 1990s till now has also been the period of reform and transition in China, during which economic restructuring and urban land reform have been the main themes. Both manufacturing facilities and industrial land have been the key subjects of reform. The issues of conservation and reuse of industrial heritage, therefore, arose in this particular background (Zhang & Chai, 2013).

Economic restructuring and industrial heritage in traditional industrial cities

In the first stage (1990s–2006), due to the influences of the global economic environment, traditional Chinese industrial cities faced a decline in manufacturing and the consequent need for economic restructuring. Many factories were closed and moved outside cities due to the need for industrial upgrading, economic restructuring, and environmental protection (Li, Zheng, & Wang, 2004). As a result, numerous industrial remnants that should be regarded as industrial heritage sites were left in urban areas. To solve the problems, a 'Develop the tertiary (service) sector instead of the secondary (manufacturing) sector' guideline was released in 2001 by the Chinese government. The state-level policy was mapped out to readjust the industrial structure of the entire country through developing the service sector after closing down or moving polluting factories away from city centers. The policies were carried out over a short period and led directly to the destruction of industrial buildings and the conversion of industrial land in many traditional industrial cities. The previous disorganized industrial layout and fast urban sprawl in China accelerated the process, as most of the old factories were in city centers, where their geographical locations made their properties potentially very valuable. Therefore, large numbers of old buildings were destroyed, and the previously industrial lands or brownfields were transformed into commercial or public green lands, reflecting their high economic value (Lu, Yang, Wen, & Long, 2010). During this process, factory buildings and machines were often left as a tangible industrial heritage, recording Chinese industrial history; however, these buildings and machines began fading away without suitable conservation and reuse, and the industrial culture as an essential part of the urban culture was overlooked.

Unlike the first stage, industrial heritage attracted more attention in the second stage (2006–now), since in 2006 the first official document on the preservation and reuse of industrial heritage in China, 'Wuxi Advice' (2006), was published, and industrial heritage was officially denoted as a form of cultural heritage. This occurred under the background of the 'Passion for Heritage' trend in China, when applying for National or World Heritage status was a trend for many local governments desiring to develop a tourism industry. Meanwhile in this stage, successful practices for the adaptive reuse of industrial heritage arose in traditional Chinese industrial cities, with representative cases being the 798 Art Zone in Beijing, Tianzifang in Shanghai, and Qijinag Park in Zhongshan (Yu & Fang, 2006). These cases are appreciated by artists and tourists for their unique postmodern industrial elements and artistic atmosphere, and have gradually become industrial tourist attractions (Fan et al., 2012). Together, the 'Passion for Heritage' and successful cases of reusing industrial heritage sites drove a wider acceptance of industrial heritage and the popularity of developing industrial heritage tourism. Following the national policy mentioned above, 'developing the tertiary sector instead of the secondary sector', some city-level policies have been issued to encourage the transformation of old factories, such as the 'three olds transformation' policy issued by Guangzhou in 2009 ('three olds' refers to old towns, old factories, and old villages). This policy aimed to transform old factories in city centers into new, environmentally friendly factories, headquarters of factories, or tourist attractions. However, most of the old buildings have been destroyed and replaced by new buildings rather than being preserved as industrial heritage sites and transformed into tourist attractions (Fan et al., 2012). Therefore, in the current period, opposing attitudes toward industrial heritage exist in traditional Chinese industrial cities, in that some tend to preserve industrial heritage sites and allow or even encourage adaptive reuse, while others tend to destroy the sites and replace them with new buildings.

From the 1990s, industrial heritage has increasingly attracted scholars' attention. However, most of the studies on industrial heritage and industrial tourism have focused on the definition of industrial heritage, development models, experiences from Western cases, and reviews of industrial heritage and industrial tourism studies in China (Li, 2002; Li & Soyez, 2003; Liu, 2012; Que, 2007), while other research has mainly studied issues of industrial heritage tourism through empirical case studies (Fan et al., 2012). It has been found that the development of industrial heritage tourism was so commercialized that the social and historical value of industrial heritage sites was overlooked, and only economic value was sought (Ning & Jin, 2008; Zhang & Chai, 2013). In general, there is scant research covering both industrial heritage and industrial tourism together; although this is increasing, most studies have been written like tourism consultation reports on how to develop industrial tourism based on current industrial heritage sites in specific cities (Zhu, Liu, & Bao, 2002). Research from a more macro perspective is necessary to explore how old industrial cities can or do make use of industrial heritage and industrial tourism.

City marketing, image reconstruction, and urban regeneration

Faced with similar problems of deindustrialization and economic transformation, many Western industrial cities in decline have applied city marketing as a technique to retune their images and improve their images in order to attract investment and tourism (Paddison, 1993; Kavaratzis, 2007). The idea that cities can be marketed like products has been employed in many cases, such that cities now increasingly apply marketing techniques as a response to economic changes, especially in those that desire to foster local economic regeneration (Kavaratzis & Ashworth, 2007). The popularity of city marketing emerged from the background of the increasing global economy, where more and more places are drawn into competition and where the built environments, infrastructure and amenities in different places tend to become more similar (Richards & Wilson, 2004). As a result, competition to attract investment has become so intense that cities need to find new solutions to distinguish themselves from their competitors, since a destination's image is able to influence people's perceptions of a place and can affect their choices and behavior (Kavaratzis & Ashworth, 2007). The competition between the old industrial cities became a competition to reconstruct unique city images through city marketing by local governments or city authorities to enhance their competitiveness (Hospers, 2009).

It is widely accepted that reconstructing images through city marketing is a central component of the urban regeneration work in many old industrial cities (Colomb, 2012). While the definition of 'image' varies among scholars, it is generally referred to as 'a compilation of beliefs and impressions based on information processing from a variety of sources over time' (Choi, Lehto, & Morrison, 2007, p. 119). City images could emerge without deliberate planning, or be created consciously by the marketing and promotion efforts of a city (induced images) or from other sources not directly associated with it, such as through books, school education, television documentaries, and the experiences of friends and family (organic images) (Gunn, 1988; Hospers, 2009). Based on this, cities, usually through local governments, attempt to change the induced image through different ways of marketing, such as by constructing signature buildings as landmarks; hosting events such as the Olympic Games, the World Cup, or a World Expo; and developing and promoting urban tourism, especially industrial heritage tourism (Richards & Wilson, 2004). Industrial heritage tourism is an important tool to improve a region's image and a significant public tool to counteract public prejudices toward industrial areas in decline: for instance, the Ruhr region in Germany, Glasgow in the UK, and Bilbao in Spain (Gómez, 1998; Hospers, 2009; Knapp, 1998).

Nowadays, the induced images of different cities can be accessed easily through their official websites, since the blurring boundaries of competition have resulted in a proliferation of destination identities being communicated through the Internet (Govers & Go, 2003). The Internet offers a new type of information source that is more dynamic, interactive, and richer in content. It has been one of the major sources of information to reduce risk and uncertainty in the decision-making of consumers (Pan & Fesenmaier, 2006). Therefore, governments at various levels build their own official websites as channels to publish news and policies as well as to project their city images. In some cities, official tourist websites are also set up to introduce tourist attractions and assist in promoting the city's image (Choi, Lehto, & Morrison, 2007).

In China, city marketing has also gained attention in recent years as a means of building attractive new city images and enhancing competitiveness (Wang & Bramwell, 2012). The transition is different from the early urbanization process, and now competition among cities has become more intense as marketing strategies are also integrated into urban development. It is observed that the transition process has been pushed in a rapid manner and that many local governments in China employ their cities' official websites as tools to promote their cities' images and tourist attractions. Plenty of information on city images and urban tourism products can be found from official websites, making it possible to utilize web content analysis as the method for this research.

Therefore, this paper selects official city and tourism websites as agents, since they link together industrial heritage tourism and city marketing. In this regard, it is possible to examine traditional industrial cities' responses to economic changes and attitudes toward industrial heritage through examining the industrial components in the cities' images along with urban tourism in order to explore whether and how far old industrial cities are making use of industrial heritage sites to reconstruct their images.

Methods

Web content analysis

The paper employs web content analysis to examine the portrayal of city images and tourism products on the official websites of traditional Chinese industrial cities. After conducting an exploratory study on the content of Ireland's promotional materials distributed in France, O'Leary and Deegan (2005) argued that content analysis of written information, such as guidebooks and travel brochures, could provide a great deal of information about the images projected by a tourism destination. With the increasingly rich and readily available text data on the web, qualitative assessments such as web content analysis of image formation and other tourism phenomena are gaining in popularity (Stepchenkova & Morrison, 2006). Some studies have employed web content analysis to identify the various images of a specific destination presented on the Internet by different authorities, such as destination marketing organizations, travel agencies, and online travel magazine and guide websites (Choi et al., 2007; Hsu & Song, 2013). Through collecting data from official websites, web content analysis has been increasingly recognized as a useful method to analyze the city/destination images projected by different authorities (Stepchenkova & Morrison, 2006; Stepchenkova & Zhan, 2013).

Sample selection

A total of 20 Chinese traditional industrial cities were selected as samples for data collection through their official websites. The cities were selected according to several criteria. First, they must all be traditional industrial cities faced with problems of a decline in manufacturing. Second, the 20 cities must be in the four main industrial districts in China: the East, West, Central, and Northeast districts (Chen & Chen, 2011), from which five cities each were selected. Third, three capital cities (municipalities) and two prefecture-level cities were chosen from each district in order to explore whether, and if so how, the various administration levels of each city influenced attitudes toward industrial heritage and city image reconstruction. Fourth, to make sure sufficient data were being collected on both city image and tourism products, all the cities selected must have substantially engaged in city marketing and have created and employed both city and tourism websites to project their city's image and promote tourism. Based these criteria, the 20 cities selected are Shanghai, Tianjin, Guangzhou, Harbin, Changchun, Shenyang, Changsha, Wuhan, Taiyuan, Chongqing, Xi'an, Chengdu, Tangshan, Luoyang, Fushun, Jilin, Zhuzhou, Datong, Baotou, and Liuzhou.

Data collection

The textual data for the 20 cities' descriptions of their images and industrial tourism attractions from the official websites were collected in three steps. The procedure will be explained by taking the city of Changchun as an example. First, the official city and tourist websites of Changchun were searched through the Baidu Search Engine using the search term 'Changchun government website (Changchun zhengfu wangzhan)' and 'Changchun tourism website (Changchun lvyou wangzhan)'. The links for the official city website[1] and tourism website[2] were put in a Word file and then entered to collect the textual data. Second, the text of the city's introduction to Changchun on the 'city overview' web page was collected from Changchun's official city website and recorded in the same Word file, since the introduction text was the description of the city's image projected by the local government. Third, to collect the textual data for the industrial tourism attractions promoted by the Changchun government, every page in the tourist attractions column of the city's official tourism website was carefully read by the author to examine whether industrial tourism attractions were recommended or mentioned. During the process of finding industrial tourism attractions on the official tourism websites, the author not only paid attention to key words such as 'industrial' or 'heritage', but also read the description of each tourism site carefully in order to avoid omitting relevant data. Once an industrial tourism attraction was found during the reading process, the attraction would be noted down in the same Word file, and then further information about the industrial tourism attraction would be searched through the Baidu Search Engine using the attraction's name as the search term. Again, all the relevant information would be stored in the Word file. The data collection process was done from 8 March 2014, to 10 March 2014, and all the collected textual data for the 20 cities, which comprised 7437 Chinese characters, were stored in one Microsoft Word file for further analysis.

Key findings

Industrial elements in city image

Table 1 displays 13 cities out of the 20 samples whose city images included industrial elements, making them cities that maintained their image as an industrial city. The descriptive sentences for the cities' images were directly translated from Chinese to English, and keywords for industrial components were marked in bold. These keywords include 'industry/industrial' (gongye), including manufacturing (zhizao ye), automobile (qiche), coal (mei), fuel (ranliao), material (yuanliao), and rare-earth metal (xitu).

The 13 cities that contained industrial elements include 5 capital/municipality cities (Shanghai, Tianjin, Chongqing, Changchun, and Shenyang) and all 8 prefecture-level cities (Tangshan, Luoyang, Fushun, Jilin, Zhuzhou, Datong, Baotou, and Liuzhou). 'Industrial' was the most frequently utilized word, being used eight times in cities' descriptions. Among the eight cities, 'industrial' was followed either by 'city' or by 'base'. In China, 'Industrial Base' refers to cities that received investment for industrial development from the national government in the 1950s and 1960s. 'Industry' appeared three times in each of the two cities' descriptions, first used for Tangshan, referring to 'the birthplace of modern Chinese industry' to reflect its position in Chinese industrial history, and also used for Fushun with 'fuel industry and material industry' to express its position as a 'Coal City'. 'Coal' was adopted twice in both Fushun and Datong to emphasize their coal reserves, with 'Coal City' for the former and 'Coal Capital' for the latter, which have the same meaning. 'Automobile' was used only in Changchun's description, since it was the national automobile base from the 1950s and had the first automobile factory in China. Baotou applied 'Rare-Earth Capital' to show its special mineral resources. 'Manufacturing' was employed once on Liuzhou's website to emphasize its position as a manufacturing base in western China. Besides industrial elements, the five capital (municipality) cities tended to emphasize their 'economic', 'political', 'cultural', or 'transportation' center positions either in their regions or in all of China. The eight prefecture cities, on the

Table 1. Cities that maintained images with industrial components.

	City	Location	Administration level	Induced City Image
1	Shanghai	East	Municipality	Municipality; biggest national **industrial** and commercial city; and World city
2	Tianjin	East	Municipality	The biggest open coastal city in the north of China; famous historic and cultural city; vital comprehensive **industrial base** and trade center
3	Changchun	Northeast	Provincial Capital	International **automobile** city; green food city; educational and cultural city; movie capital; forest city; sculpture city
4	Shenyang	Northeast	Provincial Capital	Economic, cultural, transportation and trade center in the northeast of China; national **industrial base;** and famous historic and cultural city
5	Chongqing	West	Municipality	The biggest multifunctional modern **industrial** and commercial city in the west of China; economic center of the upper Yangtze River region
6	Tangshan	East	Prefecture-level	The birthplace of Chinese modern industry; modern city
7	Luoyang	East	Prefecture-level	Important national **industrial base;** famous historic and cultural city; famous ancient capital; vital birthplace of Chinese civilization; eastern starting point of the Silk Road; famous Chinese tourist city
8	Fushun	Northeast	Prefecture-level	A comprehensive city, **industrial base** for **fuel and raw materials**; '**Coal City'**
9	Jilin	Northeast	Prefecture-level	Livable city; suitable investment city with outstanding **industrial base;** tourist and leisure city; famous historic and cultural city
10	Zhuzhou	Central	Prefecture-level	Transportation center; modern **industrial** city; open, livable city; outstanding tourist city
11	Datong	Central	Prefecture-level	Biggest national coal base; famous historic and cultural city; 'Sculpture Capital', 'Phoenix City', and '**Coal Capital'**; ancient capital
12	Baotou	West	Prefecture-level	Charming Baotou; Prosperous Baotou; Civil Baotou; Eco-Baotou; Safe Baotou; '**Rare-Earth Metal Capital'**
13	Liuzhou	West	Prefecture-level	**Industrial** center of Guangxi Province, vital western **manufacturing** base; commercial city

Source: Retrieved from the 13 cities' official city websites.

other hand, tended to stress characteristics such as 'livable' (for environment), 'prosperous' (for business atmosphere), or 'tourist city'. Overall, the 13 cities utilized words closely related to 'industry' in order to express their strengths in secondary industries. Furthermore, 'important center' positions and pleasant, cultural, commercial, and livable environments were also emphasized in constructing their new postindustrial images (Table 2).

In terms of the remaining seven capital cities without industrial descriptions (Table 3), 'political', 'economic', 'cultural', and 'center' were utilized by all, reflecting their images as important regional

Table 2. Cities that reconstructed new images without industrial components.

	City	Location	Administration level	Induced City Image
1	Guangzhou	East	Provincial Capital	International trade city; national creative city; integrated portal city; international cultural city; provincial livable city
2	Harbin	Northeast	Provincial Capital	Northern political, economic, cultural center in the northeast of China; biggest capital city; mega city with the second largest population; famous historic and cultural city; tourist city
3	Changsha	Central	Provincial Capital	Provincial political, economic, cultural, transportation, technological, financial, information center; famous national historic and cultural city; mega city
4	Wuhan	Central	Provincial Capital	Economic, technological, educational, and cultural center in the center of China
5	Taiyuan	Central	Provincial Capital	Capital city of Shanxi Province; political, economic, and cultural center; historic and cultural old city
6	Xi'an	West	Provincial Capital	Ancient capital; famous historic city; political, economic, and cultural center of Shaanxi Province; great location and transportation city; innovative technological city; fast-developing prosperous city; city with pleasant environment
7	Chengdu	West	Provincial Capital	Technological, trade, financial, and transportation center in the southwest of China; political, economic, cultural, and educational center of Sichuan Province; famous national historic and cultural city

Source: Retrieved from the seven cities' official city websites.

Table 3. The 11 cities that promoted industrial tourism.

	City	Location	Administration level	Promoted industrial tourism attractions	
				Industrial heritage tourism	Modern industrial tourism
1	Shanghai	East	Municipality	Two creative parks	Three modern museums, three factory tours
2	Tianjin	East	Municipality	One heritage site	Seven factory tours, one integrated industrial park
3	Guangzhou	East	Provincial Capital	One creative park	–
4	Harbin	Northeast	Provincial Capital	–	Three factory tours
5	Changchun	Northeast	Provincial Capital	–	One factory tour
6	Chengdu	West	Municipality	One creative park with an industrial museum	–
7	Tangshan	East	Prefecture-level	One heritage site	One integrated industrial park
8	Fushun	Northeast	Prefecture-level	One heritage site, one heritage museum	–
9	Datong	Central	Prefecture-level	One heritage site	–
10	Baotou	West	Prefecture-level	–	Three factory tours
11	Liuzhou	West	Prefecture-level	–	Three factory tours

Source: Retrieved from the 11 cities' official tourism websites.

centers for politics, economy, and culture. 'Commercial', 'financial', 'technological', 'innovative', and 'educational' were emphasized instead of 'industrial' to describe their images, which were all closely related to the service industry. One remarkable point is that 11 of the 20 sample cities described themselves with the title 'famous historic and cultural city'. This is an award title for a city with a long cultural history given by the Chinese government, whose aim was to promote urban tourism. This, to some extent, indicates that these 11 cities have all endeavored to develop tourism.

For the relationship between political-level and industrial components, it was found that among the 12 cites with a higher political administration level, only three municipalities and two capital cities still maintained the industrial components in their city image, while the eight lower political administration-level cities all kept their industrial city images. In all, among the 20 traditional industrial cities, only 7 capital cities excluded industrial elements in their images.

Industrial heritage tourism products on official tourism websites

As for industrial tourism products, 11 cities among the 20 samples mentioned or recommended them on their official websites: Shanghai, Tianjin, Guangzhou, Harbin, Changchun, Chengdu, Tangshan, Fushun, Datong, Baotou, and Liuzhou. The industrial tourism products promoted on the websites were recorded and divided into two categories: industrial heritage tourism products and modern industrial tourism products. Industrial heritage tourism attractions were defined as tourism products developed by conserving and reusing industrial heritage, while modern industrial attractions were tourism products developed based on newly built industrial factories, buildings, or industrial parks. The former category includes three sub-categories including industrial museums, industrial heritage attractions, and creative parks, while the latter contains factory tours, modern industrial museums, and integrated industrial parks. The above division of industrial tourism attractions was based on studies by Li (2002) and Yu and Fang (2006).

In total, 34 industrial tourism attractions were promoted, including 26 *modern* industrial tourism products and 8 industrial *heritage* tourism products. For the modern industrial tourism products, in all 20 factory tours were mentioned in 5 cities' official tourism websites and included 7 food factories, 3 pharmaceutical factories, and various other factories. From the corporations' websites, it could be seen that their factory tours were tools for public relations promotion. Meanwhile, three modern industrial museums built after 2000 were promoted, but all were on Shanghai's list of industrial tourism products. Integrated industrial parks, which are a particular kind of industrial park with special shopping malls and factory tours, were recommended twice. The ceramic cultural park in Tangshan was one in which the creation and history of ceramics were exhibited, and ceramics products were also offered for sale. In terms of the eight industrial heritage tourism products mentioned, industrial museums were promoted only on two cities' websites. 'Industrial museums' refers not only to museums with specific industrial themes, but also to conserved and reused industrial heritage sites. Industrial heritage attractions promoted by four cities were traditional types of tourism attractions that only protect and interpret the industrial heritage, without any other functions. Creative parks were also called cultural parks or art zones in China, and these were the most popular industrial heritage redevelopment model, with examples such as the famous 798 Art Zone in Beijing, Redtory in Guangzhou, and 82 Space in Chengdu. These sites all have become well-known and popular industrial tourism attractions.

With regard to the times the sites were originally built, all of them were constructed less than 100 years ago and mainly developed after the year 2000. Among the sites, 15 were built after 2000, 12 between 1949 and the 1990s, and 7 before 1949. Most of the industrial tourist attractions are low-level and small-scale and only include two AAAA National Tourist Attractions, two AAA National Tourist Attractions, and two AA National Tourist Attractions. The A-level National Tourist Attraction is a quality evaluation system, in which AAAAA is the highest level, while AA is the lowest level. The evaluation and selection are determined by China National Tourist Attractions Quality Evaluation Committee, an organization that belongs to National Tourism Administration. From the aspect of location, cities in the central region place less attention on industrial tourism compared with the other three areas, since only one city there recommended industrial tourism spots on its official tourism websites, while cities in the central region all promoted natural and cultural tourist attractions on their websites. The three capital cities in the central region do not maintain the image of industrial cities, and also do not promote any industrial tourism products on their official websites.

In all, eight cities both maintained industrial images and recommended or mentioned industrial tourism products, including Shanghai, Tianjin, Changchun, Tangshan, Fushun, Datong, Baotou, and Liuzhou. Although the industrial tourism attractions mentioned on the official websites were low level and small scale, focusing on modern factory tour tourism and lacking attention to industrial heritage tourism, the attention to industrial tourism generally and their industrial images still reflected these eight local governments' attitudes toward industrial culture. Therefore, it can be concluded that the eight cities recognized industrial tourism and industrial culture as important parts of their cities' cultures, worthy of recommendation and promotion.

The economic structures of each city in 1978 and 2011 were analyzed to explore the relationships between levels of industrial development and image reconstruction. The data for agriculture, manufacturing, and the service industry's proportions as percentages of Gross Rating Points (GRP) were collected from the statistical yearbook of each city in order to reflect the economic structures shown in Table 4. The data indicate that the proportion of the tertiary sector of the economy in GRP of every city increased substantially from 1978 to 2011. Specifically, the percentage of the tertiary sector of the economy to GRP was larger than that of the secondary sector of the economy to GRP in seven cities, including Shanghai, Guangzhou, Harbin, Wuhan, Taiyuan, Xi'an, and Chengdu (one municipality city and six capital cities). Meanwhile, six of those cities, with the exception of Shanghai, reconstructed their city images by excluding industrial elements, while for the eight prefecture-level cities, manufacturing was still the main component of their economies, and their industrial images were maintained. Therefore, a simple pattern can be summarized, that cities with higher proportions of manufacturing tended to keep their industrial images, while cities with a higher proportion of service industry and lower proportion of manufacturing to GRP tended to reconstruct their images.

The analysis demonstrates that all 20 cities have endeavored to project their cities' images and promote their tourism attractions. However, most of the industrial cities have reconstructed their cities' images through removing industrial components and industrial tourism, and industrial heritage tourism is especially neglected. In all, 13 cities of the 20 samples have maintained their industrial city images, and 11 of them have promoted industrial tourism products on official tourism websites.

Table 4. Economic structures of 20 cities in 1978 and 2011.

City	1978			2011		
	Agriculture Industry	Manufacturing Industry	Service Industry	Agriculture Industry	Manufacturing Industry	Service Industry
Shanghai	4.0%	77.4%	18.6%	0.7%	41.3%	58.0%
Tianjin	6.0%	69.6%	24.3%	1.4%	52.4%	46.0%
Guangzhou	12.0%	58.6%	29.0%	1.6%	36.8%	61.6%
Harbin	30.8%	51.6%	17.6%	10.5%	38.9%	50.6%
Changchun	9.0%	65.9%	25.0%	7.2%	52.3%	40.5%
Shenyang	33.3%	44.2%	22.5%	4.7%	51.2%	44.1%
Changsha	11.7%	63.1%	25.0%	4.3%	56.1%	39.6%
Wuhan	5.9%	74.9%	19.3%	2.9%	48.1%	49.0%
Taiyuan	34.6%	48.1%	17.3%	1.6%	45.6%	52.8%
Chongqing	19.1%	57.6%	23.6%	8.4%	55.4%	36.2%
Xi'an	31.9%	47.2%	20.9%	4.5%	43.9%	51.6%
Chengdu	28.7%	59.5%	11.8%	4.8%	45.8%	49.4%
Tangshan	21.3%	54.40%	24.30%	8.9%	60.1%	31.0%
Luoyang	7.0%	79.8%	13.2%	7.5%	61.3%	31.2%
Fushun	22.7%	62.8%	14.5%	6.3%	60.5%	33.2%
Jilin	33.7%	50.0%	16.3%	10.0%	50.6%	39.4%
Zhuzhou	25.5%	59.8%	14.7%	8.5%	60.5%	31.0%
Datong	10.7%	67.1%	22.2%	5.5%	50.7%	43.8%
Baotou	27.3%	49.1%	23.6%	2.7%	55.4%	41.9%
Liuzhou	4.0%	77.4%	18.6%	8.6%	63.5%	27.9%

Source: Retrieved from the 20 cities' Statistical Yearbooks.

Among the cities, only eight of them have done both. This paper also demonstrates that de-industrialization occurred in seven provincial capital cities, which means that industrial elements were excluded from the cities' images and that the tertiary sector of the economy replaced the secondary sector, becoming the pillar industry. Among the seven cities that reconstructed their images, only three have promoted industrial tourism attractions on their official websites. However, this number rose to 8 for the 13 cities that have maintained their industrial images. From this, it can be seen that cities with a higher proportion of manufacturing tended to keep industrial images, but still emphasized other components, such as 'high technology' and 'commercial center'. As well, cities whose economic structure had a higher proportion of service industry and a lower proportion of manufacturing tended to reconstruct new city images and promote their modern city images with technological, creative, financial, and educational elements. Therefore, industrial tourism in China has been distorted, changing from the original meaning of reusing industrial heritage resources to developing tourism, and has paid more attention to developing modern industrial tourism attractions instead of exploiting old industrial heritage sites. Industrial heritage tourism is being neglected, even though it could simultaneously record the industrial history and culture as well as build a sense of place for local residents (Xie, 2015).

Discussion and conclusion

In summary, through these city samples, this study sheds light on the features of city images projected by traditional industrial cities and the development of industrial heritage and industrial tourism. In general, from the analysis of the 20 city samples, it can be found that most of the traditional industrial cities are seeking to project their images on official websites, utilizing city marketing to attract external investment and tourists to revitalize their urban economies. However, while some cities paid more attention to industrial elements to highlight their urban industrial culture, others did not. Faced with similar backgrounds of deindustrialization, why do traditional Chinese industrial cities tend to destroy industrial heritage sites while their counterparts in the Western world attempt to preserve and redevelop industrial heritage sites? Below are some possible explanations.

First, China is involved in the globalization process, and Chinese traditional industrial cities have to compete with other intra-national and international cities. As a result of the increasing integration of the global economy, traditional Chinese industrial cities are involved in the globalization process as well as a competition process. This is different from the situation before the reform beginning in the 1990s, during which there was seldom competition with other cities since industrial cities were mainly dependent on national government investment and locally based investment. However, with increasing global competition and dependence on transnational investment opportunities, industrial cities that have lost their traditional manufacturing industries have had to attract external sources of funding or new direct investments in order to regenerate their local economies (Chen & Chen, 2011). Some cities have adopted a new form of governance, urban entrepreneurialism, as a reaction to deindustrialization and a means for economic restructuring and regeneration (Xu & Yeh, 2005), and cities are now engaged in self-marketing just like corporations market their products. Hence, the intensity of city competition has accompanied the rise of city marketing as a strategy to improve their competitiveness. Content analysis of the cities' images indicates that these 20 traditional industrial cities have all expended much effort in building unique, attractive, and 'modern' images through the use of terms such as 'creative' and 'high-technology'. Some of them have reconstructed their images through removing the industrial components from their city images and neglecting their industrial culture and industrial history. Their image reconstruction efforts reflect a repositioning in which looking forward to catch up and compete is the key theme for local governments, instead of recording the past to commemorate their industrial cultures.

Second, there is a reliance on the real estate economy in China in urban areas, and Chinese urban economic development has been characterized as the 'real estate economy' (Zhu, 1999). Before the land reform, beginning in 1988, land was excluded from economic transactions in China, since the public, through the government, supposedly owned all land under the socialist principle. The central planning system that allocated urban land to users through administration channels spared land users monetary payments for land occupation, but the users also had no rights to transfer the land. After the land reform, however, the right-of-use of land, separated from ownership, could be transferred to developers or users for a fixed period after a rental payment. In the same year, reflecting the large demand for land and housing, the national housing reform was enacted, aiming to increase housing consumption through creating a housing market and enabling housing privatization (Li & Huang, 2006). Urban residents could no longer stay in social welfare housing with low rents, but now needed to buy their own properties in the open housing market. Within this background, from the 1990s, once industrial buildings were destroyed, the brownfields could be immediately transacted at a high price and reused to develop real estate, and so the huge demand for land made it more difficult to protect and reuse industrial heritage sites. This is different from the case in the Western context, where one result of the 1970s oil crisis was a degree of deindustrialization resulting in many factories and mines closing down, triggering an economic recession. Much land and many factories and mines were left abandoned, and no one wished to redevelop those brownfields. Other than turning the leftover buildings into tourist attractions, there were few solutions (Taylor & Landorf, 2015).

Third, in the transition to a socialist market economy, labor and industrial culture eroded along with the rise of consumption culture. Before the 1990s, Chinese people, of whom the majority were working class, respected working people and even had the saying 'labor is glorious', such that the working class, including workers and farmers, could feel proud of themselves (Li & Soyez, 2003). However, with the rise of consumerism in China, the public could make their own choices and pursue their own individual desires and unique pleasures. This, to some extent, led to the degradation of social norms and values in Chinese society (Fung, 2009). Compared to being a worker with a low salary, people became more proud of taking professional positions with high salaries that would allow them to afford more fashionable commodities. In the current transition to a socialist market economy, the consumption culture in China has been increasingly replacing labor and industrial culture. Labor and industrial culture have become belittled, and most Chinese people now do not admire the beauty of industrial heritage at all (Li, 2002). In contrast, in Germany, respect for labor and industrial culture is promoted through the development of industrial museums and industrial heritage tourism attractions. Students are organized by their schools to experience the coal-mining process in industrial museums and are educated to respect labor and their industrial history. Tourists are also interested in this particular tourism experience; for instance, the UNESCO World Heritage Site Zollverein Coal Mine Industrial Complex in Essen attracted 1.5 million visitors in 2015 (Stiftung, 2016). The German case indicates that industrial heritage and industrial culture can be preserved and transformed into popular tourist attractions, contributing to local economies.

The paper reveals that Chinese traditional industrial cities, in the context of transition and economic restructuring during the process of urban development, have become participants in global competition rather than reflecting and preserving their pasts. For numerous reasons, industrial heritage and industrial culture have been eroding in China, and the culture of consumption has begun to dominate. Although for traditional industrial cities, transition in the urbanization process is unavoidable, industrial culture as a vital part of urban culture and urban history should be given more attention. Important industrial heritage sites should be preserved in order to record the memory and urban structures of cities, and what is more, developing industrial heritage tourism could also enrich the types of tourism products, attract tourists, protect industrial culture, and regenerate local economies. These advantages would help in the transition period in the urbanization progress.

Traditional industrial cities in China are undergoing great changes due to their restructuring from manufacturing to the service sector. This study is only an exploratory look into the features of industrial heritage tourism development and image reconstruction, since existing studies and policies have paid limited attention to the implications of cultural shifts during this transition, and further research through empirical case studies should be undertaken on the decision-making processes of local governments regarding industrial heritage preservation and image reconstruction. In addition, how to integrate industrial culture into Chinese urban development should be given more attention in the future, both in academic research and in practice.

Notes

1. Official city website of Changchun. http://www.ccszf.gov.cn/ccszf/4/tindex.shtml, accessed on 3 March 2014.
2. Official tourism website of Changchun. http://www.ccta.gov.cn/you.html, accessed on 3 March 2014.

Acknowledgements

I would like to express my gratitude to Professor Xu Honggang for her support and supervision of this research project.

Disclosure statement

No potential conflict of interest was reported by the author.

References

Bramwell, B., & Rawding, L. (1996). Tourism marketing images of industrial cities. *Annals of Tourism Research, 23*, 201–221.

Caffyn, A., & Lutz, J. (1999). Developing the heritage tourism product in multi-ethnic cities. *Tourism Management, 20* (2), 213–221.

Chen, Y., & Chen, Y. (2011). Analysis of China's industrial layout adjustment and industry transfer. *Contemporary Economy & Management, 33*(10), 38–47.

Chen, Y., & Song, Y. (2004). Regeneration and rejuvenation of traditional industrial city of Harbin. *City Planning Review, 28*(4), 81–83.

Choi, S., Lehto, X. Y., & Morrison, A. M. (2007). Destination image representation on the web: Content analysis of Macau travel related websites. *Tourism Management, 28*(1), 118–129.

Colomb, C. (2012). Pushing the urban frontier: Temporary uses of space, city marketing, and the creative city discourse in 2000s Berlin. *Journal of Urban Affairs*, *34*(2), 131–152.

Dong, L., & Zhang, P. (2008). Industrial transformation and employment change of old industrial city: The case of Shenyang, China. *Scientia Geographia Sinica*, *28*(2), 162–168.

Edwards, J. A., & Coit, J. C. L. (1996). Mines and quarries: Industrial heritage tourism. *Annals of Tourism Research*, *23*(2), 341–363.

Fan, X., Soyez, D., & Dai, S. (2012). Social construction and tourism development of industrial heritage: Comparative study between China and Germany. *Thinking*, *38*(6), 123–128.

Firth, T. M. (2011). Tourism as a means to industrial heritage conservation: Achilles heel or saving grace? *Journal of Heritage Tourism*, *6*(1), 45–62.

Fung, A. Y. (2009). Fandom, youth and consumption in China. *European Journal of Cultural Studies*, *12*(3), 285–303.

Garcia, B. (2005). Deconstructing the city of culture: The long-term cultural legacies of Glasgow 1990. *Urban Studies*, *42*(5–6), 841–868.

Gómez, M. V. (1998). Reflective images: The case of urban regeneration in Glasgow and Bilbao. *International Journal of Urban and Regional Research*, *22*(1), 106–121.

Govers, R., & Go, F. M. (2003). Deconstructing destination image in the information age. *Information Technology & Tourism*, *6*(1), 13–29.

Gunn, C. A. (1988). *Vacationscape: Designing tourist regions*. New York, NY: Van Nostrand Reinhold.

Hospers, G. J. (2002). Industrial heritage tourism and regional restructuring in the European Union. *European Planning Studies*, *10*(3), 397–404.

Hospers, G. J. (2009). Lynch, Urry and city marketing: Taking advantage of the city as a built and graphic image. *Place Branding and Public Diplomacy*, *5*(3), 226–233.

Hsu, C. H., & Song, H. (2013). Destination image in travel magazines a textual and pictorial analysis of Hong Kong and Macau. *Journal of Vacation Marketing*, *19*(3), 253–268.

Kavaratzis, M. (2007). City marketing: The past, the present and some unresolved issues. *Geography Compass*, *1*(3), 695–712.

Kavaratzis, M., & Ashworth, G. J. (2007). Partners in coffeeshops, canals and commerce: Marketing the City of Amsterdam. *Cities*, *24*(1), 16–25.

Knapp, W. (1998). The Rhine-Ruhr area in transformation: Towards a European metropolitan region? *European Planning Studies*, *6*(4), 379–393.

Li, C., Zheng, W., & Wang, X. (2004). Study on the tendency of interactive development of urbanization and industrial structure evolvement in China. *Human Geography*, *19*(4), 50–54.

Li, L. (2002). De-industrialization and development of industrial heritage tourism: The actual process and development model of Ruhr in Germany. *World Regional Studies*, *11*(3), 57–65.

Li, L., & Soyez, D. (2003). Evaluation of industrial tourism development of China: From a western perspective. *Human Geography*, *18*(06), 20–25.

Li, S., & Huang, Y. (2006). Urban housing in China: Market transition, housing mobility and neighborhood change. *Housing Studies*, *21*(5), 613–623.

Liu, B. (2012). Industrial heritage conservation: A literature review. *Architectural Journal*, *2012*(1), 12–17.

Lu, C., Yang, Q., Wen, F., & Long, Y. (2010). Study on the relationship between urban land use structure and industry structure: Chongqing as an example. *Urban Development Studies*, *2010*(1), 102–107.

Ning, Z., & Jin, S. (2008). An inspection of 798 artistic zone: A cultural tourist attraction in Beijing. *Tourism Tribune*, *23*(3), 57–62.

Oevermann, H., Degenkolb, J., Dießler, A., Karge, S., & Peltz, U. (2016). Participation in the reuse of industrial heritage sites: The case of Oberschöneweide, Berlin. *International Journal of Heritage Studies*, *22*(1), 43–58.

O'Leary, S., & Deegan, J. (2005). Ireland's image as a tourism destination in France: Attribute importance and performance. *Journal of Travel Research*, *43*(3), 247–256.

Paddison, R. (1993). City marketing, image reconstruction and urban regeneration. *Urban Studies*, *30*(2), 339–349.

Pan, B., & Fesenmaier, D. R. (2006). Online information search: Vacation planning process. *Annals of Tourism Research*, *33*(3), 809–832.

Que, W. (2007). Chinese traditional industrial heritage in the scope of world heritage. *Economic Geography*, *28*(6), 1040–1044.

Richards, G., & Wilson, J. (2004). The impact of cultural events on city image: Rotterdam, cultural capital of Europe 2001. *Urban Studies*, *41*(10), 1931–1951.

Stepchenkova, S., & Morrison, A. M. (2006). The destination image of Russia: From the online induced perspective. *Tourism Management*, *27*(5), 943–956.

Stepchenkova, S., & Zhan, F. (2013). Visual destination images of Peru: Comparative content analysis of DMO and user-generated photography. *Tourism Management*, *36*, 590–601.

Stiftung, Z. (2016). *Press release tourism*. Retrieved from https://www.zollverein.de/uploads/assets/56ec2a456954983de800017d/160308_Tourismus_engl.pdf

Taylor, T., & Landorf, C. (2015). Subject–object perceptions of heritage: A framework for the study of contrasting railway heritage regeneration strategies. *International Journal of Heritage Studies, 21*(10), 1050–1067.

Wang, Y., & Bramwell, B. (2012). Heritage protection and tourism development priorities in Hangzhou, China: A political economy and governance perspective. *Tourism Management, 33*(4), 988–998.

Xie, P. F. (2006). Developing industrial heritage tourism: A case study of the proposed jeep museum in Toledo, Ohio. *Tourism Management, 27*(6), 1321–1330.

Xie, P. F. (2015). A life cycle model of industrial heritage development. *Annals of Tourism Research, 55*, 141–154.

Xu, J., & Yeh, A. G. (2005). Repositioning and competitiveness building in regional development: New development strategies in Guangzhou, China. *International Journal of Urban and Regional Research, 29*(2), 283–308.

Yu, K., & Fang, W. (2006). Exploring China's industrial heritages. *Architectural Journal, 2006*(8), 12–15.

Zhang, Y., & Chai, Y. (2013). Interpreting the cultural connotation of Beijing's modern industrial heritages: From the perspectives of danwei in urban China. *Urban Development Studies, 20*(02), 23–28.

Zhu, H., Liu, Y., & Bao, J. (2002). The exploration of the Old industrial cities' tourism planning: A case study of Huangshi city in Hubei province. *Economic Geography, 22*(S1), 252–257.

Zhu, J. (1999). Local growth coalition: The context and implications of China's gradualist urban land reforms. *International Journal of Urban and Regional Research, 23*(3), 534–548.

Spatial–temporal distribution characteristics of industrial heritage protection and the influencing factors in a Chinese city: a case study of the Tiexi old industrial district in Shenyang

Xiaojun Fan and Shanshan Dai

ABSTRACT

In this article, the temporal and spatial distribution of industrial heritage protection was presented, using the Tiexi old industrial district of Shenyang as a typical case. An explanatory framework was constructed to explain the selected process of industrial heritage. The findings indicate that the highly selective process and the temporal spatial transformation of industrial heritage have been driven by economic, cultural and institutional factors. Tiexi old industrial district is not a single case, but reflects the history and general problems of conserving industrial heritage in China. The case of Tiexi contributes to understanding Chinese industrial heritage in three aspects. First, as to temporal character, there is an excessive concentration ignoring modern and contemporary industrial heritage. Second, from the perspective of space, the fragmented protection mode makes industrial heritage an 'enclave' like lonely islands, thus affecting the overall image of industrial culture. And third, as far as institutional factors are concerned, the government plays the leading role while the workers and other important stakeholders are missing.

Introduction

A city is the main carrier of economic, social, and cultural development. Over the past century, great changes have taken place in China's cities, especially after the founding of the People's Republic of China and China's reform and opening up. Along with the high-speed development of the economy, urbanization is moving forward rapidly. In 1949, there were only six large cities with a population of more than one million, 191 cities with more than 50,000 people and the urban population was 57.65 million, accounting for 10.6% of the total population of China. During the 30 years of reform and opening up, the urban space of China expanded 14 times. According to the National Bureau of Statistics, by the end of 2015, China's urban population was 771.16 million. There were 15 mega-cities with populations of more than 10 million (Shanghai the largest with more than 33 million), totaling almost 260 million inhabitants, and another 90 cities with populations of more than 1 million. Urbanization not only dramatically increased the number and size of China's cities, but also transformed city functions and spatial layout. Therefore, the Chinese urban landscape changed substantially in a very short period.

The rapid process of urbanization brought a great impact on cultural heritage protection, because the contradiction between cultural heritage protection and the massive increase in urban populations requiring expanded land and associated resources, inevitably aggravated environmental conditions and conservation efforts. Old city areas became major renewal zones with the development of real estate, especially as land in the city center gradually became a scarce resource. Many traditional historic sites disappeared rapidly in this progress, urban cultural heritage was destroyed and cities lost their original character.

The protection of urban cultural heritage lags far behind the pace of urban development. The initial protection of cultural heritage was mainly focused on cultural relics. Until the early 1980s, the scope of protection was expanded from tangible heritage to intangible heritage, from single buildings to the historical and cultural city or blocks, but the evaluation still followed the standard of time. While the main protected objects of historic and cultural cities and towns are traditional agriculture cities, the modern industrial city has not been incorporated into the scope of protection and the overall protection ideas have not been used in the industrial city. There are only 29 modern sites from the nineteenth to twentieth centuries, accounting for 3.2% of the total (Li, 2008). Until 1994, the World Heritage Committee proposed putting together a more representative, and balanced world heritage list (Que, 2007), and only since then has modern heritage gradually been incorporated into the scope of protection, including industrial heritage.

Industrial heritage represents industrial civilization. Relevant research began in the discipline of industrial archaeology. Wider studies from other disciplines have focused on it in recent years. Interpretations given to industrial heritage have been as varied as the disciplines and authors interested in the subject: technical complexity of restorations (Stratton, 2000); sustainable use of installations (Bramwell & Lane, 1999; Butler, 1999; Jansen-Verbeke, 1999); economic and social revitalization (Loures, 2008; Summerby-Murray, 2002); as an integral part of a territory and landscape (Benito & Alonso, 2012; Jansen-Verbeke, 2009); tourism value (Saurí-Pujol & Llurdés-Coit, 1995; Synnestvedt, 2006; Wanhill, 2000), and so forth. Research in China has been application oriented, primarily for the purpose of development and utilization, from the perspective of architecture, landscape design and environmental transformation, and heritage protection. The research contents include the definition of concept and value, the introduction of foreign industrial heritage tourism and the case study of the northeast old industrial base (Han & Tong, 2010; Luo Gaoyuan, 2008; Shan, 2006; Wu, 2002). At present, there is little research on the formation process, the influencing factors, the value of the industrial heritage and the underlying causes of these problems especially within Chinese political, economic and cultural contexts.

In the formation process of industrial heritage, how are sites and buildings selected and protected and what are the factors that influence their selection? Some researchers have suggested that the formatting process of industrial heritage is one very discerning selection. Elements of industrial heritage are only selectively preserved. Firstly, it has been pointed out that selection of some sites is in effect 'creating the heritage', which has certain subjective, empirical and descriptive characters. Heritage is re-constructed through the creation of memories and the commercialization process of consumption (Xu, Wan, & Fan, 2014). The formatting process of industrial heritage is thus a process of heritage meaning construction. It is selected by mainstream culture, that is, the process is affected by public comprehension, social culture, economic structure and political institution during a specific period (Peng & Lin, 2008). The blurred and indistinct definition of industrial heritage, absence of institutional protection and inconsistent standard of identification and assessment have resulted in a highly selective process of industrial heritage preservation. In addition, Graham, Ashworth, and Tunbridge (2000) point out that the heritage has dual attributes of internal contradiction, that is, the contradiction between economic attributes and cultural attributes. On the one hand, heritage carries rich cultural meaning, on the other hand, the past is modified and packed by growing commercialization and industrialization into products and experience as a part of modern entertainment consumption.

Industrial heritage has economic attributes, which may constitute an important strategic factor of economic development and recovery of a city, becoming the capital in the economy of the heritage and culture industry and providing a mechanism for economic development (Summerby-Murray, 2007). It is increasingly valued as a result of the growing interest in heritage in general and production-related heritage in particular, and offers significant opportunities as a tourism resource. Xie (2015) proposes a life cycle model of industrial heritage development, consisting of territorialization, deterritorialization, and reterritorialization to illustrate the intricate interplay of identity, landscape and socio-spatial changes. In the stage of territorialization, postindustrial sites are identified as an important heritage source. Deterritorialization denotes the stage in which forces of tourism infuse new meanings into these sites. Reterritorialization indicates a burgeoning phenomenon of repurposing the industrial landscape for the use of creative industries and consequently generating a different territorial identity (Xie, 2015). Industrial heritage conservation involves not only adaptive re-use but also the creation of cultural values of obsolete spaces. If cultural initiatives that aim to create cultural values are operated as a tool for redevelopment and financial revenue-making, they might not play their best role in conservation (Cho & Shin, 2014).

However, many people who have lived through processes of industrial ruination focus on imminent regeneration rather than mourning or celebrating the industrial past (Mah, 2010). More effective political engagement is required to ensure that this is understood by those with power and influence over the historic environment (Oglethorpe, 2014). While actual planning processes have been led by private investors and real estate developers, case studies have shown that participation from the public sector via funding is vital to ensure long-term solutions (Swensen & Stenbro, 2013). Community participation with the relevant authorities, and local initiatives in the reuse of industrial heritage sites have exerted an influence on the development of such areas (Oevermann, Degenkolb, Dießler, Karge, & Peltz, 2016).

When it comes to China, a completely different context should be mentioned. The economic attribute, the cultural attribute and the institutional factors behind it are different. In terms of cultural attributes, Western industrial heritage contains a rich cultural meaning. The feeling of loss caused by deindustrialization promoted the cultural identity of industrial heritage at the end of the 1960s to the early 1970s. To deal with this situation of deindustrialization, (Western) local governments carried out urban economic recovery and reconstruction plans to increase the attractiveness of local culture and leisure. 1975 as European Heritage Year was a key event in changing the concept of cultural heritage. The notion of heritage protection maintained that cultural heritage could retain historical memory to reflect on the present and future development from consideration of the past. In the 1970s, the emergence of the protection movement 'On site' focused on the history of ordinary people's daily life, emphasized the coexistence of history and the surrounding environment, and resulted in innovations such as ' Dg where you stand' in Sweden and Deutsches Museum in Germany. Industrial heritage is an important part of the process which has protected the memory of local societies through such avenues as industrial history, technology, and so on. The rise of the European Industrial Heritage Museum is rooted in civil society, with community playing an important role in the re-use of industrial heritage (Howard, 2002).

The history of industrial development and the process of industrialization in China and Western countries are different, which leads to differences in identification of industrial civilization and industrial heritage. With a 300–400 year-long history of transforming their societies from a rural, agrarian base to manufacturing and urbanization, industrial civilization is the pride of the nation in many Western countries. On the contrary, Chinese industrialization has obvious characteristics of external forces involved in its development, the main force of its modern industry arising from the economic colonial powers of the capitalist countries. The early industrialization process is together with colonial history (Yu & Fang, 2006). After the founding of the People's Republic of China in 1949, the process of industrialization was rapid and short, and it has experienced the modernization process in only 30 to 40 years, in stark contrast to the several hundred years' experience of the west. In China there is no equivalent counterpart to the glory of the industrial revolution in Europe and profound accumulation of industrial culture.

In terms of economic attributes, there are various ways of industrial heritage reuse with a high degree of specialization, which has formed a regional integration in Western countries. The understanding and transformation of industrial civilization together with a conscious focus of onsite protection are emphasized. Although there are components of economic value re-use forms, economic and cultural attributes tend to be more balanced. Attention is not only paid to the material preservation of machines and equipment, but also to the production process of intangible heritage. However, in China, economic-oriented re-use of industrial heritage while meeting the market demand of its consumer society, also brought financial benefits for industrial heritage protection. Compared with protection by government, the financial advantage of a marketing approach is obvious. Therefore, the Chinese re-use mode is one which displays a convergence characterized by a lack of industrial civilization and heritage values, with real estate development strategies assuming the mantle of 'heritage'.

On the other hand, there is a tradition of heritage protection penetrating into culture in Western countries. Industrial heritage is an important driver of place identity, sense of place, and cohesion. Social movements from the lowermost level of workers promoted the discourse of industrial heritage. Individual and non-governmental organizations also played an important role. Its combination makes a good social basis for industrial heritage protection with a balance of driving forces from both top-down and bottom-up. Unlike the Western trajectory, industrial heritage in China reflected more commercial and political values, mainly promoted by government with a lack of participation, of social consensus and social forces.

Industrial heritage can be classified into single industrial heritage sites or places and industrial towns (industrial area) by scale (He & Liu, 2010). Tiexi old industrial district in Shenyang city is a typical industrial town (industrial area). The industrial heritage of Tiexi old industrial zone carries most of the historical memory of the northeast industry. It is the concentrated expression of community spirit, reflecting the historical process of the old industrial base, its development and cultural changes. Since 2002, Tiexi old industrial district has experienced great changes. It presents the development process of cities in the industrialization and urbanization processes in China, influenced by political and economic forces. It demonstrates how political and economic power affect the development of the city. Industrial heritage lost or retained in this process reflects understanding and the processing mode of industrial heritage in the Chinese context under the pressure of economic development. In this article, the characteristics of the industrial process of Tiexi old industrial district are revealed, and the temporal and spatial distribution of industrial heritage is presented. An explanatory framework is constructed to explain the temporal and spatial transformation in industrial heritage.

Research method and background of Tiexi

This article adopts the case study method. Case studies try to research one or several cases to understand one kind of phenomenon. Case studies try to arrive at general conclusions through the analysis and expansions of one specific case (Wang, 2002). Specifically, this study uses literature analysis, participatory observation and interview methods to collect data. In June 2008, February 2010, September 2010, and May 2011, field research was conducted in Tiexi involving the district government, Tiexi tourism bureau, Tiexi archives, Shenyang Foundry Museum, and Shenyang workers' village. Qualitative methods including observation and interviews were used to collect information about the attitudes of different stakeholders such as officials, local residents, and tourists. Total number of interviewees was 32 chosen by the purposive sampling method, including 5 officials, 2 museum staff, 17 local residents, and 8 tourists. As policy-makers, the government which is responsible for decision-making of industrial heritage selection, is an important stakeholder of industrial heritage producers representing the national interest. Community residents and tourists represent the social forces in the industrial heritage selection. Their attitudes and cognition constitute a general public understanding of industrial heritage. During the field research, sampling of interviews with residents and visitors was done according to the research purpose. The open interview and semi-structured interview method was undertaken to ascertain attitudes about industrial heritage.

There are some typical characteristics of this research justifying Tiexi district as a study case. Shenyang is a typical industrial city with rich industrial heritage resources and containing abundant historical value, social and cultural value, and science and technology value. As an old industrial district, the city's boundary, railway line and railway crossing distribution, and street names of Tiexi have distinct industrial features. In October 2008, the 'old factory story of Tiexi' became a municipal non-material cultural heritage project of Shenyang city, Liaoning Province, which is the only oral literature heritage that currently reflects the industrial age (He & Liu, 2010).

Tiexi is an administrative district in Shenyang City, founded in 1938. The first mint, first arsenal, first truck, first use of mechanical porcelain production in China all occurred in Tiexi during 1900–1929. After the founding of the People's Republic of China, Shenyang became known as a 'Department of Industrial Equipment of China', which was a heavy industry base developed in the first and second Five-Year Plans. Tiexi is called 'the hometown of machine tools', and the birthplace of the metallurgical industry, and the nation's largest foundry enterprise was also located there.

After 2002, Shenyang established Tiexi New District and carried out the development strategy of 'Move the East and Construct the West', which meant relocating the industrial enterprises in the eastern part of the old industrial zone to the West zone and the eastern region focused on new developments of service industry. Two hundred and fifty-four factories were moved out, and 8.6 km^2 of industrial land was used to build commercial and residential buildings (Zhang, Hu, & Xiong, 2011). Due to the large-scale renewal mode of demolition and reconstruction, the urban style and culture of Tiexi have undergone tremendous changes. The former 'South living and North working' pattern was broken and the former integrated industrial landscape gradually changed its distribution points and lines. The industrial buildings decreased significantly from 16.9% in 1997 to 7.83% in 2008. The proportion of commercial buildings exhibited the fastest growth with an average annual growth rate of 20.22% over the past 11 years, while, the proportion of industrial buildings reduced at a rate of 4.88% per annum (Zhang et al., 2011). Factory historical sites have been very vague and difficult to identify. The disappearance of industrial plants and buildings meant that the Tiexi industrial culture lost its material carrier. Due to the lack of awareness of industrial heritage at that time, the government did little to protect the industrial heritage of the city.

After the wide acceptance of the concept of industrial heritage by domestic authorities and the importance of the protection of industrial heritage was recognized in 2006, the central government began to implement heritage protection policies. Local government began to take some protective measures. Since then, Shenyang Foundry Museum, Shenyang Workers Village Living Museum and other public cultural facilities have been built. In this process, Tiexi was transformed from a single industrial area into a modern service center which integrates trade, real estate, and financial services, etc. The proportion of manufacturing and service industries changed from 95:5 to 75:25. Industrial heritage and industrial culture in Tiexi received more attention from then on (The people's Government of Tiexi District, 2010). In 2008, Tiexi district became one of the 18 typical regions of the country in 30 years of reform and opening up and won the Demonstration Prize for the UN Global Best Livable Area Award. The inherent progress of Tiexi Old Industrial District was not only a result of the influence of international heritage protection standards but also the need for Tiexi itself to conserve its urban culture. China's industrial heritage work has progressed from massive demolition to rescue and protection and the case of Tiexi reflects this progress typically and clearly. The research scope of this study is the old industrial area of Tiexi, a district which covered an area of 39.48 km^2 before 2002.

The spatial and temporal characteristics of selected items of industrial heritage in Tiexi

Spatial distribution characteristics

Before 2002, as noted the residential buildings of Tiexi were located in the south while factories were located in the north. Tiexi is surrounded by railways and intersected with high density roads and railways. There are 8 railway lines, length 19,553 m, 70 railway crossings and 5 railway overpass bridges distributed throughout this area. They constitute a unique city and space image of Tiexi and can be regarded as certain forms of intangible industrial heritage. In addition, the street names retain and reflect the industrial cultural history of Tiexi. The south residential and north industrial working pattern is distinct with Jianshe Road named in 1946 and meaning 'construction of industrial zone'. The streets named in 1957 still in use today retain the mark of the industrial age with the two suffixes 'gong' and 'ye' included in their nomenclature. The combination of 'gong' and 'ye' is 'gongye' which means 'industry.' There are 68 streets named 'gong' and 20 roads named 'ye' in Tiexi, such as Xinggong Street, Baogong Street, Zhaogong Street, Weigong Street, Zhonggong street, and Weiye Road, Daye Road, Gongye road, and Xunye road. Despite great changes in the city, the street names in Tiexi still reflect its original industrial history.

After 2002, the impact of new economic development and urban construction disrupted the industrial era spatial pattern of 'south house-north factory'. The historical and cultural sites, industrial museums, urban cultural square and creative industry park constitute the line-point spatial distribution pattern. The industrial heritage sites are distributed in linear mode along Jianshe Road from east to west and Weigong River park from north to south. The isolated industrial heritage sites consist of four categories: 15 historical and cultural sites, 3 industrial museums (Industrial Museum of China, Shenyang Workers Village Living Museum, Tiexi Figures Museum), an industrial cultural square (Heavy Machinery Plant Square) and 1 creative industrial park (Tiexi 1905 Cultural and Creative Industrial Park). Industrial museums, the Industrial Cultural Square and the Creative Industrial Park are co-located and overlap in space. For example, the historical building group of Tiexi Workers Village is in the same location as the Shenyang Workers Village Living Museum and the Tiexi Figures Museum. Shenyang Foundry No.1 Workshop (foundry casting) is located in the same place as the Industrial Museum of China (Figure 1).

The Casting Museum, the Workers Living Museum, the Heavy Industry Cultural Square, and the Weigong River Lineal Park have become prominent symbols of industrial heritage. The re-use mode of industrial heritage is combined with the citizen's leisure and entertainment public space. Industrial museums began to carry out industrial heritage tourism in 2007, then to charge an entry price in May 2009 and the visitors are mainly packaged tourists. Labor Park, Weigong River Lineal Park, and Tiexi Heavy Industry Cultural Square provide public space for people to rest and relax. The urban planning of Shenyang combines industrial heritage with public space where citizens may relax and be entertained, thus emphasizing the function of industrial heritage in the shaping of the city's characteristic style and cultural experience space. The rich types of industrial elements constitute the overall image of the industrial heritage of Tiexi (Figure 2).

Temporal distribution characters

The temporal distribution of Tiexi's industrial heritage is concentrated in two periods. Among the 15 historical and cultural Sites, 7 are the legacy of 1930–1945 and eight originated in the 1950s.The temporal distribution characteristic is consistent with the industrial development history of Tiexi. It also reflects the industrial heritage cognition and value evaluation attitude which focuses on the important historical period (Table 1).

Figure 1. Some features of selected industrial heritage in Tiexi. Source: Authors own.

Influencing factors of industrial heritage retained in Tiexi

The process of heritage formation is affected by public comprehension, social culture, economic structure, and political institution during a specific period. Graham et al. (2002) pointed out that the heritage has the dual attributes of internal contradiction, that is, the contradiction between economic attributes and cultural attributes. Both economic and cultural factors are important influential factors in the heritage forming process.

The highly selective process and the spatial transformation of industrial heritage in Tiexi have been driven by economic factors, institutional factors, and socio-cultural factors. The most important driving force is economic development and consequential adjustment of the city's functions. Industrial structure adjustment and change of urban functions re-combine the spatial framework of urban land use. Due to differences in land prices, commercial, financial, and other industries gradually agglomerated to the center of the city, and the original industry located in the central area gradually transferred to the outskirts. Retention of industrial heritage is an up-down process by government in the historical and cultural site system. In this process, a few industrial heritage sites become industrial museums, while others are consumed by economics to become cultural products. Therefore, most industrial places were replaced by high-rise buildings to meet the functional requirements of the city center. The highly concentrated temporal distribution shows the obvious

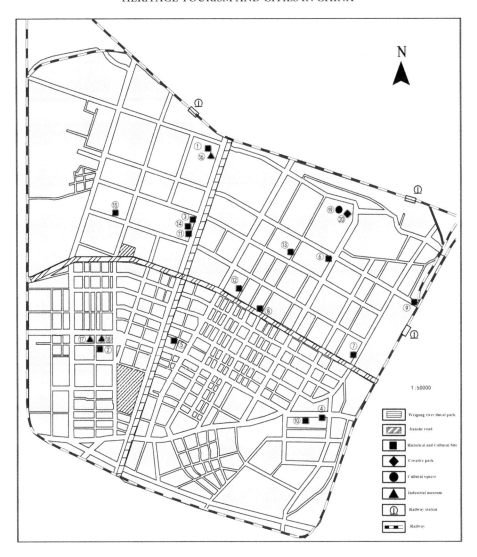

Figure 2. Distribution chart of selected items of industrial heritage in Tiexi old industrial area.

evaluation standard tendency decided at the institutional level. The social and cultural factors reflect the lack of industrial identity and heritage values in China as a result of the problem of short history, special process of industrialization, and the negative influences of industrialization.

Economic factors: impact of capital on culture

The transformation of Tiexi stems mainly from economic reasons. In the mid-1990s, Tiexi was in a period of recession; the average rate of asset-liability ratio of enterprises was as high as 90%, debt accumulated to 26 billion Yuan, nearly 100,000 workers were retrenched, 40% of the enterprise was in a semi shut-down state and 50% of the plants were idle (Zhang, 2006). The economy began to recover after the initiation of the project for 'Moving heavy industrial factories from east to west' in 2002. By 2006, the GDP of the Tiexi new district reached 27.6 billion Yuan which was 2.63 times greater than 2002 and the local fiscal revenue was 2.615 billion which was 3.5 times more than 2002 (Dong, 2007). The original industrial zone has become the city's center area with

Table 1. Industrial heritage of officially protected site/entity in Tiexi.

No.	Name	Period of construction	Protection type	Protection (year)
1	Shenyang Foundry No.1 Workshop (foundry casting)	1956	Historical and cultural site protected at the provincial level	2008
2	Historical group of Tiexi Workers Village buildings	1952	Historical and cultural site protected at the city level	2013
3	Decomposition Filtering Workshop of Manchuria Agricultural Chemical Industry Company Fengtian factory	1945	Not evaluated historical and cultural site	2011
4	Aviation repair factory site of Fengxi airport	1933	Not evaluated historical and cultural site	2011
5	Shenyang Workers Cultural Palace	1957	Not evaluated historical and cultural site	2011
6	Club of Shenyang Cable Factory	1956	Not evaluated historical and cultural site	2011
7	Manchuria Ale Company well site	1930	Historical and cultural site protected at the district level	2011
8	Workshop of Xinhua Printing Factory	1950s	Not evaluated historical and cultural site	2011
9	Water tower of Shenyang Water Supply Station	1950	Not evaluated Historical and Cultural Site	2011
10	Hangar of Fengxi Airport	Republican period	Not evaluated historical and cultural site	2011
11	Plant site of vapor factory, Branch of Shenyang Chemical Limited	1957	Not evaluated historical and cultural site	2011
12	Shenyang No.4 Rubber Factory	1957	Not evaluated historical and cultural site	2011
13	Shenyang High Voltage Switchgear Factory	1937	Not evaluated historical and cultural site	2011
14	Shenyang Chemical Plant	1938	Not evaluated historical and cultural site	2011
15	Shenyang Coking Gas Plant	1930s	Not evaluated historical and cultural site	2011
16	Industrial Museum of China	1956	Industrial museum	2007
17	Shenyang Workers Village Living Museum	1952	Industrial museum	2007
18	Tiexi Figures Museum			
19	Heavy Machinery Plant Square	1937	Industrial cultural square	2009
20	Tiexi 1905 Cultural and Creative Industrial Park	1937	Creative industrial park	2013

higher land prices, with the price increasing to 2000–3000 RMB per square meter from the original 500 RMB, while commercial land has risen to 4000 RMB per square meters. The location advantage and rising price of the land attracted economic capital to pursue profit-making in Tiexi.

The reconstruction pattern of Tiexi is to use real estate projects to replace the original industrial land. The urban renovation projects aim to maximize the economic benefits, which is disadvantageous to the protection of industrial heritage. In the process of the transformation of Tiexi, two viewpoints have been in fierce collision (He, Yang, & Ru, 2007). The critics believe that the symbol of the old industrial age were largely obscured by tertiary industries, they proposed that the treatment of industrial heritage should not only consider economic value but also consider its cultural value, and should explore and use the original industrial and cultural landscape to continue the industrial cultural atmosphere (Zhang, Zhang, & Chen, 2004). On the contrary, some others believe that compared to the city's economic development and the people's livelihood issues, nostalgia for the protection of industrial heritage is unwarranted (Yuan, 2008, p. 82). In the reconstruction process of Tiexi, economic interests are the most decisive factors, since reconstruction programs that can obtain high returns are more likely to be adopted. Even though the cultural value of industrial heritage can be changed into economic value through material reconstruction and re-use, the economic value is often invisible and unpredictable and difficult to recover. Because of the large volume and occupied area of industrial heritage sites, huge

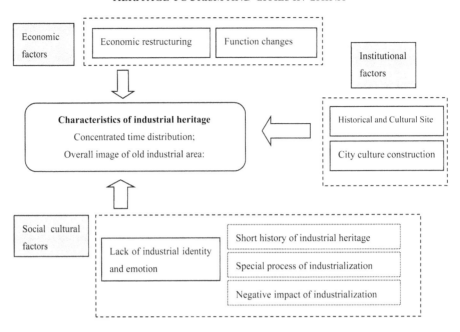

Figure 3. Influencial factors in the industrial heritage selected process in Tiexi.

protection funds have to be invested. For example, Tiexi needs to invest about 15 million Yuan to collect industrial heritage waste annually, and even when collected at the price of scrap metal it would cost up to about 12 million Yuan. The shortage of funds has accelerated the deterioration of industrial heritage protection. Ultimately, the imbalance of economic and cultural interests in competition led to the fragmentation of Tiexi's industrial heritage, the industrial structure of the 'South House-North Factory' was broken, and the characteristics of the city's industrial culture atmosphere gradually faded. The hard-working and dedicated spirit of labor model as the core of Tiexi industrial heritage formed a simple but strong industrial heritage environment. After large-scale urban renewal, the cultural ideas have transformed from industrial to commercial. It is no longer the ideal of 'Industry prospering, Tiexi thriving', but rather that the commercial urban cultural milieu has strengthened and the industrial characteristics have gradually weakened (Figure 3).

Socio-cultural factors: lack of industrial identity and supportive sentiment/attachment to supporting values

Attachment to supporting values for identification of industrial history in China is lacking because of the characteristics of China's industrial heritage itself. Firstly, as a modern concept, the history of valuing industrial heritage in China is very short compared with other types of heritage. The value of industrial heritage has often been neglected because of a general valuation based on standard of time. City residents know less about industrial heritage compared to, for example, literary heritage, art heritage, the heritage of calligraphy and so forth, and generally believe that industrial remains are so recent and lack aesthetic value that they do not qualify as heritage (Li & Soyez, 2003). The concentrative time-distribution characteristics of industrial heritage also reflect this viewpoint clearly. Interviews with community residents and visitors confirmed this point, such as one interviewee who said: 'It seems the history of industrial things is not so long, I don't know what value they have'. Secondly, China's industrial society has had little influence on understanding its cultural attributes because of its short development time. The main driving force of modern industry arose from the Western capitalist countries; the early stage of industrialization of China carried the stamp of Western colonial powers, which could not be avoided but difficult to accept emotionally. Thirdly, many people tend to have a negative impression of industrialization. It is often related to production processes, which are perceived to cause the destruction and/or of the degradation of the environment and the landscape and are antithetical to romantic aesthetic connotations. They think that industrial heritage has a 'black' side, such as pollution, environmental destruction and colonial invasion. So people have mixed feelings of 'like and dislike' and think 'industry is ugly' (Alfrey & Putnam, 1992). The demolition of chimneys in the Shenyang smelting factory founded in 1936 is a typical case. The destruction of the chimneys and the relocation of the factories brought about perceived improvements in the living conditions and most local residents supported their removal. Now on the former site of the smelting factory, modern high rise buildings have replaced the industrial structure. In addition, the reason why Tiexi's industrial buildings were demolished was due to inade-quacies in functional design and construction. Most industrial buildings of Tiexi were built in the 1950s–1960s, limited by the engineering technology and architectural standards of that time, so that construction technology, structure, spacial layout and quality were not high. Since it often costs more to upgrade the structure of an old industrial building than to rebuild it, they were torn down and replaced. These narrow ideas often hamper confidence in the transformation and re-use of old buildings (Chen, 2007).

Institutional factors: single model dominated by government

In Tiexi, government plays a very important role in industrial heritage conservation. The histori-cal and cultural sites and the city cultural squares are promoted and financially supported by gov-ernment. Other re-use forms combined with public leisure space to improve the cultural image of the city are also affected by government policy. The government-dominant model is a common characteristic of Chinese industrial heritage conservation and re-use. On one hand, it reflects the characteristics of industrial heritage as public property. On the other hand, it reflects the absence of participation of community residents, industrial enterprises and other stakeholders. This simple top-down approach has hindered the diversification of industrial heritage. At the same time, due to an excessive tendency to apply evaluation based on standards of certain periods at the institutional level, the temporal distribution of preserved industrial heritage appears highly concentrated, and cannot fully reflect the transition of the processes of industrialization and modernization.

The situation in Tiexi reflects the lack of integral protection measures and narrow time evaluation criteria of industrial heritage protection. This has led to a dramatic reduction of old buildings, changes of the industrial city pattern, disruption of community structure and the diminution of Tiexi's industrial cultural atmosphere. Many reasons have led to the current situation. Firstly, the protection of industrial heritage mainly exists in the form of historical and cultural sites at present, and this form of protection has neglected the diversification of industrial heritage. The value assess-ment system of industrial heritage is imperfect, and the definition and the technical standards are not unified; thus, it is difficult to protect and re-use industrial heritage. Secondly, industrial sites that could qualify as heritage often belong to industrial enterprises, and once there is an application to become a historical and cultural site, it means not only stripping ownership from the enterprises but also having to bear the subsequent responsibility of repair and maintenance. The imbalance of rights and responsibilities has resulted in companies being reluctant to take the initiative to apply for industrial heritage as official historical and cultural sites (Dai & Que, 2011). In addition, existing ideas of urban renewal (manifested is such slogans as *The city changing face as soon as poss-ible is the symbol of development*) and the potential role of overemphasizing political achievements (e.g. *Speedy changes in investment promotion and city appearance are the most obvious, direct and simple reflections of political achievement*), make protecting of industrial heritage difficult.

Discussion and conclusion

Tiexi is a microcosm of Chinese industrial heritage conservation and re-use, and urban gentrification. In the last 100 years, momentous changes have occurred in this city. It has experienced rapid urbanization and the function and nature of the city are changing all the time. 100 years ago, Shenyang was the regional political and commercial center, and now it has been transformed into an economic and cultural center. During the century, industrial development laid the pattern and foundation of many cities in China, and to a certain extent also constituted the characteristics of urban culture. Under the impact of economic development and urban construction, Tiexi's industrial area's spatial pattern of 'south house-north plant' has been broken. Historical and cultural sites, industrial museums, the urban cultural square and the creative industry park constitute the line-point spatial distribution pattern instead of overall old industrial area protection.

The case of Tiexi contributes to an understanding Chinese urban industrial heritage in at least three ways. As to temporal character, there is an excessive concentration ignoring modern and contemporary industrial heritage. From the perspective of space, the fragmented protection mode makes industrial heritage an 'enclave' like lonely islands, which affects the overall image of industrial heritage. As far as institutional factors are concerned, the government plays the leading role while the workers and other important stakeholders are missing.

First of all, the temporal distribution of industrial heritage in Tiexi is very concentrated, mainly spread over the colonial and semi-colonial period, and the early national industrial period, so that these time spans do not fully reflect the changes of industrial civilization in the process of industrialization and modernization. This kind of spatial and temporal distribution fully reflects the great salient changes taking place in Chinese cities, especially industrial cities. The formatting process of industrial heritage is different from the heritage ancient villages and ancient towns. It lacks integrated protection. Industrialization in China has existed for a relatively short time and is so infiltrated into daily life that residents are still living it; as a result, many people neglect the existence of industry as heritage. According to most people's perceptions, only representative imperial palaces, symbolic art, architecture, glorious, and historical heritage is cultural heritage. In industrial heritage is just a product of social development transition with no depth of meaning or cultural value. Industrial heritage is a part of industrialization and modernization processes along with other features of everyday 'living' heritage. This kind of heritage is not only confined to history and the past, but also includes the 'now'. Industrial estates should not be frozen to fit into a specific historical period like a museum piece, but should take full account of the time and space continuum. To avoid time and space fragmentation, different periods of industrial heritage, including the present-day 'living' heritage could be selected. Industrial heritage can reflect the changes of an industrial civilization and the connotation of industrial culture comprehensively.

Secondly, from the perspective of inheritance, the old industrial zone in Tiexi is a complete industrial heritage area the plant and environment of the factory 'owns' unique industrial language, they have their own charm and value'. The preservation of industrial heritage cannot rely on the construction of a number of museums to display a few pictures; the great dignity and momentum of heavy industry can be felt by people only when personally standing in front of a huge plant or machinery (Yuan, 2008). In spite of the advantages of only choosing an individual old plant and old factory with particularly important significance, the fragmented protection approach makes industrial heritage like a lonely island, being separated away from the overall environment. Incidentally, the highly selective nature of protecting historical objects will inevitably bring about a one-sided value judgment, causing the separation of the industrial heritage from it's surrounding community, forming a binary opposite 'heritage island'. The fragmented heritage protection mode or the use of museums impact the representative and real value of industrial heritage, and from the perspective of heritage protection it is not recommended. But the integral protection mode is more difficult to operate; it will take more time and energy and will cost more. Therefore, a feasible way of protecting heritage is to combine the points, lines and faces heritage. Through lineal protection, coordinate the solitary building with the whole industrial zone, while giving consideration to both the intangible cultural heritage such as plant construction, and non-material heritage such as industrial culture and the image of the city.

Thirdly, the protection of Chinese industrial heritage occurs mainly through external promotion without forming a general social consensus or involvement of key stakeholders. In such a situation lacking independent positive feedback, the promotion of industrial heritage protection is very limited. How to expand the social consensus of industrial heritage, to mobilize the participation of social forces, to achieve relative balance between economic attributes and cultural attributes, -- all these factors are needed in order to pay more attention to studying Chinese industrial heritage. The localization of industrial heritage is very important and worthy of additional research.

Disclosure statement

No potential conflict of interest was reported by the authors.

Funding

This work was supported by Liaoning Provincial Federation Social Science Circles [Grant No. lslgslhl-144], Liaoning Planning Office of Philosophy and Social Science [Grant No. L16BGL040].

References

Alfrey, J., & Putnam, T. (1992). *The industrial heritage: Managing resources and uses.* London: Routledge.

Benito, P., & Alonso, P. (2012). Industrial heritage and place identity in Spain: From monuments to landscapes. *The Geographical Review, 102*(4), 446–464. doi:10.1111/j.1931-0846.2012.00169.x

Bramwell, B., & Lane, B. (1999). Sustainable tourism: Contributing to the debates. *Journal of Sustainable Tourism, 7*(1), 1–5. doi:10.1080/09669589908667323

Butler, R. W. (1999). Sustainable tourism: A state-of-the-art review. *Tourism Geographies, 1*(1), 7–25. doi:10.1080/14616689908721291

Chen, B. C. (2007). On Shenyang Tiexi industrial district: The existing situation and transformed prospects. *Urban Space Design*, (5), 21–23. doi:10.3969/j.issn.1672-9080.2007.05.005

Cho, M., & Shin, S. (2014). Conservation or economization? Industrial heritage conservation in Incheon, Korea. *Habitat International, 41*, 69–76. doi:10.1016/j.habitatint.2013.06.011

Dai, X. Y., & Que, W. M. (2011). Temporal–spatial distribution of mining heritages in China: The perspective of officially protected site/entity. *Geographical Research, 30*(4), 747–757.

Dong, F. (2007). The path selection and basic experience of the revitalization of the industrial zone in Tiexi, Shenyang. *Macroeconomic Management*, 7, 67–69. Retrieved from http://www.cnki.net/KCMS/detail/detail.aspx?QueryID=0&CurRec=1&recid=&filename=HGJG200707023&dbname=CJFD2007&dbcode=CJFQ&pr=&urlid=&yx=&v=MDk1MTVUcldNMUZyQ1VSTHlmWStacEZ5bmtVTDdPTFNyQmFiRzRIdGJNcUk5SFo0UjhlWDFMdXhZUzdEaDFUFUM3E=

Graham, B., Ashworth, G. J., & Tunbridge, J. E. (2000). *A geography of heritage: Power, culture, and economy.* New York, NY: Oxford University Press.

Han, F. W., & Tong, Y. Q. (2010). The investigation of industrial heritage protection and tourism use in Shenyang. *Territory & Natural Resources Study*, (1), 77–79. doi:10.3969/j.issn.1003-7853.2010.01.037

He, J., & Liu, L. H. (2010). The construction of industrial heritage conservation system – From the traditional industrial heritage on Chinese intangible cultural heritage lists. *Urban Studies, 17*(8), 116–122. doi:10.3969/j.issn.1006-3862.2010.08.019

He, R., Yang, C. M., & Ru, J. H. (2007). Interview on Tiexi district. *Time Architecture*, (1), 132–135. doi:10.3969/j.issn.1005-684X.2007.01.024

Howard, P. (2002). The eco-museum: Innovation that risks the future. *International Journal of Heritage Studies*, *8*(1), 63–72. doi:10.1080/13527250220119947

Jansen-Verbeke, M. (1999). Industrial heritage: A nexus for sustainable tourism development. *Tourism Geographies*, *1*(1), 70–85. doi:10.1080/14616689908721295

Jansen-Verbeke, M. (2009). The territoriality paradigm in cultural tourism. *Tourism*, *19*(1–2), 25–31. doi:10.2478/V10106-009-0003-z

Li, C. X. (2008). *Heritage: Origin and rule*. Kunming: Yunnan Education Publishing House.

Li, L. L., & Soyez, D. (2003). Evaluation of industrial tourism development of China: From a western perspective. *Human Geograhpy*, *18*(6), 20–25. doi:10.3969/j.issn.1003-2398.2003.06.005

Loures, L. (2008). Industrial heritage: The past in the future of the city. *Wseas Transactions on Environment and Development*, *4*(8), 687–696. Retrieved from http://www.wseas.us/e-library/transactions/environment/2008/27-696.pdf

Luo, G. Y. (2008). Industrial heritage and its tourism value in China. *Economic Geography*, *28*(1), 173–176. Retrieved from http://d.wanfangdata.com.cn/Periodical/jjdl200801037

Mah, A. (2010). Memory, uncertainty and industrial ruination: Walker riverside, Newcastle upon Tyne. *International Journal of Urban & Regional Research*, *34*(2), 398–413. doi:10.1111/j.1468-2427.2010.00898.x

Oevermann, H., Degenkolb, J., Dießler, A., Karge, S., & Peltz, U. (2016). Participation in the reuse of industrial heritage sites: The case of oberschöneweide, Berlin. *International Journal of Heritage Studies*, *22*(1), 43–58. doi:10.1080/13527258.2015.1083460

Oglethorpe, M. (2014). The Rolt Memorial Lecture 2013: The public benefit of industrial heritage - taking a positive view. *Industrial Archaeology Review*, *36*(2), 85–96. doi:10.1179/0309072814Z.00000000032

Peng, Z. R., & Lin, Y. Q. (2008). Interpretation of heritage. *Guizhou Social Sciences*, *218*(2), 13–18. doi:10.3969/j.issn.1002-6924.2008.02.002

Que, W. M. (2007). On international protection and research of industrial property. *Acta Scientiarum Naturalium Universitatis Pekinensis*, *43*(4), 523–534. doi:10.3321/j.issn:0479-8023.2007.04.014

Saurí-Pujol, D., & Llurdés-Coit, J. C. (1995). Embellishing nature: The case of the Salt Mountain Project of Cardona, Catalonia, Spain. *Geoforum*, *26*(1), 35–48. doi:10.1016/0016-7185(95)00016-E

Shan, J. X. (2006). Focus on protection of industrial heritage, a new form of cultural heritage. *China Culture Heritage*, *4*(4), 10–48. Retrieved from http://www.cnki.net/KCMS/detail/detail.aspx?QueryID=1&CurRec=1&recid=&filename=CCRN200604003&dbname=CJFD2006&dbcode=CJFQ&pr=&urlid=&yx=&v=MjY5NjIxTHV4WVM3RGgxVDNxVHJXTTFGckNVUkx5ZlkrWnBGQ3ZoV3JyTEppN1pZTEc0SHRmTXE0OUZaNFI4ZVg=

Stratton, M. (2000). *Industrial buildings: Conservation and regeneration*. London: Taylor & Francis.

Summerby-Murray, R. (2002). Interpreting deindustrialised landscapes of Atlantic Canada: Memory and industrial heritage in Sackville, New Brunswick. *The Canadian Geographer*, *46*(1), 48–62. doi:10.1111/j.1541-0064.2002.tb00730.x

Summerby-Murray, R. (2007). Interpreting personalized industrial heritage in the mining towns of Cumberland County, Nova Scotia: Landscape examples from Springhill and River Hebert. *Urban History Review*, *35*(2), 51–59. doi:10.7202/1015921ar

Swensen, G., & Stenbro, R. (2013). Urban planning and industrial heritage – A Norwegian case study. *Journal of Cultural Heritage Management and Sustainable Development*, *3*(2), 175–190. doi:10.1108/JCHMSD-10-2012-0060

Synnestvedt, A. (2006). Who wants to visit a cultural heritage site? – A walk through an archaeological site with a visual and bodily experience. In L. Russell (Ed.), *Images, representations and heritage* (pp. 333–351). New York, NY: Springer.

The people's Government of Tiexi District. (2010). Economical and intensive use of land resources to promote the transformation and revitalization of old industrial bases in Tiexi. *Land & Resources*, *12*, 18–19. doi:10.3969/j.issn.1671-1904.2010.12.006

Wang, N. (2002). Representative or typical? – The logical basis and the method of case study. *Sociological Studies*, (5), 123–125. Retrieved from http://www.cnki.com.cn/Article/CJFDTotal-SHXJ200205010.htm

Wanhill, S. (2000). Mines - A tourist attraction: Coal mining in industrial South Wales. *Journal of Travel Research*, *39*(1), 60–69. doi:10.1177/004728750003900108

Wu, X. L. (2002). Main characters and experience of British industrial tourism. *World Regional Studies*, *11*(4), 73–79. doi:10.3969/j.issn.1004-9479.2002.04.011

Xie, P. F. (2015). A life cycle model of industrial heritage development. *Annals of Tourism Research*, *55*, 141–154. doi:10.1016/j.annals.2015.09.012

Xu, H. G., Wan, X. J., & Fan, X. J. (2014). Rethinking authenticity in the implementation of China's heritage conservation: The case of Hongcun Village. *Tourism Geographies*, *16*(5), 799–811. doi:10.1080/14616688.2014.963662

Yu, K. J., & Fang, W. L. (2006). Industrial heritage in China. *Architectural Journal*, (8), 12–15. doi:10.3969/j.issn.0529-1399.2006.08.003

Yuan, Z. (2008). Industrial culture and its inheritance dilemma – land use and industrial culture inheritance in the transformation of Tiexi District Shenyang City. *Theory Horizon*, *9*(9), 80–83. doi:10.3969/j.issn.1003-6547.2008.09.036

Zhang, P. F., Hu, Y. M., He, H. S., Xiong, Z. P., & Liu, M. (2010). Dynamic changes of urban architecture landscape based on Barista: A case study in Tiexi District of Shenyang City. *Chinese Journal of Applied Ecology*, *21*(12), 3105–3112. Retrieved from http://d.wanfangdata.com.cn/Periodical/yystxb201012015

Zhang, P. F., Hu, Y. M., & Xiong, Z. P. (2011). Spatiotemporal variation characteristics and related affecting factors of architecture landscape in Tiexi district of Shenyang. *Chinese Journal of Ecology*, *30*(2), 335–342. Retrieved from https://www.researchgate.net/publication/283756102_Spatiotemporal_variation_characteristics_and_related_affecting_factors_of_architecture_landscape_in_Tiexi_District_of_Shenyang

Zhang, P. Y. (2006). Institutional and cultural factors for the reconstruction of Shenyang Tiexi industrial zone. *Human Geograhpy*, (1), 45–48. doi:10.3969/j.issn.1003-2398.2006.02.010

Zhang, Y. F., Zhang, M. H., & Chen, B. C. (2004). On the transform of industrial landscape of Old district: A New task during renovation of Tiexi Industrial District, Shenyang. *Modern Urban Research*, *11*(11), 34–38. doi:10.3969/j.issn.1009-6000.2004.11.008

Transnationalizing industrial heritage valorizations in Germany and China – and addressing inherent dark sides

Leilei Li and Dietrich Soyez

ABSTRACT

Industrial heritage valorizations are usually characterized by two pervasive trends: *Firstly*, there is an understandable, but extremely narrow, focus on national histories of industrialization, thus excluding what has always been a constitutive element of any industrialization path after the initial industrial revolution in England: transboundary flows of hardware, capital, knowledge, people or power. *Secondly*, there is an almost exclusive concentration on the individual achievements of entrepreneurs, engineers and architects in times of peace and industrial progress. Current industrial heritage valorizations only rarely adequately reflect the other side of industrialization phases or patterns, that is, their disquieting stories of war, occupation, other forms of imposed foreign influence, disasters, social unrest and the suffering of individuals or groups triggered by, or leading to, crises, failures, relocations and destruction. Taking these blind spots as its starting point, this paper explores more inclusive ways of representing industrial heritage. Based on the concept of geo-historically entangled processes of transnationalization and case studies from Germany and China, the authors argue that the industrial landscapes reflect both former and current transboundary industrialization processes representing two or more nations' painful and dissonant, but common, heritage. This should be mirrored more appropriately and consistently in industrial heritage tourism approaches and interpretation strategies.

Preface

On 5 July 2015, during the 39th session of the UNESCO World Heritage Commission at Bonn, Germany, the legacy of a potentially highly important industrial tourist destination complex was inscribed into the list: 23 sites mirroring the establishment of iron and steel, shipbuilding and coal mining of the Japanese Meiji industrial revolution between 1850 and 1910 (Japan World Heritage Nomination, 2014). They testify to 'what is considered to be the first successful transfer of Western industrialization to a non-Western nation' (http://whc.unesco.org/en/list/1484).

Thus, the political, diplomatic and media tug-of-war between Japan, Korea and China preceding the inscription was put to an end by a trade-off: During the preparatory work and, in particular, since the official nomination of the sites in 2014, Korea had formally contested the inscription, contending that the hardships of Korean forced labour at some of the sites during mid-twentieth-century periods of war and annexation should be regarded as a clear reason for exclusion. Immediately prior to the vote, Japan agreed in an official statement to develop interpretation strategies allowing an under-standing of 'the full history of each site,' that is, addressing the suffering of a large number of Koreans and others who were brought to the industrial facilities against their will, and to remember the victims (cf. the adoption of an amendment in the form of a footnote submitted by Germany to paragraph 4g, cf. WHC-15/39.COM/INF.19).

At the same time, the inscription for the first time sheds light at the global level on the fact that both transnational and dark facets mark many industrial sites all over the world, thus setting the scene for the main thrusts of the following paper as well as the necessity to develop appropriate interpretational strategies at such sites.

Introduction

For more than two centuries, industrialization paths anywhere in the world, with the possible exception of the initial period in England, have been characterized by transboundary patterns of interaction in times of both peace and war. Yet, traditional industrial heritage approaches in Europe, North America and Asia indulge in decidedly national narratives and achievements, thus reproducing what a political geographer denounced two decades ago as the 'territorial trap' of international relations theory (Agnew, 1994).

Starting from these apparent blind spots in traditional heritage approaches to industrialization and industries, this paper aims to explore more inclusive and complementary ways of (re)constructing the historical industrial facts. It thereby searches for alternative ways of thinking about and (re) presenting industry, ways that do not exclude the transboundary and/or dark sides of the use of industrial resources, industrialization processes and locational decision-making. In the course of this search, this paper draws heavily on concepts, reasoning and examples from a burgeoning general geography of heritage, for instance, Graham, Ashworth, and Tunbridge (2000), Ashworth, Graham, and Tunbridge (2007) as well as on own earlier work on specifically industrial (heritage) tourism, mainly Li and Soyez (2003, 2006), Soyez (2009a, 2009b, 2013a,b) and Leung and Soyez (2009).

This paper is deliberately focused on conflict- and war-related cases, as these facets of industrial reality are under-researched and under-represented in both domestic and international industrial heritage approaches. Yet, it goes without saying that comparable, let alone less painful but still highly shameful, situations and outcomes can also affect transnationally active industrial companies in times of peace. Such issues are abundantly addressed under the heading of 'barriers to entry' in the international economics and economic/industrial geography literatures, that is, highlighting the difficulties resulting from differences in countries of origin and host countries respectively as regards legal systems, bureaucratic behaviour, business routines and, even more crucial, actors' incapability to cope appropriately with cross cultural gaps and risks (e.g. Caves, 1971; Hayter, 1981 as well as more recent textbooks such as Coe & Yeung, 2015; Dicken, 2015 or, specifically addressing international business blunders with a number of highly illustrative examples, Ricks, 2006).

Relevant examples will be referred to briefly in the following where deemed convenient. The comparative Sino-German approach will reveal both similarities and differences, and due to these countries' embeddedness in much wider spatial contexts, this approach enables us to shed new light on both European and Asian issues in the field of heritage appreciation. These perspectives should lead to the emergence – or creation – of new heritage and tourism geographies, potentially offering new directions for landscape potential, land use and economic opportunities.

The line of reasoning is as follows: After this brief introduction, illustrative and particularly painful examples from Europe are presented in order to clarify the issues at stake. This chapter is followed by a discussion of relevant topical and conceptual approaches in social sciences at large, allowing for a better understanding of current shortcomings in industrial heritage realizations. Next, characteristic patterns and phases of China's industrialization are outlined and the current status of industrial heritage approaches in China is explained and evaluated. A brief conclusion will wind up the paper.

Clarifying the issues at stake: dark industrial legacies of Germany's third Reich

Peenemünde military test site

In early 1992, a number of respected German institutions (both industrial and public interest R&D associations, such as DLR/*German Air and Space Agency*), as well as governmental representatives, prepared to celebrate an important anniversary for the development of space technology: the first ever launch at Peenemünde on the northeast German Baltic coast in 1942 of a missile to reach space, or more precisely with a potential maximum altitude of approximately 85 km and a horizontal reach of 190 km (for more detailed information, cf. Bode & Kaiser, 2004). Immediately before the planned event, however, international protest and pressure had become so strong that the celebration had to be cancelled (New York Times, Sept. 29, 1992). Obviously, the German organizers had totally underestimated the sensitive feelings that both site and missile touched upon outside Germany, in particular, in Great Britain and many East European countries (see below): Peenemünde was a *military test site* where both the army and air force were developing, constructing and testing the A4 rocket, later baptised V2 (*Vengeance weapon* No. 2) by Nazi propaganda. V2 missiles were mainly launched from locations in the Netherlands and France to attack London and later also Antwerp during the last months of Second World War in 1944/1945. They claimed the lives of thousands of civilians in these cities and, because of their lack of precision, brought random terror and havoc to many parts of the city centres and suburbs. And although the intended celebration at Peenemünde clearly had to be seen against a background of what Ashworth and Hartmann (2005, pp. 259–260) call *apologetic stances* (far removed from the usual strategies typical of perpetrators, i.e. *denial, concealment* or *blame shift*), this did not soothe the feelings of the victims.

After the devastating British air raid on Peenemünde during the night of 17/18 August 1943, the V2's multi-local production sites were increasingly placed underground, and the main assembly lines were relocated to a former mining site, called *Mittelwerk GmbH*, the factory's code name, close to the town of Nordhausen in the Harz mountains. The V1 production system developed in a similar manner and as of November 1944, the flying bomb's final assembly was also relocated to Mittelwerk's underground facilities (originally, V1's main assembly line was located at the Volkswagen plant at what became the town of Wolfsburg after the war).

While these relocations of the production facilities were going on, a concentration camp was established, called *Mittelbau-Dora*, consisting at the end of the war of more than 40 branch camps. Here, thousands of workers, mainly Prisoners of War and forced labourers, had to live and work in appallingly de-humanized conditions, leading to the death of thousands (for details cf. Mommsen & Grieger, 1996; Wagner, 2001). *Mittelbau-Dora* is now an important site of holocaust remembrance, organized and interpreted by the Buchenwald and Mittelbau-Dora Remembrance Site Foundation, but strangely enough, it is not shown on any European industrial heritage map (for more details, see htpp://www.erih.net; http://www.dora.de).

Past industrial archipelagos of tragedy and trauma

European maps are dotted with a disturbing multitude of Holocaust sites, which represent a particularly distressing legacy of the German Third Reich in both Western and Eastern Europe (Graham et al., 2000, p. 71).

Both Death Camps and Concentration Camps were generally combined with so-called 'Work Camps' ('Arbeitslager'), and towards the end of the war, these were split up into hundreds of so-called 'branch' or 'subsidiary camps' (Außenlager' or 'Nebenlager'), located at or close to industrial production sites (see below). Due to the almost total allied control of Germany's air space as of 1944, most of these sites (and some camps), as shown above, had to be relocated to former underground mines or storage sites, thus being converted into true, if sometimes makeshift, manufacturing sites. Increasingly, but not exclusively, under the control of SS (as was the case at *Mittelwerk*), all these sites both in Germany and in many countries occupied by German armies, had to bear the brunt of Germany's arms production. Millions of forced labour from more than 20 European countries were cruelly exploited under completely inhuman conditions, often resulting in what German historians qualify as 'death by work' (in German: 'Tod durch Arbeit').

All this corroborates the historical fact, not sufficiently acknowledged in industrial heritage contexts, that our pasts are in foreign countries and their pasts in ours, statements especially but far from exclusively true of Europe and its recognized, potential, concealed or forgotten heritage (Soyez, 2013a).

Thus, these sites constitute a past (industrial) archipelago of transnational trauma and tragedy, not only interconnected by the same historical burden, but also in a clear 'manufacturing' sense: Many of these sites constituted transnationally interlinked elements of complex production chains and networks, particularly obvious in the case of advanced weaponry, such as the mazes of late war aircraft production or the flying bomb V1 and the missile V2 (they can be regarded, from a purely organizational point of view, as early predecessors of the sophisticated global production networks that industrial geography focuses on today, cf. Coe & Yeung, 2015; Dicken, 2015; Hayter & Patchell, 2016). Currently, the identification of the latter group of sites and its readability of arms production systems as a whole for heritage purposes are overshadowed almost to invisibility by the factual impact and emotions called for by the magnitude of losses of lives at these former places of horror.

Thus, Peenemünde and its assembly site *Mittelwerk* only represent a particularly painful, multifaceted and visible example of sites commemorating wars and war crimes. These evoke highly controversial meanings and memories and lead to what is called in the literature a *contested heritage*.

Likening Europe's industrial landscapes to a *palimpsest*, we only have to scratch the surface to discover a deep, multi-layered history, marked by pervasive processes transcending former and current national boundaries, that is, *transnationalization* (see below), be it by means of ideas, information, knowledge, people, innovations, patents, capital or hardware. Dark memories and (potentially) contested heritages can be traced, providing examples of intrinsic dissonances, today subject to very selective politics of representation all over continental Europe. These politics only rarely expose or more fully explain the sites' histories, and, more often than not, their darker sides remain hidden, concealed, inaccessible or have simply been sanitized (cf. Li & Soyez, 2006, on this aspect of many industrial heritage sites; Foote, 2003 on America's landscapes of violence and tragedy).

While this is particularly true at most sites belonging to corporations that were involved in the arms production during the Third Reich, the most impressive contrasts between dark pasts and bright present mark the most recent developments in Germany's industrial (heritage) tourism destinations: the automotive brand worlds of Volkswagen AG (Autostadt/Wolfsburg), Daimler AG (Mercedes-Benz Museum/Stuttgart), AUDI (Audi Forum/Ingolstadt) or BMW AG (BMW World/Munich). Although their main function is marketing, they undoubtedly represent some of the most comprehensive industrial heritage realizations in Germany (cf. Soyez, 2013b, 2015): The past and the present are celebrated, but these firms' pervasive entanglements in the Third Reich and its arms production systems are mentioned in passing only, not really explained or buried in silence.

In order to find alternative ways of dealing with these deficits, the specific issues of heritage dissonances and existing approaches for dealing with them need to be conceptualized more consistently.

Terminological and conceptual discussion

The main objective of the following discussion is to draw up a generalized tableau of current social sciences topical and conceptual environments in which industrial heritage approaches are embedded, thus illustrating the serious deficits and the considerable lagging behind of even its most recent realizations.

Facets of transnationalization

To start with, it must be emphasized that the first key term in this paper's title – transnationalization (and its derivatives) – carries two meanings, the first being descriptive, the second prescriptive: *Transnationalizing heritage* should (1) be a reminder of the fact that most industrial sites, in one way or another, came into being as a result – or under the influence – of processes and actors that transcend national boundaries, and (2) can be understood as an admonition to dissolve national categories in heritage thinking by making industrial heritage sites transnational sites of remembrance wherever appropriate.

It is particularly appropriate to conceptually embed these issues in the field of *transnationalization*. The understanding of the term varies considerably but a widely accepted basis in the international literature comprises pluri- and trans-local social, political, cultural or economic interactions and processes transcending international boundaries. In contrast to many concepts of globalization (not least in the field of economic transactions), the transnational approach also more consistently addresses transboundary flows of systems of symbols and meanings as well as boundary-crossing everyday social practices, trans-local identities, hybridities or discourse spaces that are still *firmly anchored in national states and solidly grounded geographically* (for a thorough discussion of different concepts cf. in particular Jackson, Crang, & Dwyer, 2011; Vertovec, 2009).

The second key term – dark – is understood as specifying events, objects, sites or destinations that are marked by the fact that their controversial history has left at least one party affected with strong feelings of injustice, pain or even trauma, due, for instance, to natural disaster or human-induced oppression, humiliation, violence, atrocities or death.

Taking this as a starting point, the central ideas and suggestions presented here tap into a most valuable body of literature that has recently developed in fields such as *economic, social* and *urban geography* (Dicken, 2015; Hayter & Patchell, 2016; Krätke, Wildner, & Lanz, 2014; Pacione, 2009; Smith, 2001; Thrift & Kitchin, 2009; Werlen, 1997), the *geography of heritage* (here, in particular, Ashworth et al., 2007; Graham et al., 2000; Macdonald, 2009; Storm, 2014), *dark tourism* in its different manifestations (Ashworth & Hartmann, 2005; Hartmann, 2013; Lennon & Foley, 2006; Logan & Reeves, 2009), transnational social sciences (Faist, Fauser & Reisenauer, 2013; Wimmer & Glick Schiller, 2002) and, finally, history, be it labelled crossed, connected, transfer or entangled history (Budde, Conrad, & Janz, 2006; Conrad, 2016; Olstein, 2015; Osterhammel & Petersson, 2009; Pernau, 2011; Werner & Zimmermann, 2006).

In the current context, we prefer the latter term: *entangled history*. Better than any other of the approaches listed above, it makes clear how transnationally active actors, be they individuals, organizations, institutions or states, are inextricably and inevitably linked to and mutually dependent on one another. Furthermore, a central idea in *entangled history* is that processes of mutual and multidirectional influences, absorption and hybridization are pervasive not only in times of peace, but – and maybe even more so – also in times of colonization and war (Frevert, 2005).

Heritagization: from local to global processes of remembrance

Originally, processes (and concepts) of remembrance were mostly bound to a clearly defined locality, as mirrored by the emblematic *lieu(x) de mémoire* coined by Nora (1984 and later), a concept including, however, also tangible and intangible objects, events or symbols, collectively remembered in a national context.

Since then, François (2006), among others, has advocated strategies for transcending international boundaries by thinking about what are, or could become, European *lieux de mémoire*, theorizing issues of transnationally *shared, split* (and contested) or *implicit* sites of remembrance (cf also François and Schulze, 2001; Jarausch and Lindenberger, 2011, linking such processes in conflictual European settings).

Thus, new transboundary facets have been added to traditionally discussed issues of, for example, identity and place, which can evolve in different directions over time. Particularly impressive shared heritage sites transcending European boundaries include the battlefields of First and Second World Wars, Verdun or Normandy D-day beaches, respectively, today jointly remembered by former enemies in war and their descendants (Petermann, 2007, 2011). The recently re-opened Verdun Memorial explicitly addresses the soldiers of all the countries involved as victims, thus downplaying the traditional antagonism between France (including its allies) and Germany in particular, and becoming an actively shared or quietly accepted implicit site of transnational reconciliation instead of national remembrance (http://www.centenarynews.com/article/museum-honouring-verduns-fallen-reopens-after-125m-centenary-renovation).

More specifically in the current context, a typical industrial heritage site in Europe displaying a comparable evolution over time is the 'Park of blast furnace no. 4' at Uckange in France, part of a former iron-producing facility established by German industrialists in annexed Lorraine at the end of the nineteenth century. For decades, it represented 'the other's' legacy, but has now become a transnationally shared tourist destination (http://www.moselle-tourisme.com/visiter/culture-et-histoire/ficheproduit/F845149153_parc-du-haut-fourneau-u4-uckange.html).

An impressive (heritage) fusion resulting from a transboundary, peacetime interaction between Germany and Japan is Yawata Ironworks, constructed at the turn of the nineteenth and twentieth century by the German corporation Gutehoffnungshütte (Oberhausen, Ruhr industrial area) in what is now Kitakyushu/Japan.

On the one hand, recent studies carried out in Germany at the Rhine-Westphalia Economy Archive/RWWA in Cologne testify to the fact mentioned earlier that even peacetime transboundary processes, in this case transnational technology transfer from Germany to Japan, can be marked by highly problematic and dark facets that deserve much broader research efforts (Soyez, 2014). Many details of the Yawata story, now regarded as an unusual, almost hybrid Japanese–German industrial heritage, are clearly acknowledged, valued and highlighted from a Japanese perspective as remarkable assets in the context of the recently awarded World Cultural Heritage status of the Meiji Industrial Revolution.

On the other hand, mid-twentieth-century war-time events at this site have resulted in highly contested dark facets, and the discussions and decisions around it must be regarded as a hitherto unique occurrence in transnational heritage contexts, alluded to in the introductory preface of this paper and potentially serving as an illustrative example of the most recent shift in international trends of remembering (Japan World Heritage Nomination, 2014):

This fundamental turning point (and spatial extension) has taken place with the development of concepts embracing even global or cosmopolitan sites as well as circulations of memory. They are mirrored by terms such as transnational or 'global memoryscape', representing a fusion of heritage and space at a new level, exploring the intersection between public memory and globalization processes by tapping into concepts originally developed by Appadurai (1996), Assmann and Conrad (2010), de Cesari and Rigney (2014) and Phillips and Reyes (2011).

These latter approaches offer rewarding interconnections with geography. Examples of such links include its current multi-scale, conceptions of *place* within unfolding – and (transnationally) *stretched* – geographies of identity and heritage in their historical depths and spatial extensions/extents, or as Massey puts it (2005, p. 130, but developed as a concept from the early 1990s): an understanding of place as ' … open ("a global sense of place") as woven together out of ongoing stories, as a moment within power-geometries, as a particular constellation within wider topographies of space, and as in process, as unfinished business … .'

These approaches offer a wide variety of fruitful research topics where transboundary, pluralized and multi-scale geographies, histories, identities, places, meanings and linkages intersect and are played out, as are their intrinsic dissonances. According to recent research in this field, however, (industrial) heritage can be redefined as a *contact zone,* that is, as a place 'where different pasts and experiences are negotiated, a site of mutual translation' (Peckham, 2003, p. 57), an idea very close to Tunbridge and Ashworth's (1996) earlier suggestion that contested pasts and addressing their omissions can become 'a resource in conflict'.

The idea of intrinsic heritage dissonances with the resulting 'mismatches' between heritage and people in space and time can serve as an illustrative example (Graham et al., 2000, p. 24, 93). Such mismatches result mainly from the movement – in domestic as well as transnational spaces – of people, borders and spheres of influence (more rarely of the heritage object itself), bringing all parties into touch with others' heritage and distancing them, at least partially, from their own. If a perspective from a given homeland/nation state is adopted, there are several categories with broad implications for industrial production systems, caused by specific time–space paths in state systems, such as:

- temporary occupation/annexation during, or as a result of, armed conflicts, – negotiated or imposed border shifts (more often than not after a war), – voluntary or forced migration (such as deportation) and, as a special case,
- colonization in its different forms, be it through occupation (see above) or any form of unwelcome (political, economic, social …) influences on another country,
- de-colonization, that is, the departure of those who held colonial power, followed by the emergence of new elites and new states, possibly also of new borders.

Most of these events/processes represent extremely painful periods in a nation's and/or individual's lives and confront people with the depreciation or even the erasure of their traditional heritage, and the construction of a new one as well as a whole gamut of ensuing heritage dissonances, making it difficult, if not impossible, to appreciate, let alone to protect, the *other's* heritage.

To summarize: The terminological and conceptual tableau drawn up in the foregoing has provided ample evidence for the fact that industrial heritage approaches trapped in national 'container thinking', more recently addressed in other social sciences as 'methodological nationalism' (Amelina, Nergiz, Faist, & Glick Schiller, 2011; de Cesari & Rigney, 2014; Wimmer & Glick Schiller, 2002), have to be replaced by concepts integrating processes and impacts induced by transboundary interactions in peace and war. As many, but far from all, of these are characterized by a gamut of dark events, periods and experiences, reaching from the unpleasant to the traumatic, they have also to be addressed more consistently, if necessary, in approaches mirroring a plurality of contested or contradictory narratives.

Widening the view to Asia

While this paper's first part and its findings are empirically based on a wide range of European case studies, a growing documentary basis testifies to the fact that both the thrust and the necessity of addressing transnationalism and darker facets of industrialization processes can be transferred to South and East Asia (cf. af Geijerstam, 2004; Japan World Heritage Nomination, 2014 and the introductory *PREFACE*).

The transfer of this paper's conceptual thrust to China is, to date, both tentative and explorative, that is, it is not yet based on dedicated field studies (cf., however, Li, 2009). Nevertheless, the current documentary base in China, and in Western literature, is as broad as it is varied: The cases presented in the following are mainly taken from standard academic knowledge, mostly in the fields of economics and economic history, to a lesser extent from industrial geography. Most of the data presented here can also be found in a variety of Asian and Western internet sources, so that methodological triangulation and crosschecking are possible. More intensive field studies are planned in some of the case studies presented in the following.

Starting from the above-mentioned concept of transnationalism, the (re)search focus is on characteristic events, facts and processes in China reflecting pluri- and trans-local social, political, cultural or economic interactions that transcend international boundaries but are still firmly embedded in nation states. The final selection, however, is mainly based on the following categories with wide-ranging implications for industrial production systems in periods of both peace and war, while being strongly influenced by historical contexts that imposed, enforced or allowed for desired and unwanted transboundary flows of people, hardware and knowledge:

- the transfer of industrial hardware, from single engines to complete industrial facilities ready for use,
- the transfer of knowledge in its most varied forms, but mostly in the form of the education of Chinese citizens abroad or by importing foreign experts
- capital transfer from abroad leading to investments, takeovers and so on.

China's modern industrialization from a transnational and dark perspective

China's modern industrialization, starting from the mid-nineteenth century, was mainly a process triggered or strongly influenced by exogenous factors, as very early Chinese forms of paper, silk or iron production never led to a western-style endogenously fuelled industrial revolution . At the beginning of China's modern industrialization when China was declining and becoming a semi-colonial country in the late Qing Dynasty, two 'paths' of transnationally influenced industrialization intermingled (for a general overview, see, e.g. Spence, 1991, in particular, the chapter 'The Industrial Sector', pp. 325–333 as well as Feuerwerker, 1958): *Firstly*, domestically fuelled catching up processes, triggered by a both real and perceived lagging behind compared to Western countries, and initiated by Chinese bureaucrats such as Li Hongzhang. *Secondly*, industrialization processes started, imposed and often financed, or at least influenced, by foreign colonial powers, actually accompanied by a lot of wars and conflicts with many international implications.

After the establishment of the Peoples' Republic of China (PRC) in 1949, there are still two sub-periods of China's transnationally triggered industrialization with some dark aspects. One is the cold war period with its so-called planned economy dominated by Mao, and the other is after the opening policy triggered by Deng Xiaoping in the late 1970s.

The following three sections will offer some descriptive examples in order to illustrate the kinds of transnationalism or dark sides that are embedded in China's modern industrialization history, though – as underlined earlier – transnationalism is not automatically identical with dark periods. The first section is based on Li Hongzhang's so-called *Yang Wu Yun Dong*, or 'Self-Strengthening Movement' and its transnational industrial establishments. Since they represent national icons of the People's Republic of China, some of these are still well known today and have been controversially discussed in the context of China's industrial heritage. The second section is mainly related to war-time industrial establishments with Japanese and Russian occupation as well as colonial impacts with number of dark facets. These two periods are historically intertwined and considerably influenced the subsequent socialist industrialization. The third section introduces socialist industrialization from 1949 with transnational and dark features in both the cold war period and under the current globalization processes leading to Guangdong's world factory status since the late 1980s. These three sections and paths of industrialization demonstrate clear aspects of regionalization and transnational aspects shaping a wide variety of characteristic industrial landscapes over time in China.

National industrialization characterized by transnationalism and dark sides in the mid-nineteenth and early twentieth century

The most spectacular elements of Li Hongzhang's Westernization Movement (or *Self-Strengthening Movement*) were (1) the so-called *Machinery Bureaus* of the 1860s: Jiangnan Machine Manufacturer, now Shanghai Jiangnan Shipyard (Group) Co. Ltd., has been relocated from the original site and partly demolished due to the space requirements of Shanghai EXPO2010, (2) Jinling Machinery Bureau, now Nanjing Chengguang Machinery Factory, now under reconstruction and will be named 1865 creative space and (3) Foochow Arsenal/Mawei Shipyard, now Mawei Shipbuilding Ltd., also in a reconversion process into a museum area. A fourth Bureau at Tianjin no longer exists.

While representing the first national factories in China, their establishment was only possible through reliance on foreign resources (e.g. imported iron ore or pig iron), foreign technology, foreign capital and foreign expertise. The first Machinery Bureau, *Jiangnan Machine Manufacturer* was built in Shanghai in 1865 in order to produce mostly military equipment (firearms, steamboats, artillery). The ironworks consisted of a facility originally located in Hongkou in Shanghai, built with American capital, and further equipped with machinery bought in the United States. China's first steamboat, baptised *Tian Ji* and later renamed *Hui Ji,* was launched here. Only in 1890 were small converters imported from England – and produced China's first batch of steel. Another typical indicator of ongoing transnationalism in this field was the establishment of a 'translation house': Here, future translators of technical books, instructions and so on were trained, and a Technical School, with the Osaka Institute of Technology in Japan serving as a model, was established to train future engineers (Xu & Huang, 1998). In 1938, the whole site was taken over and run by Japanese until 1945. It was later taken over by the Kuomintang – who eventually destroyed most of the facilities when they had to retreat from Shanghai.

The history of *Jinling Machinery Bureau*, also established by Li Hongzhang in 1865 in what is today Nanjing, is very similar. The workshop was designed and built by an English engineer, and some years later, an American born in Scotland became the director. He travelled to Europe, buying machinery in the UK, Germany and Switzerland, which then enabled the factory to produce guns and cannons designed after American and German models. In 1948, Kuomintang moved most of the equipment to Taiwan, leaving nothing but some machines and mostly empty buildings. Production resumed later in what was known as 307 Ordnance Factory, later becoming what is now the Chenguang Group.

Another famous example is the *Foochow (or Mawei) Arsenal* in what is now Fuzhou. It was also built on the orders of Li Hongzhang (together with Zuo Zongtang), then leaders of the Qing government's Self-Strengthening Movement. Production started in 1866 with imported technology, facilities and engineers from Europe, supervised by a French naval officer. Simultaneously, a renowned Naval School was built, mainly using foreign textbooks, courses and management systems. It produced under complete foreign supervision for some years until the 1870s when Chinese supervisors were able to build ships without foreign help. China's first steel warship, the *Pin Yuan,* was constructed here. The Arsenal was almost completely destroyed during the Sino-French War of 1883–1895, but was rebuilt and a few years later became the cradle of China's airplane industry (in the beginning run by Chinese engineers having graduated from MIT in the US). After it had been destroyed and reconstructed several times during the Sino-Japanese War between 1937 and 1945, the Arsenal was taken over by the State in 1949. It got a technological boost from the Osaka Shipyard in Japan after the opening policy, and now cooperates closely with shipyards in the Netherlands and Germany.

The late nineteenth-/early twentieth-century history of two more China's most famous industrial establishments, the *Kailuan Coal Mining* company in Tangshan, Hebei Province, and the *Hanyang Ironworks* in Wuhan, Hubei Province (Feuerwerker 1958; Wang, 2007; Yan, 2007), is very similar from a transnationalism point of view.

Industrial establishments in war-time periods from 1895 to 1949

Dark heritage perspectives are often related to unsettled historical periods. As mentioned above, China's modern industrialization was accompanied by number of wars and colonial-like experiences (Liu, 2013). This pattern can be linked, for example, to:

- the Opium Wars of 1839–1842 and 1856–1860 and their aftermaths (in particular, Treaty of Nanjing, Treaty of Tianjin) with the period of 'unequal treaties', treaty ports and so on,
- the Sino-Japanese War in 1895 and the ensuing Treaty of Shimonoseki (giving Japan the privilege of building factories),
- the Yihetuan (Boxer War) and the ensuing military operations of eight Western countries (*Ba Guo Lian Jun*), including Germany, 1900/1901,
- the growing influence of Russia and Japan in northeast China in the second half of the nineteenth century, followed by the occupation of northern Manchuria by Russia and southern Manchuria by Japan,
- the Japanese annexation of northeast China with the establishment of its colony Manchukuo in 1931,
- the Sino-Japanese War of 1937–1945 (also leading to the partial re-location of many industries, in particular of the iron and steel industry, to Szechwan and Yunnan provinces by Kuomintang National government),
- the civil war 1945–1949.

Around the end of the nineteenth century, that is, after the Sino-Japanese War in 1895, Japan became the most influential foreign actor in large parts of China, especially with regard to the further development of industry. Its role continued to increase until the end of Second World War in 1945. Landmark events include the establishment of the Southern Manchuria Railway Co. in 1906. It was particularly important with regard to its role in opening up access to the resources of Northeast China for the development of an important cluster of coal mining and the iron and steel industry, thus preparing this large region to become a resource colony in the decades to come.

Important industry clusters in Northeast China, such as iron and steel works in Anshan and Benxi, coal mining in Fushun and manufacturing industry in Dalian and Shengyang developed fast (Wei, 1982), intensified after the creation of the Japanese puppet state of Manchukuo in 1931. Soon, the whole of northeast China became a raw material supply base for Japan as well as providing a huge market for Japanese manufactured products and a very important military base (Zhao, 2003, pp. 365–371). Haizhou coal mine in Fuxin, Liaoning Province, for instance, is now regarded as one of the chief symbols of China's industrialization and listed as the first experimental city for the recent policy of reconstructing problem-ridden resource-dependent cities by the State Department of China. This coal mine was run by Japanese interests from 1931 to 1945, heavily relying on Chinese forced labour. In 1951, Fuxin coal mine was listed as one of 156 important industrial projects in the PRC and was modernized with the aid of experts from the Soviet Union – and even a Japanese specialist. Much of the modernized machinery in Haizhou coal mine came from the Soviet Union, [East?] Germany and Czechoslovakia.

The role of Russian and German knowledge and capital transfer was dwarfed by Japanese influences, but was not insignificant. After the Sino-Russian Secret Treaty signed in 1896, for example, the Russians built the 2500 kilometre-long Zhongdong railway in Northeast China connecting Russia and China with three sub-lines in the Harbin junction. There were also a lot of associated factories along the railroad, where Tsarist Russia contended with Japan for supremacy and invaded northeast China. Another similar example is Germany's colonial industrial development in Qingdao for 17 years since 1898, although the German zone of influence was taken over by Japan in 1914.

Only a few examples could be presented in the foregoing. It is evident, however, that there are very few Chinese industrial establishments dating from the nineteenth and earlier twentieth centuries that do not demonstrate massive transnational influence, very often in several 'layers' and interactions between Europe, North America and Asia over time. Moreover, the turmoil of recent Chinese history has meant that most of these industrial establishments, sites and landscapes have experienced a multitude of dark events, many, even though not all, of which are linked to transnational processes.

Socialist industrialization after 1949

This third pattern mentioned above derives from Deng Xiaoping's open door policy, which created what is now called the 'factory of the world' and represented a more 'normal' industrialization path, that is, heavily influenced by Foreign Direct Investment/FDI by both overseas Chinese and mostly circum-Pacific countries. It is very similar to what has been experienced by many industrial or industrializing countries worldwide, but still with typical elements that can be characterized as dark. For example, the 156 industrial projects, which were planned to develop New China industrialization from 1953 to 1957 with the help of the former Soviet Union and some East European socialist countries, were actually either a failure or could not continue because of the political rupture between China and Russia in 1958. These specific cold war industrial projects, partly established with the help of socialist 'brother countries' in the 1950s, had to be relocated to the so-called 'Third Line' (i.e. interior sites in middle and western China) (Chen, 2003) in the 1960s in order to put them out of reach of military attacks, which were considered possible during the Sino-Russia and Vietnam War. This kind of industrial relocation has been proved a wrong decision because the Third Line industries were economically not efficient at all and had to be closed, stopped, merged or reconstructed in the later market economy period. This caused much emotional and economic hardship and dark memories for the first generation of socialist working-class people, persisting until today (Li & Wang, 2014).

Another example heavily overshadowed by dark facets is related to the period of the so-called 'great leap forward' from 1958 to 1960. Directed by the ultra-left line in the communist party of the time, and today regarded as disastrous, the whole country was engaged in all kinds of iron and steel production in order to exceed that of developed countries like UK and USA. This resulted in the production of substandard products. The specificities connected to this particular path of industrialization and failure constitute a very special example of dark facets in a domestic context, as do many of those pressures, hardships and exploitation patterns that characterize the most recent phase of China's industrialization, that is, the development of the 'factory of the world'. However, while most of the negatively affected people are part of the local workforce, the responsibilities for shortcomings of regulation and organization lie in both the national and international arenas, including not only local and foreign entrepreneurs but, in a less direct way, also international customers. Such implications are well documented, although in an extreme example, by the highly deplorable – and widely discussed – events at Taiwanese Foxconn's Shenzhen factories (series of workers' suicides allegedly caused by work pressure).

Thus, if future industrial heritage preservation strategies are to be aimed at mirroring China's industrial history in all of its most important facets, both its transnational past and its darker sides have to be represented more consciously and more consistently – just as is the case in Europe. For example, most corporations with a Japanese past are state-owned enterprises today, including iron and steel works and coal mines such as the current Benxi Iron and Steel Group. This group was actually established by the Qing government in cooperation with Japanese capitalists in 1905, but this point is not even mentioned on the Group's current website (http://www.bxsteel.com/dongshizhang.jsp) for the image of nationalism narrative. The following chapter contains a further discussion of the extent to which the darker facets of China's industrialization are represented at heritage sites today.

Industrial heritage preservation in China: current status – future enrichment

To date, there are hardly any consistent attempts to formally protect industrial heritage in China, and it was only at the Wuxi Forum on Industrial Heritage held in 2006 that the importance of preserving this part of China's history was acknowledged for the first time by high-ranking government officials. The main reason, of course, is that most citizens, decision-makers and institutions in China are preoccupied with rapid development and modernization. Furthermore, the predominant view is that any remnant from China's industrialization phases, in particular those of the twentieth century and especially from the post-1978 period, are too 'young' to have any heritage value.

However, there are a few exceptions: the third National Heritage Survey of 2007 lists, for the first time, 11 industrial heritage sites, including a selection of buildings in Dasheng cotton mill in Nantong, Qingdao brewery and Shilongba hydro-electricity plant in Kunming. Furthermore, at both provincial and local levels, awareness of the specific character and potential value of old industrial remnants is clearly growing. This is also attested to by the fact that preservation issues and strategies are now being discussed at all of the historic industrial sites mentioned in the previous chapter, and plans to develop both Kailuan and Haizhou coal mines into National Mining Parks have already been made.

A critical perspective on current industrial heritage valorizations and inventories in China, however, reveals some characteristics very similar to the situation in Europe, thus confirming the main introductory theses: (1) As this paper illustrates, most officially or informally acknowledged industrial heritage sites in China testify to a decidedly transnational history of industrialization. However, almost without exception, all of these sites are embedded in distinctly national narratives, and some of them have even become national symbols; the transnational implications of their origin, function, development, destruction and reconstruction are almost never addressed explicitly, let alone emphasized as constitutive of their existence and their (potential) value. (2) Due to China's turbulent history since the start of industrialization, and because the industrialization process itself is constitutive of many of these historic turbulences and disruptions, a multitude of dark events and memories are linked with most industrial sites. Many of these are rarely addressed, mostly just ignored, sometimes consciously hidden or intentionally erased.

As was stressed above, all of these comments are also true for the current industrial heritage situation in Western countries, especially with regard to its transnational and dark implications. However, there are two aspects, that are currently very different in China, and which from a Western point of view lead to considerable problems in the process of valorizing existing potential: (1) There seems to be a largely undisputed policy of 'empty factories' (cf. Liu, 2009), that is, the heritage concept is only or mainly focused on the chief industrial architectural remnants of industry, their 'outer shell' so to say, while other tangibles and intangibles of former production facilities and systems attract hardly any attention; and, (2) any re-use strategy seems to be under the absolute imperative of profitability, resulting in the use of former industrial buildings as sites for cultural industries or their conversion into 'bar and restaurant streets' in most cases, just as has happened with Factory 798 in Beijing. In other words, neither the integrity nor the authenticity of the former industrial site nor its intrinsic industrial value is appreciated in the way that has become characteristic for most European and North American contexts.

Conclusions

Industrialization processes all over the world, and in particular in China, can only be understood in the context of innumerable transboundary flows of machines, people, capital, ideas, innovations and so on, not only in periods of peace, but also, and sometimes even more so, in periods of war. An appropriate way of conceptualizing both these processes and their spatial impacts is the perspective of transnationalism, which highlights the boundary-transcending criss-crossing of movements, on the one hand, and the sedimentation of material layers over time, on the other, while mapping and trying to understand the seemingly inextricable (transnational) entanglement of all actors involved. Any attempt at appropriately mirroring this reality in the selection and interpretation of industrial heritage is incomplete if neither the transnational fact itself nor the darker sides of industrialization processes in both unruly and peaceful times are addressed.

Against this backdrop, we recommend the adoption of a perspective of *entangled industrial (heritage) geographies* in order to chart these still largely unknown territories both in Europe and in China, while pursuing two main objectives: (1) to explore more appropriate ways of representing and interpreting past industrial worlds and production systems, including their transnational and dark implications, and, (2) to valorize this past in ways that allow for multiple narratives, transcending the national and not covering up but using existing intrinsic dissonances as a resource to capitalize on, with regard to culture, education, identities and the economy.

In the long run, the adoption of consistent strategies aimed at valorizing authenticity and intrinsic values could even become a much better – and more profitable – use of the existing cultural capital of former industrial sites, especially with regard to appropriate city (and regional) marketing strategies and a burgeoning domestic and international heritage tourism as well. These strategies could potentially lead to the development of transnational sites of remembrance, either shared or split but still common, pluralizing our pasts and making them understandable in increasingly transnationalizing multicultural societies.

Acknowledgement

We would also like to thank two the reviewers for their helpful comments.

Disclosure statement

No potential conflict of interest was reported by the authors.

Funding

This paper is supported by the Natural Science Foundation of China (the project code is 41471124).

References

Agnew, J. (1994). The territorial trap: The geographical assumptions of international relations theory. *Review of International Political Economy, 1*(1), 53–80.
Amelina, A., Nergiz, D. D., Faist, T., & Glick Schiller, N. (2011). *Beyond methodological nationalism: Research methodologies for cross-border studies*. New York, NY: Routledge.
Appadurai, A. (1996). *Modernity at large: Cultural dimensions of globalization*. Minneapolis: Minnesota University Press.
Ashworth, G., Graham, B., & Tunbridge, J. E. (2007). *Pluralising pasts. Heritage, identity and place in multicultural societies*. London: Pluto.
Ashworth, G. & Hartmann, R. (Eds.). (2005). *Horror and human tragedy revisited: The management of sites of atrocities for tourism*. New York, NY: Cognizant Communication Corporation.
Assmann, A., & Conrad, S. (Eds.). (2010). *Memory in a global age. Discourses, practices and trajectories*. Basingstoke: Palgrave Macmillan.
Bode, V., & Kaiser, G. (2004). *Raketenspuren. Peenemünde 1936-2004*. Berlin: Ch. Links Verlag.
Budde, G., Conrad, S., & Janz, O. (Eds.). (2006). *Transnationale Geschichte: Themen, Tendenzen, Theorien*. Göttingen: Vandenhoek and Ruprecht.
Caves, R. E. (1971). International corporations: The industrial economics of foreign investment. *Economica, 38*, 1–27.
de Cesari, C., & Rigney, A. (Eds.). (2014). *Transnational memory: Circulation, articulation, scales*. Berlin: de Gruyter.
Chen, D. (Ed.). (2003). *Third line construction: West development preparing for the war*. Beijing: The Central Party School Publishing House.
Coe, N. M., & Yeung, H. W. C. (2015). *Global production networks: Theorizing economic development in an interconnected world*. Oxford: Oxford University Press.
Conrad, S. (2016). *What is global history?* Princeton, NJ: Princeton University Press.
Dicken, P. (2015). *Global shift: Mapping the changing contours of the world economy* (7th ed.). London: SAGE Publications.
Faist, T., Fauser, M., & Reisenauer, E. (2013). *Transnational migration*. Cambridge, MA: Polity Press.
Feuerwerker, A. (1958). *China's early industrialization: Sheng Hsuan-huai (1844–1916) and Mandarin enterprise*. Cambridge, MA: Harvard University Press.
Foote, K. E. (2003). *Shadowed ground: America's landscapes of violence and tragedy*. Austin: University of Texas Press.
François, É. (2006). Europäische lieux de mémoire. In G. Budde, S. Conrad, & O. Janz (Eds.), *Transnationale Geschichte: Themen, Tendenzen, Theorien* (pp. 290–303). Göttingen: Vandenhoek and Ruprecht.

François, É., & Schulze, H. (2001). *Deutsche Erinnerungsorte*. (Vols. 3). München: Oldenbourg.

Frevert, U. (2005). Europeanizing German history. *Bulletin of the German Historical Institute Washington, D.C.*, *36*, 9–24.

af Geijerstam, J. (2004). *Landscapes of technology Transfer. Swedish ironmakers in India 1860-1864.* Stockholm: Jernkontorets bergshistoriska skriftserie 42/Stockholm Papers in the History and Philosophy of Technology.

Graham, B., Ashworth, G. J., & Tunbridge, J. E. (2000). *A geography of heritage: Power, culture and economy*. London: Arnold.

Hartmann, R. (2013). Dark tourism, thanatourism, and dissonance in heritage tourism management: New directions in contemporary tourism research. *Journal of Heritage Tourism*. doi:10.1080/1743873X.2013.807266

Hayter, R. (1981). Patterns of entry and the role of foreign-controlled investments in the forest product sector of British Columbia. *Tijdschrift voor Economische en Sociale Geografie*, *72*, 99–113.

Hayter, R., & Patchell, J. (2016). *Economic geography: From an institutional perspective*. Don Mills, ON: Oxford University Press Canada.

Jackson, P., Crang, P., & Dwyer, C. (2011). *Transnational spaces*. New York, NY: Routledge.

Japan World Heritage Nomination. (2014). *Sites of Japan's Meiji industrial revolution: Kyushu-Yamaguchi and related areas.* Tokyo: Cabinet Secretariat.

Jarausch, K. H., & Lindenberger, T. in cooperation with Ramsbrock, A. (Eds.). (2011). *Conflicted memories: Europeanizing contemporary histories*. Oxford: Berghahn.

Krätke, S., Wildner, S., & Lanz, K. (Eds.). (2012). *Transnationalism and urbanism*. New York, NY: Routledge.

Lennon, J., & Foley, M. (2006). *Dark tourism: The attraction of death and disaster*. London: Thomson.

Leung, M. W. H., & Soyez, D. (2009). Industrial heritage: Valorising the spatial-temporal dynamics of another Hong Kong story. *International Journal of Heritage Studies*, *15*(1), 5–75.

Li, L. (2009). Industrial heritage conservation in China: Seen from an actor analysis perspective. In B. Liu (Ed.), *China industrial heritage building survey and research* (pp. 4–11). Beijing: Qinghua University Press.

Li, L., & Soyez, D. (2003). Evaluation of industrial tourism development of China from a western perspective. *Human Geography*, *18*(6), 20–25.

Li, L., & Soyez, D. (2006). Industrial tourism destination management in Germany: A critical appraisal of representation practices. In J. Bao, H. Xue, & A. Lew (Eds.), *Community tourism and border tourism* (pp. 408–429). Beijing: China Travel and Tourism Press.

Li, L., & Wang, S. (2014). China industrial heritage and the emotional heritage of working class: Based on the analysis on China industrial literature works. In W. Zhu, and B. Liu (Eds.), *China modern industrial heritage building survey, research and protection* (Vol. 4, pp. 414–424). Beijing: Qinghua University Press.

Liu, B. (2013). China modern industrial development and industrial heritage – a colonial and post-colonial rethinking. In W. Zhu, & B. Liu (Eds.), *China modern industrial heritage building survey, research and protection* (Vol. 3, pp. 89–98). Beijing: Qinghua University Press.

Liu, S. (2009). An importance case representing modern China new system industrial architecture – researching the former Zhongdong railway Harbin main workshop. In B. Liu (Ed.), *China industrial heritage building survey and research* (pp. 156–167). Beijing: Qinghua University Press.

Logan, W., & Reeves, K. (2009). *Places of pain and shame: Dealing with 'difficult' heritage*. London: Routledge.

Macdonald, S. (2009). *Difficult heritage: Negotiating the Nazi past in Nuremberg and beyond*. London: Routledge.

Massey, D. (2005). *For space*. London: SAGE.

Mommsen, H., & Grieger, M. (1996). *Das Volkswagenwerk und seine Arbeiter im Dritten Reich*. Düsseldorf: ECON.

New York Times. (2002, September 29). Germans plan, then cancel, celebration of a Nazi Missile, p. 1992.

Nora, P. (Ed.), (1984/1986/1992). *Les lieux de mémoire* (Vols. 7). Paris: Gallimard.

Olstein, D. (2015). *Thinking history globally*. Basingstoke: Palgrave Macmillan.

Osterhammel, J., & Petersson, N. P. (2009). *Globalization: A short history*. Bognor Regis: University Press Group Ltd.

Pacione, M. (2009). *Urban geography: A global perspective* (3rd ed.). London: Routledge.

Peckham, R. S. (2003). Mourning heritage: Memory, trauma and restitution. In R. S. Peckham (Ed.), *Rethinking heritage. cultures and politics in Europe* (pp. 205–215). London: I.B. Tauris Publishers.

Pernau, M. (2011). *Transnationale Geschichte*. Göttingen/Oakville, CT: Vandenhoeck & Ruprecht.

Petermann, S. (2007). *Rituale machen Räume: Zum kollektiven Gedenken der Schlacht von Verdun und der Landung in der Normandie*. Bielefeld: transcript Verlag.

Petermann, S. (2011). Places and spaces: The remembrance of D-Day 1944 in Normandy. In P. Meusburger, M. Heffernan, & E. Wunder (Eds.), *Cultural memories (= knowledge and space 4)* (pp. 233–247). Heidelberg: Springer.

Phillips, K. R., & Reyes, G. M. (2011). *Global memoryscapes: Contesting remembrance in a transnational age*. Tuscaloosa: University of Alabama Press.

Ricks, D. A. (2006). *International business blunders* (4th ed.). Oxford: Blackwell Publishing.

Smith, M. P. (2001). *Transnational urbanism. Locating globalization*. Malden, MA: Blackwell Publications.

Soyez, D. (2009a). European heritage – in Europe and beyond. *Geographische Zeitschrift*, *97*(1), 1–5.

Soyez, D. (2009b). Europeanizing industrial heritage in Europe: Addressing its transboundary and dark sides. *Geographische Zeitschrift, 97*(1), 43–55.

Soyez, D. (2013a). Our pasts are in foreign countries and their pasts are in ours: The challenge of transnationalising industrial heritage. *TICCIH Bulletin, 61*(3), 1–2.

Soyez, D. (2013b, July 10–14). *Uncomfortable landscapes of our industrial pasts: Transnationality and trauma*. Paper presented at conference proceedings "Rust, regeneration and romance – iron and steel landscapes and cultures". Ironbridge, Telford, UK.

Soyez, D. (2014). Transnational geoheritage: Yawata Steelworks (Japan) and its German roots. *International Journal of Geoheritage, 2*(1), 1–22.

Soyez, D. (2015). Automobile Industrieerlebniswelten – Stätten der Industriekultur? *Industriekultur, 1*(15), 18–19.

Spence, J. D. (1991). *The search for modern China*. New York, NY: W.W. Norton & Company.

Storm, A. (2014). *Post-industrial landscape scars*. New York, NY: Palgrave Macmillan.

Thrift, N., & Kitchin, R. (2009). *The international encyclopedia of human geography* (Vol. 1). Amsterdam: Elsevier.

Tunbridge, J. E., & Ashworth, G. J. (1996). *Dissonant heritage: The management of the past as a resource in conflict*. Chichester: Wiley.

Vertovec, S. (2009). *Transnationalism*. London: Routledge.

Wagner, J.-C. (2001). *Produktion des Todes: Das KZ Mittelbau-Dora*. Göttingen: Wallstein Verlag.

Wang, J. (2007). *The economic history of modern China (1895-1927)*. Beijing: Economy and Management Publishing House.

Wei, X. (1982). *Industrial geography*. Beijing: Peking University Press.

Werlen, B. (1997). *Sozialgeographie alltäglicher Regionalisierungen. Band 2: Globalisierung, Region und Regionalisierung*. Stuttgart: Steiner.

Werner, M., & Zimmermann, B. (2006). Beyond comparison: Histoire Croisée and the challenge of reflexivity. *History and Theory, 45*(1), 30–50.

Wimmer, A., & Glick Schiller, N. (2002). Methodological nationalism and beyond: Nation–state building, migration and the social sciences. *Global Networks, 2*(4), 301–334.

Xu, X. & Huang, H. (Eds.). (1998). *Modern industrialization history of Shanghai*. Shanghai: Shanghai Social Science Publication.

Yan, Z. (2007). *The economic history of modern China (1840–1894)*. Beijing: Economy and Management Publishing House.

Zhao, D. (2003). *The economic history of modern China (1842–1949)*. Zhengzhou: Henan People's Publishing House.

Impacts of urban renewal on the place identity of local residents – a case study of Sunwenxilu traditional commercial street in Zhongshan City, Guangdong Province, China

Ding Shaolian

ABSTRACT

This paper studies the impacts of urban renewal on local residents' place identity by examining the changes in local residents' place identity in Sunwenxilu, a traditional commercial street in downtown Zhongshan City, Guangdong Province, China, which carried out urban renewal relatively early in modern China. Applying Breakwell's [(2015). Risk: Social psychological perspectives. In J. D. Wright (Ed.), *International encyclopedia of the social & behavioral sciences* (2nd Ed.). New York, NY: Elsevier] identity process model and using the renewal process as a starting point, data concerning local residents' place identity in Sunwenxilu were collected through in-depth interviews, observations, and literature analysis. The results reveal that local residents had established a strong place identity on Sunwenxilu before it changed to be a community of "incompetents" in the 1990s. In the late 1990s, Sunwenxilu was transformed into a cultural tourism pedestrian street. Right after the transformation, local residents regained their self-esteem with the improvement of the physical environment and intensification of cultural symbols, and re-established their place continuity by maintaining their collective memories. However, a failure to improve the local residents' self-efficiency of place during the "superficial" renewal had resulted in vulnerability of the local residents' place identity in terms of self-esteem, continuity and distinctiveness, thus causing another crisis of place identity. Obviously, the construction of place identity results from the interaction of all elements, so too much emphasis on only one element may trigger a new identity crisis.

Introduction

At the end of the 1970s, China began to implement a reform and opening up policy to cope with globalization, which accelerated the progress of urbanization and modernization in China. Except for economic growth and improvements in efficiency, urbanization has also reshaped China's urban spaces. That is to say, the urban historic elements are being replaced by modern mainstream landscapes, which have posed an increasingly severe challenge for the continuation of a sense of place in the city. Urban renewal for the purpose of protecting urban historic elements has become a strategy generally implemented by China's city administrators to reshape the sense of place. However, for more than 30 years, although many cultural tourism pedestrian streets have been built, they are widely questioned due to their monotonous streetscapes and weakened cultural functions. What role these urban renewal projects, based on the protection of historic elements, play in the construction of place identity has become an unavoidable topic in academic circles.

Research background

Influence of urban renewal

Since World War II, urban renewal has been a continuous concern of Western scholars. In the early stages, environmental scholars proposed that urban renewal should be promoted by improving the environment (as cited in Ding, 2008), which functioned as the theoretical basis for large-scale renewal in the form of demolition for redevelopment. In the 1960s, Jane Jacobs (2005) began to criticize the damage of such a simple and crude renewal model on urban diversity, and proposed that a more effective way to realize the revitalization of urban centers was to implement pedestrianization and provide more public spaces. After being introduced to China, the theory was of great significance for China's urban renewal practices under the leadership of planning and designing circles (Chen, 2007; Zhang, 1988). Although Noll and Zimbalist (1997), Bright (2000), Dickens (1999), and others discussed problems such as the social inequity caused by the industrial urban renewal and gentrification phenomena, in addition to changes in employment opportunities, their ideas were not as influential as the previous theory (as cited in Ding, 2008).

In the early stages, the theoretical study of China's urban renewal mainly focused on Western experiences in planning and design (Chen, 2007; Zhang, 1988). After entering the twenty-first century, with the continuous increase of problems exposed in renewal projects, some scholars began to propose that the "organic renewal" model should be adopted (Tan, 2006; Ye, 2003), but the aforesaid proposition of adoption of the organic renewal model cannot restrain large-scale renewal from damaging the historic culture (Wang & Deng, 2009). In this period, some scholars also proposed that social cost and the value of cultural veins should be also appraised carefully during the renewal process and that a public participation mechanism should be introduced during the process of planning and constructing (Bai & Chen, 2008; Chen, 2009; Deng, 2011; Guo, 2006; Hu, 2013; Wan, 2006; Zhao, Lu, & Qi, 2012). China has now been implementing urban renewal for many years, and the influence of those practices on the development of China's cities has become an unavoidable problem that needs to be solved in academic circles. On the whole, the problem has not attracted enough attention from academic circles, and additionally, few scholars have studied the influence of urban renewal from the perspective of sense of place.

Urban renewal and place reconstruction

With the continuous acceleration of the globalization process, local social and cultural boundaries are being continuously threatened, and anti-globalization momentum has become stronger and stronger, causing "creation of place" activities such as heritage protection to be carried out in response (Creswell, 2006, p. 88). When delocalization is realized, "place" is redefined and endowed with new meaning in the new global relationship system (Zhu & Liu, 2011). From the perspective of political economics, Harvey proposed that urban redevelopment produces strained relations between fixedness of place and mobility of capital. In order to compete for mobile capital, places market themselves, which brings about an urban renaissance (as cited in Creswell, 2006, pp. 90–103). He also pointed out, from the perspective of political economics, that "place" is a form of resisting global capitalist forces. Place is often regarded as the "whereabouts of collective memories" (Harvey, 2000, p. 302), that is, the identified site is constructed by connecting a group of people and their past memories. Hence, place is preserved or constructed during the journey from memories to visions, from the past to the future. The construction of place can reveal hidden memories and help in planning prospects for different futures (Harvey, 2000, p. 302). During this process, place identity plays a key role. With the transformation of identity, changes occur during the process of place creation, the political track leading to the future is redefined, some memories are suppressed, and other memories are saved from being lost, and thus the remodeling of place and the place development path (expected space) is completed (Harvey, 1996, p. 306). In this sense, city renewal based on historic cultural protection is essence in a place-recreation process in old cities as the main battlefields where place and globalization meet. Thus, a more reasonable explanation for the urban renewal process can be gotten from studies on urban renewal from the perspective of place. However, until recently in China, no scholars introduced concepts related to "place" for studying urban renewal or proposed that a historic district should be studied as a living space (place) as an essential base, or that city and district development should be emphasized from the perspective of place identity (Liao & Yang, 2014; Sik, Ping, & Raymond, 2005).

Place and place identity

In the 1970s, place was one of the main concepts that distinguished humanistic geography from positivistic geography. Based on the perspectives of phenomenology and existential philosophy, humanistic geographers believe that place is not only an object, but also an existing worldly form. It is regarded as a core element in constructing the meaning, intention or value for a person (Creswell, 2006, p. 35). Each person requires to be positioned as an identified place. For both individuals and groups, place is the source of identity, and place identity refers to the partial knowledge of the self-perception of an individual's social role in a given place. A person can distinguish themselves from others through place identification; that is, place can play a role in social categorization, and is equivalent to some kinds of social identification (Tang, 2013, pp. 54–55). Attachment to one's native land is a common human emotion, and special natural objects, landmarks, historical events, heroic figures and markers such as temples can enhance people's sense of identity and encourage their awareness of and loyalty to a place (Zhu, Qian, & Chen, 2010).

Dimension of place identity

Williams and Roggenbuck (1989) pointed that place identity reveals how a place represents an individual and how an individual distinguishes themselves from others (as cited in Zhu & Liu, 2011). In short, place identity refers to a process whereby an individual interacts with a place, enabling socialization. This socialization involves multiple complex processes, such as the emotional process, perceptual process, and cognitive process. Through these processes, the individual and the group define themselves as a part of a specific place (Stedman, 2002) and determine their positions and roles in the society via that place (Proshansky, Fabian, & Kaminoff, 1983). In such a context, place is no longer only the physical background where human activities occur, but also becomes a constituent part of oneself (Lewicka, 2011). In other words, place identity is a constituent part of individual identity which is developed from the distinctive elements of a place and the essence of the interaction between the individual and the place (Bernardo & Palma, 2005).

Proshansky (1978) believed that place identity is a complex multi-dimensional concept. The multiple dimensions refer to the connections between the individual identity and the physical environment and defining oneself accordingly; for example, ideas of consciousness and unconsciousness, beliefs, preferences, feelings, values, goals, behavioral tendencies, and skills. He also emphasized that the physical environment is very important in shaping people's place identity (Proshansky et al., 1983). As place identity is characterized in pluralism and changefulness, the concept of multiple dimensions is helpful for people to understand the generation and development processes of place identity. Breakwell systematically analyzed the concept of place identity and proposed the theory of identity process; that is, the theory that place identity consists of four aspects: self-esteem, self-efficacy, distinctiveness and continuity (Breakwell, 2015). The model derived from the theory has been widely recognized by scholars and used in newer studies (Breakwell, 2015; Knez, 2005).

Factors influencing place identity

Twigger-Ross and Uzzell (1996) used Breakwell's identity dimension model to study the perceptions and attitudes of residents in an area of the London Docklands toward their residential environment, and their study revealed that those with an emotional attachment to the local residential environment are more inclined to give positive evaluations. A study by Bres and Davis (2001) revealed that festival activities play a positive role in enhancing the place identity of residents in a community (as cited in Zhu et al., 2010). Mazanti and Ploger (2003) performed a case study on urban renewal and found that the place identity of residents in poor areas features a differentiation between inside and outside such areas. The interviewed persons inside this area did not feel that the number of unemployed residents, the share of refugees and immigrants, etc. would justify calling their neighborhood problematic or deprived as the negative public image represented made by the outside. A study by Clark and Stein (2003) revealed that natural landscapes are the most important constituent part of community identity and those residents who frequently visit those natural landscapes identity highly with the cultural elements of the community (as cited in Tang, 2013, pp. 55–56). In addition, urban historical and cultural landscapes reflect the unification of diachronism and synchronicity and function as signs of urban historic memories. Landscapes interact with memories to shape the cultural characteristics of a place and form the place identity (Li, Zhu, & Huang, 2010).

Methods

Selection of research object

Study site

Zhongshan City, formerly Xiangshan County, was originally an island on Lingdingyang Bay. As early as the Neolithic Age 5000 years ago, there were inhabitants living there who were occupied in fishing. In the 22nd Year of Shaoxing in the Southern Song Dynasty (1152 CE), the Guangzhou government combined Nanhai, Fanyu, Xinhui, and Dongguan counties into Xiangshan County, with Macao included. In April 1925, in honor of Mr Sun Zhongshan (also known as Sun Yat-sen), the great forerunner of the revolution, Xiangshan County was renamed Zhongshan County. In 1983, Zhongshan County was upgraded to a county-level city, and in 1988, a prefecture-level city. Zhongshan City is located at latitude 22°11′ ˜ 22°46′ N, longitude 113°09′ ˜ 113°46′ E. It is in south-central Guangdong, with Fanyu District in Guangzhou and Shunde District in Foshan to the north, and the city's center is 86 km away from Guangzhou. Across Lingdingyang Bay on the Pearl River waterfront to the east are Dongguan, Shenzhen, and the Hong Kong Special Administrative Region. To the southeast, Macao is 65 km away and Hong Kong 52 km away, as shown in Figure 1. Since the reform and opening up policy was implemented, Zhongshan City has become an important manufacturing base in the Pearl River Delta Region (Local Compilation Committee of Zhongshan City [LCCZC], 2006, pp. 2–14).

Sunwenxilu is a traditional business center in Zhongshan City. As early as the establishment of the county in the Southern Song Dynasty, local markets formed around Shiqi Port. Up to the Hongwu period in the Ming Dynasty, 18 fixed shops appeared in this region, historically named the "Shibajian" (meaning 18 Shops) (Yin, 1995). In the late Qing Dynasty and the early Republic period, "Shibajian" developed into a comprehensive traditional business street integrating residences, commerce and services in one area (Ding, 2008, p. 19). In the early Republic period, the government of Zhongshan County transformed four traditional alleys into a new "Shiqi Main Road". After this transformation, the business street attracted many merchants to operate their shops there, which brought business prosperity to Sunwenxilu (Construction Committee of Zhongshan City [CCZC],1996, pp. 35–38). After the founding of PRC, under the planned economy system, businesses in Sunwenxilu became stagnant, and it became merely a main road with heavy traffic. After the reform and opening up policy, business there boomed again(LA14). However, in the mid- to late 1990s, business on Sunwenxilu street declined. In order to revive the street, the government of Zhongshan City implemented a pedestrianized transformation of Sunwenxilu from 1997 to 1998, turning it into the current cultural tourism pedestrian street of Sunwenxilu (Zhao, 1997, p. 513, pp. 894–895).

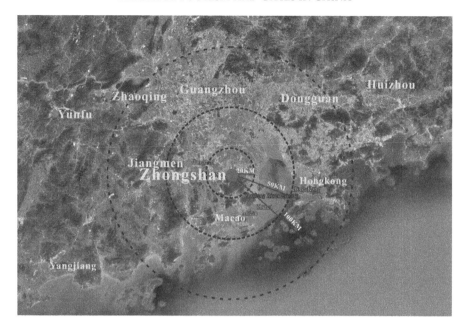

Figure 1. Geographic sketch map of Zhongshan City.

Representativeness of the case

Since the Portuguese leased Macao in the sixteenth century, Macao in Xiangshan has become a center where Chinese and Western cultures blend, and therefore Xiangshan has become the forefront for the fusion of Chinese and Western cultures (Wang, 2006, pp. 1–3). Especially after the Opium Wars, Chinese and Western culture interacted more and more frequently because of the increasingly frequent commercial exchanges. During the process of the blending and clashing of Chinese and Western cultures, many "elites", represented by Sun Zhongshan, appeared in Zhongshan City. Confronted by the culture clashes, they began to think about the development of their "homeland" in the future, and concepts like "Save the Nation by Engaging in Industry", "Business War Theory", etc. were proposed by them for "homeland" development at the national level. Then, in order to respond to the call of "Business War" by Zheng Guanying, Wu Tiecheng, and others, the head of Zhongshan County put forward the slogan "Dismantle the city wall and build roads to develop the business" and transformed traditional "Shibajian" into the "Shiqi Main Road": that is, the predecessor of current Sunwenxilu (CCZC,1996, pp. 35–38).

After the reform and opening up, Zhongshan City again became an important manufacturing industry base in the Pearl River Delta Region and the forefront for the fusion of Chinese and Western cultures, and Zhongshan City entered a stage of rapid globalization. Nowadays, Zhongshan City presents a picture of globalization depicted by Massey (as cited in Creswell, 2006, pp. 104–116), and Michael Jackson, a music superstar from the USA, traveled there to perform. Commodities from all over the world can now be bought in grocery stores there, and most families there have overseas relatives may send their children go to universities abroad after graduating from high school. Before pedestrianization was implemented for the Beijing Road in Guangzhou (2002), the Nanjing West Road in Shanghai (2000) and Wangfujing Street in Beijing (1998), at the beginning of 1997 the government of Zhongshan City began transformation of the old district into the Cultural Tourism Pedestrian Street of Sunwenxilu, which was the beginning of the urban renewal of Zhongshan City. Nowadays, Shiqi(administrative center, location of the case under study), Nanlang, Huangpu, Xiaolan, etc. in Zhongshan City have all preserved many historical buildings and settlement landscapes, and the inner city has also preserved a 2 km^2 area reflecting the style of the old city. There were a number of dialects (e.g. the Shiqi dialect, Xiaolan dialect, Shaxi dialect, etc.) in Zhongshan City several hundred years ago, and folk customs such as

Shagangxu, Chrysanthemum Show, Piao-se, etc. that have prevailed for several hundred years are still very popular among people in Zhongshan. In 2011, Zhongshan City was rated as a Chinese famous historical and cultural city (China News: http://www.chinanews.com/gn/2011/03-17/2912319.shtml, retrieved September 4, 2016). At the beginning of 2015, Sunwenxiluin the old city center of Zhongshan (i.e. the case in this study) became the only district to be rated as one of the "first batch of 30 Chinese historical and cultural districts" in Guangdong Province (*People's Daily* Online: http://politics.people.com.cn/n/2015/0422/c1001-26884209.html, retrieved September 4, 2016).

As stated by Massey, a place is not closed, but defined through its interactions with the outside world. Thus, "place" is a process, and place identity is a collection of multiple elements (as cited in Creswell, 2006, pp. 104–116). Accordingly, we shall study a place at a larger scale than the local scale and from a dynamic and plural perspective. Ever since Macao became a port for Chinese and Western exchanges, Zhongshan City, once a "small place" in the border area of China reflecting the characteristics of Chinese culture, has become a place where Chinese and Western cultures blend. Such globalization continues today. Thus, based on Breakwell's (2015) place identity theory and with the old city renewal time nodes as the starting point, the study aims to analyze the changes in the place identity of local residents in the early, middle and late stages from a dynamic perspective, give more reasonable explanations for the local efforts of China's cities under the background of globalization, and provide references for the evaluation of such efforts.

Data collection and analysis

In this study, in-depth interviews, observations, and second-hand data analysis are used to obtain the necessary data. The author conducted field investigations from June 2006 to January 2007, from July 2014 to September 2014, January 2015 to March 2015, and on weekends from March 2015 to May 2015, as well as from July 2015 to September 2015. Through snowball sampling, the author collected first-hand data via semi-structured and open-ended face-to-face in-depth interviews with residents who have lived continuously in the old urban area, residents that lived there before but have now relocated, newcomers (mainly including the wealthy in addition to migrant workers that came to work in Zhongshan recently but have local residence cards), Chinese people from overseas, and other outsiders familiar with Zhongshan. The interviewees included government officials, enterprise operators, retired people, self-employed persons, informal economic operators, and job hunters, and the basic information of the interviewees is listed in Table 1. Local residents includes residents that lived here before the place declined but have now relocated: that is, the first type of residents are "escapers" (LAi) and the second type of residents that still live here now are "left-behind persons" (LBi). The topics involved in the interviews with 34 local residents generally included the history of their personal residence, their histories of operating and working there, changes in the local practical activities before and after the old city renewal, and changes in their recognition and emotions toward the place. Other nonlocal residents are designated as MAi, MBZi, MBQi, MCZi, and MCZQi; local business managers and social elites are designated as Ei; overseas Chinese and overseas returnees are designated as Ii; and other samples are designated as Oi. The interviews were mainly for the purpose of defining the natives' place identity through their interactions with those nonlocal residents. As stated by Massey, direct interaction with them can enable the natives of Zhongshan to define their sense of place (as cited in Creswell, 2006, pp. 113–114). In the interviews, the author tried her best to establish good relationships with the interviewees by frequently participating in their activities and actively integrating herself into their social circles, as well as ensuring the authenticity and reliability of the data through comparison with other interviews, on-site observations and reviewing second-hand data: that is, the triangulation method. The author also specifically observed the festival activities of the local residents during traditional Chinese festivals such as the Spring Festival, Lantern Festival, Tomb-sweeping Day and Mid-autumn Festival, and Western festivals such as Valentine's Day and Christmas Day, with offline long-term participatory observation of the Zhongshan Book Exhibition, Urban Renewal Salon and Reading Experience Sharing Session and online platforms such as Funny Longdu, Zhongshan Release,

Table 1. Basic information of interviewees.

Type	Code	Number of interviewees	Basic characteristics
Escapers	LA1–LA15	15	Residents who moved away from old city proper
Left-behind persons	LB1–LB19	19	Left-behind local residents in the old city proper
Immigrants	MA1–MA9	9	Technical people working in government departments, enterprises and institutions
	MBZ1	1	Employees from Zhongshan township who have purchased local houses
	MBQ1–MBQ7	7	Employees from other regions who have purchased local houses
	MCZ1	1	Employees from Zhongshan township who have not purchased local houses
	MCQ1–MD15	15	Employees from inland who have not purchased local houses
Operators and managers	E1–E13	13	Government administrators, operators and managers of enterprises and institutions and technicians such as painters.
Overseas Chinese and overseas returnees	I1–I3	3	Chinese who moved overseas and returned after studying abroad
Others	O1–O4	4	Outsiders familiar with the region

and Shiqi Activity Society. In this study, 120 interviewees were involved in all, and about 200,000 characters of interview records and more than 20,000 characters of observation notes were noted down. The second-hand materials involved in the study are mainly from local treatises, government papers, program documents, online forums, news report, WeChat platform, etc.

Analytical framework

Taking the old city renewal process as the starting point, and with Breakwell's identity process model, this paper studies the place identity of local residents on Sunwenxilu under the circumstance of old city renewal. Breakwell (2015) proposed four processes of place identity: distinctiveness, continuity, self-esteem and self-efficacy, and constructed an identity process model. The distinctiveness dimension reflects the lifestyle and specific relationship between the individual and their home. People distinguish themselves from others through place identification, and in this sense, place is similar to social categorization, so place identification is equivalent with social identification. The continuity dimension directly relates to the maintenance and development of self-identity continuity, which is divided into place-referent continuity and place-congruent continuity. For place-referent continuity, place functions as the referent of past selves and actions, and people can gain self-identity by maintaining a relationship with a place, while self-esteem relates to an individual's perception of self-value or social value. For example, people who live in historic towns tend to gain a sense of pride through their perceptions of that place. Self-efficacy refers to people's trust in their environmental adaptiveness, and people will have a sense of self-efficacy when the environment benefits or at least does not hinder the people's daily lives. And people tend to be more successful inside such manageable environment (as cited in Breakwell, 2015). With the old city renewal time nodes as the starting point, this paper studies changes in distinctiveness, continuity, self-esteem, and self-efficacy of the local residents' sense of place before the decline, in the period of decline, in the early stage of renewal, and in the late stage of renewal, clarifies the construction of local residents' sense of place under the background of old city renewal, and analyzes the interrelationships of these four dimensions during the process of the local residents' identity construction.

Research findings

Place identity before the decline

Identification of "City dwellers"

Twigger-Ross and Uzzell (1996) indicated that place distinctiveness can be defined from the following four perspectives: residential environment (urban or rural), region (some specific place), local place (a part of the local community), and personal experience (life history). This study found that when it came to the history before the town's decline, nearly all interviewees defined their own identity as being related to the distinctiveness of their residential environment; that is, self-styled "city-dwellers" can be distinguished from "country folks" from towns.

Strong self-esteem

As previously mentioned, since the late Ming Dynasty, frequent commercial activities in Sunwenxilu have laid the foundation for the district to become an economic and cultural center in the Daxiang-shan area. At the beginning of the reform and opening up policy, as a forerunner for implementing "Three-plus-one" trading-mix (custom manufacturing with materials, designs or samples supplied by oversea clients), Zhongshan City built the earliest hot springs hotel for overseas Chinese, and two major stores, the Overseas Chinese Commercial Mansion and People's Department Store, have been top commercial ventures in the Pearl River Delta Area, and So Sunwenxilu became the first area to embrace globalized urbanization. All the residents from towns go sightseeing and shopping there on New Year's Day or other festivals. Local residents are regarded as enviable civilized "city dwellers" by themselves and the others outside the city.

High self-efficiency

Since the Republic period, Sunwenxilu has become an important hub that connects China and other countries. Most city dwellers there were rich and had overseas Chinese relatives, and almost all of them advocated the Western lifestyle and could purchase modern Western consumer goods through overseas Chinese relatives, for example, gramophones and record players, skin care products, kerosene stoves, etc. (as shown in Figure 2). They not only watch traditional dramas, but also movies and even the performances of international magicians. In addition, both traditional home-cooked food and Western food and snacks can be found there. As stated by some residents, this is a hopeful place, where even "Mr. Sun Zhongshan operated a pharmacy" there previously (LA6, LA15).

> One of my distant relatives lived here before. On each spring festival, my parents will take me to the city. Here were many things that I have never seen. All department stores are beautiful and sold lots of delicious snacks. (MBZ1)

> Here was once named as "inland Macao" before. During the Republic period, four major Chinese department stores set up outlets here and even Mr. Sun Zhongshan opened a pharmacy here. (LA6)

> Here was the most prosperous before. Many fashionable things can be only bought here. Once our relatives came, we will take them to go to the department stores, which sold things that they had not seen in the countryside then. (LA14)

> Then foreign cigarettes, watches, clocks, chocolates and cosmetics all can be bought here (Overseas Chinese Store). It is really terrific. Many outsiders will come to buy those things and many things had not been seen by them. (LB3)

Figure 2. Cosmetics (left) and gramophone (right) imported from the West by Zhongshan City in the republic period. Source: Xiangshan Commercial Museum.

Stable continuity

Before the reform and opening up policy, traditional Chinese rural society changed slowly, so the place identity attached to the residents' home areas and family was strong and stable (Li et al., 2010). This study finds that since the late Ming Dynasty, "Shibajian", the predecessor of Sunwenxilu, has developed into the center of the Daxiangshan Area. During the Republic period, Sunwenxilu was transformed into the Shiqi Main Road, along which many modern industries and businesses gathered. Thus, it became representative of advanced urban civilization, and its position as a cultural center continued till the old city's renewal. All the interviewees said that they were "indigenous" inhabitants and were proud of living there (LB1, LB4, LB8).

Identity crisis before renewal and the response method

Loss of the sense of self-esteem of place identity

In the late 1990s, as the center of Zhongshan City began to move eastward, the business circles of the Yihua Department Store in the eastern area gradually replaced Sunwenxilu and became the main business center, enticing the rich in Zhongshan City to shop there (Ding, 2008, pp. 63–67). Meanwhile, the development of manufacturing in villages and towns driven by the "Three-plus-one" policy also promoted the rapid spread of business in Zhongshan City into those towns. Then, the famous One-Plus–One Supermarket set up outlets in the villages and towns, which attracted residents from those places to shop. In addition to the decline in the physical environment, the "city center" that once flourished was re-labeled as the "old city proper" and was described as being shabby, crowded, dirty and disorderly; the competitive persons who can afford to buy a new apartment all left and those remaining were labeled "incompetents". When it comes to Sunwenxilu, they are not as proud as before, but feel more melancholy and helpless (LB3, LB6, LB7, LB9).

Continuous decrease in self-efficacy

Before renewal, Sunwenxilu was confronted by environmental deterioration, narrow roads, insufficient parking, aging buildings and other safety hazards. In order to reduce the fire risk, open fires were not allowed in the Sunwenxilu business street (LA14). In addition, due to the insufficient electric power supply, some large shopping malls' electricity demand could not be met, so they installed illegal power generation devices (E9). On the one hand, the physical environment and infrastructure of Sunwenxilu were on the decline, and on the other, the increasing modernization of residents' homes in addition to the consumption and travel demands driven by the reform and opening up policy continuously reduced the self-efficacy of Sunwenxilu.

> At that time, Sunwenxilu was always crowded and noisy. Especially on the market days of Shagangxu, we could not even ride a bicycle. (E8)

Helplessly staying behind, and actively leaving due to the fracture of self-identity of place

Continuity is an important dimension of place identity, and is divided into place-referent continuity and place-congruent continuity. Here, place-congruent continuity refers to general and transferable local characteristics, for example, people select a place to reside that can represent their own values, or change their residential environment to make it consistent with their current identities (as cited in Tang, 2013, p. 55). Before renewal, Sunwenxilu was obviously on the decline, and the residents there were not only bothered by low self-efficacy, but also confronted by challenges to their continuity of self-identity posed by stigmatizations such as "decline", "backwardness", "incompetence", etc. In the interviews, the left-behind persons expressed their helplessness.

> Now here is not so good as before. Only the poor like us live here. No rich persons are willing to live here. (LB16-LB19)

It was said that the place would be dismantled, but later we heard that this place was protected, and the dismantlement was not allowed. Alas, we can do nothing but to stay here, because we have not enough money to buy houses in other places! (LB3)

During this process, to construct a harmonious sense of identity, persons with strong competence and good opportunities took the initiative to leave Sunwenxilu and go to other zones, such as the east zone of Zhongshan City, to find residences corresponding with their identities.

I had no choice. Then it was too old and shabby there, without convenient transportation, so I took the opportunity of housing allotment of my work unit and moved away. (LA5, LA12)

Elimination of place distinctiveness and the blurring of place boundaries

With the loss self-esteem of place identity, local residents of Sunwenxilu no longer emphasize that they are natives (in Shiqi), and even deliberately conceal the fact. For example, they will deliberately avoid speaking in the local dialect in public, and instead speak Cantonese in order to eliminate the place distinctiveness and blur their place boundaries so as to avoid the stigmatization of the old city.

We were ashamed of speaking in Shiqi dialect that was regarded to be out of fashion to outsiders before, and generally, we spoke Cantonese. (LA9, LA11)

Identity reconstruction at an earlier stage

Duality of place self-esteem of left-behind persons: traditional culture spokespersons in outsiders' eyes and "incompetents" in their own eyes

In the early stage of renewal, with the beautification of the environment and landscape as well as outsiders enhancing the traditional culture, Sunwenxilu became a clean, orderly and fashionable place rich in historical and cultural heritage. The old local lifestyle, residential environment, customs, habits, etc. were all reported by media abroad. The local residents' hidden collective memories were activated, local cultural phenomena appeared, and place self-esteem regained a positive affirmation at the cultural level, which made local residents become traditional cultural spokespersons as defined by the media, and they also became willing to narrate the past as such spokespersons. However, when they took off attractive "cultural" coats, they could still not get away from the stigmatization associated with the self-labeled "incompetents". In this research, only one retired person who was engaged in Chinese affairs overseas stated that although she had bought a new house in eastern area of Zhongshan City , the cultural heritage motivated her to stay (LB1), while other left-behind persons still thought that living there was a choice of "incompetents".

Maintenance of continuity: imagining a homeland

With the beautification of the physical environment and improvements in the environment and sanitation, Sunwenxilu became an ideal place for left-behind residents to relax, and they can be seen resting on seats in the pedestrian street and on the steps outside of windows of the shops. Meanwhile, with the protection of the historical landscape and the reappearance of historical icons, the left-behind persons' memories were activated and the continuity of place identity appeared again. Then, the local residents again began to see their "homeland" through symbols and memories.

When I see the cloth seller, I remember that my mom took me to the cloth store to buy cloth for making clothes when I was a child. And I liked the small pedicab installed with a stove when I was young and the seller's shouts often attract us children to buy many delicious snacks, Especially in winter, it was very warm near the pedicab (with sweet smile on the face). (LB3, LB4)

I went back to have a look at that place when its transformation was just completed; then it indeed became very beautiful and buildings there were still previous arcades. Afterwards, I went back to my old school and felt a special closeness. (LA11)

I went back when its transformation was just completed and felt a special closeness. Afterwards, the museum was opened and I took my child to go there once. There were many lifelike wax figures in the museum. In addition to the lamplight and sellers' shouts, it's just like a return to the old days. (LA15)

Intensification of distinctiveness: "we are natives in Shiqi"

As mentioned above, although the left-behind residents still face stigmatization as "incompetents", when facing outsiders, the native-dwellers, especially the left-behind residents, naturally emphasize their own cultural distinctiveness. They are willing to claim to be "natives in Shiqi" and intensify this image by sharing their old stories and customs. Interestingly, during this process, "speaking in the Shiqi dialect" has become the most effective means to reveal their distinctiveness and abandon the feeling of shame for speaking the dialect.

Differentiation of self-efficacy

Sunwenxilu became a good place for relax and also a "food desert" for those who are left-behind. At the end of the 1990s, in order to address the decline of the Sunwenxilu business street, the government of Zhongshan City advocated that Sunwenxilu be transformed into a cultural tourism pedestrian street. The new commercial pedestrian street took on a brand-new look and attracted many citizens and tourists to go shopping and sightseeing (LA2), which increased the popularity of the street and promoted the development of the retail industry (E6). Since the old city's renewal, the environment, sanitation, landscape and public security in Sunwenxilu have all been improved. As local residents said, it has now become a "park".

However, the renewal also produced new troubles for local residents. Sunwenxilu is positioned as the "cultural tourism pedestrian street", and during the process of renewal, the service facilities that served low-income groups in local communities have become objects to be renovated. Some are affordable, but ugly and untidy traditional snack shops, teahouses in the community, grocery stores, and hardware stores are all being eliminated. Old people in the community have to go to surrounding areas, or even farther, to Shaxi, Dachong, etc., to drink morning tea and seek services originally provided in the community.

Now it is very inconvenient, even it is difficult for my old friends and I to find a place to drink tea. Last week, we just take a bus to Shaxi to have tea. It's just as well we can take the bus free of charge. (LB4)

There were many small shops on Sunwenxilu, but they were dismantled at the time of renewal. Even we must walk a long way to buy only a tap. (LB3)

Sunwenxilu became a reminiscent recreational area of escapers . In the early stage of renewal, many historical and cultural landscapes in Sunwenxilu were renovated and represented. This street was turned into a symbolic place for the city of Zhongshan as a memory of its glorious commercial history. This symbolic meaning was frequently reported and emphasized. As the results, those who left the street in the earlier stage gradually came back to live there. In addition, they also like to show their relatives and friends from out of the city the place as the authentic home town for the people of Zhongshan, This street became the root of all people of Zhongshan. And words like "I", "we", "my", or "our" appear frequently in the interpretations such as in "I was born here" or "That's how we used to be." A strong place identity was developed among local people.

I was born there before and lived there for many years. When friends from other places came, I often show them around Sunwenxilu and let them see the place that I lived before. (LA12)

Identity crisis in the late stage of renewal and the response method

Crisis of distinctiveness: arcades and homogeneous commodities

As early as 1998, the first phase of renewal of Sunwenxilu had been completed. At that point the renewal of pedestrian streets such as Shangxiajiu and Beijing Road in Guangzhou had not yet started, so the project attracted government officials from all over the country to conduct an investigation (LA2). Afterwards, many projects with identical buildings and landscapes were carried out nation-wide. Only in Guangdong Province, there were several pedestrian streets of the same style in Xinhui, Jiangmen, Taishan and Guangzhou (see Figure 3). In addition, after renewal, with the sharp increases in property management fees and rent for stores (property management fees were increased to RMB 3/m2, which made it a block of which the property management fees is highest in the city) (E4), time-honored stores gradually moved away from Sunwenxilu, and the original characteristics of the area were further lost. As one interviewee said, "Sunwenxilu is of no characteristics, because commodities there can be bought everywhere." (LA1).

Crisis of self-esteem and continuity of place: hypermarket where low-price commodities are sold to others

With the increasingly intense business competition and changes in the macro commercial pattern in Zhongshan, the original tourist resource market of Hong Kong and the local high-end tourist resource market have gradually shrunk, and the renewal cannot reverse the decline of Sunwenxilu (E9, E10), but accelerate the departure of time-honored branded stores. The century-old Juxiangyua-nanchor store has moved away, and more than 100-year-old business history of the Fushoutang Pharmacy in Sunwenxilu has also come to an end. Sunwenxilu has evolved into a district where mainly low-end clothing for migrant workers is sold.

> We, local persons, don't buy things here, and only migrant job-hunting boys and girls that don't understand the market go there. (LB3, LB6, LB7)

Delocalization of self-efficacy

Local consumption vs. international commodities and services. After the renewal, Sunwenxilu has been frequently questioned over the lack of services such as catering and recreation. In 2008, Zhong-shanXingzhong Group Co., Ltd. invested in the construction of a linear urban complex: Xingzhong Square along the river in Sunwenxilu's west end. Mid- and high-end commodities and services are

Figure 3. Commercial pedestrian streets with identical landscapes.

provided in the square, and many brand clothing stores, large restaurants, cinemas and amusement parks have gathered there. It has become a modern urban product, and local residents are an unwelcome audience.

> Xingzhong Square is beautiful, but commodities sold there are expensive. Sometimes, we will go in and have a look. However, the sellers know we cannot afford commodities there just at a glance, so usually they are not responsive, which makes us feel uncomfortable. (LB3)

> I myself have never been there to go shopping. Only once on a holiday, my child came to see us and invited us to dinner. It is too expensive to have a dinner there and I really cannot afford it! (LB3)

To seek commodities and services that match their daily needs, local residents have to go to other areas. For example, they have to walk across two districts to Tingzixia Street to buy time-honored brand-name almond cakes, walk for 20 minutes to Shun De Chi on Taiping Road or Hongguang on Hubin Road to have breakfast, etc.

Delocalization of consumptions of escapers. After the construction of Xingzhong Square, local residents who had left were attracted to go back for shopping. Especially with regard to cinemas and large restaurant chains, for example, Shanxi's Nighty-nine Cents, Venice Western Restaurant, etc. have become the most popular restaurants in Zhongshan City, and booking in advance is required to have dinner in them. However, although these high-end commodities and services are available in Sunwenxilu, due to the modern appearance and operating patterns of those stores and restaurants, consumers cannot connect them with Sunwenxilu, and the consumption is characterized in delocalization.

> I have not been to Sunwenxilu for more than 10 years. Now we go to Lihe (former commercial circles of Yihua Department Store and CBD at the highest level in Zhongshan) for shopping. Sometimes we also go to Xingzhong Square to watch movies or have western food. My child like having a meal in Venice Western Restaurant there and on his last birthday, we just had a meal there. It is convenient for parking there. (LA8)

In the interviews, I found that the interviewees did not cognitively connect Xingzhong Square with Sunwenxilu, and that Xingzhong Square is seen as just a delocalized modern urban commercial complex.

Identity reconstruction over local scale of place

In the late stage of renewal, with the departure of the time-honored branded stores, the cultural function of Sunwenxilu was increasingly weakened, and the local residents of Sunwenxilu were threatened by crises of distinctiveness, continuity, self-esteem, and self-efficacy of place. Confronted by the disruption of cultural image and the concept of "home", local residents started redefining the boundaries of "home", and blurred the original boundary defined at the community level. They began to collectively call themselves "Zhongshan people", and the scope of their identity was extended from the community to the city. Seemingly, such an extension produced no influence on the strength of identity, which can be seen from the Zhongshan people's attachment to "home". In the globalized environment, Zhongshan people tend to buy houses or work near their homes, and during this process, non-material symbols and texts such as language, historical stories, old photos, old albums, etc., gradually replaced the physical symbols and concept of place and became the new standard for their identity. The group reconstructed their own identity by speaking in the Shiqi dialect and sharing their common past living experiences and other historical events in Sunwenxilu.

> We were ashamed of speaking in Shiqi dialect and avoided speaking in Shiqi dialect before. However, we feel a special closeness when speaking in Shiqi dialect to Shiqi people now. (LA11)

> I like Zhongshan Story program (A public welfare program introducing the history and culture of Zhongshan on Zhongshan TV) very much. Many past stories are narrated in the program, which delivers a special closeness. (LA11)

I like it very much, too! (LA9, LA10)

I like these old photos and I just lived there before. It is too long time since I moved away from there and I couldn't recall anything there without these photos. I saved them in my mobile phone and feel a special close-ness each time I see them. I often show them to my children to let them know the place where their father lived before. And I also share them with my friends and they all think the place is special, ho ho! (LA14)

Discussion and conclusion

Discussion

By adopting Breakwell's theory of identity process, the author conducted an exploratory study on the construction process of place identity of local residents in the traditional business street of Sunwen-xilu under the background of urban renewal. Narin (1965) believed that nearly everyone is born with a demand of living in an identifiable place (as cited in Tang, 2013, p. 54). Tuan (1977) also proposed that whether for an individual or a group, "place" is a source of sense of security and identity. Place identity refers to the recognition that a given place is part of the self-perception of a social role, which is proved in the case of Sunwenxilu. The study has revealed that Sunwenxilu, as a place where local residents were born and grew up, plays an important role in the identity process of local residents. However, various elements of place play different roles in the construction of place identity, and they also influence each other, and place self-esteem is the most important element of place identity. Once a place endows an individual with self-esteem, the individual will voluntarily demonstrate the distinctiveness of the place in identifying themselves.

In contrast, if a place cannot endow an individual with self-esteem, and threatens the continuity of the individual with respect to place-congruent continuity, the individual will tend to eliminate the distinctiveness of the place, blur the boundaries of the place, and even escape to some other place that can deliver more self-esteem. However, place self-esteem alone is not sufficient. Place self-esteem cannot directly convert to the individual's self-esteem. If a place can only endow an individual with self-esteem, but the place's self-efficacy is low, the self-cognition brought by the self-esteem of place may put the individual in a conflicting state. In this circumstance, the individual would suffer from a different external identity and internal identity. Therefore, they are lack of motivation for initiatively manifesting and maintaining the distinctiveness, and may even deliberately eliminate the distinctiveness to relieve the pressure brought by inconsistency of internal identity and external identity. Obviously, the urban renewal focusing on the material level only reconstructed the self-esteem of place to some degree and activated the continuity of place. However, since place identity is multi-dimensional, the conversion of the self-esteem of place to the individual self-esteem and the maintenance of place continuity shall be also supported by the place distinctiveness and self-efficacy.

A high self-efficacy of place can effectively mobilize local residents to maintain their self-esteem, distinctiveness, and continuity of place, but low place self-efficacy may accelerate the deconstruction of placeless, for example, delocalization of consumption. Thus, during the process of renewal, intensified place self-efficacy was of great significance in motivating local residents to actively support their place identity. In addition, when the self-esteem, continuity and self-efficacy of place are threatened, the individual will reconstruct their identity over the normal level of placeless at the cost of low-level placeless.

Conclusion

This study reveals that the renewal of the old city influenced the place identity of the local residents in all four processes: self-esteem, distinctiveness, continuity, and self-efficacy.

Before its decline, as the area in China earliest influenced by globalization, Sunwenxilu became the representation of Western urban civilization in Zhongshan's people's eyes. Based on such distinctive-ness, local residents called themselves "civilized urban people" and constructed a place identity that distinguished them from residents of villages and towns. Meanwhile, relatively well-developed external transportation and commodities and services also greatly promoted the local residents' place-based self-efficacy. In addition, stable continuity also plays an important role in the place identity of local residents, and both place-referent continuity (i.e. "we live here from generation to generation") and place-congruent continuity have contributed to the construction of the residents' place identity.

Before the renewal, the sudden occurrence of globalization caused the Sunwenxilu district, originally the city center representing "advanced civilization", to became the "old city proper", representing "backwardness". Challenged by the loss of place self-esteem and self-efficacy, and confronted with the subsequent identity crisis with regard to continuity, the "competent" persons all left the area to go to the "new city proper" to seek modern dwelling environments that corresponded with their perceived identities, while the others became the "left-behind" residents.

In the early stage of renewal, with the transformation of Sunwenxilu into a cultural tourism pedestrian street, local residents again found their self-esteem of place, and continuity of place was once again found; local residents again started thinking of their home as being based on symbols and were themselves symbolized as "spokespersons" of the local culture, and the distinctiveness of the local culture became a basis for the residents to reposition themselves in the context of globalization. However, the renewal was carried out in the context of globalization, and during the process of renewal, old facilities were eliminated because they did not meet the demands of tourists. The previous users then become onlookers themselves, and saw objects in the park such as "food deserts", which caused them to be troubled by the old image of "incompetents".

In the late stage of renewal, with the homogenization of commodities and the landscape and with reduced commodity quality, Sunwenxilu gradually became a business street where low-end clothing were sold to migrant workers and where counterfeit and substandard goods became prevalent, so local residents tried their best to break their perceived ties with the pedestrian street to rid themselves of the influence of that bad image on their self-esteem. In this period, the government continuously improved the service facilities in the area, but because of the internalization and modernization of service facilities, local residents' localized consumption seems awkward. There are many kinds of commodities of good qualities offered by the modern shops in Xingzhong Square near them, the local people had to purchase the commodities they can afford outside the community. Although these internationalized commodities and service facilities also attract people who have previously left to come back to shop, that is a type of delocalized consumption which cannot contribute to place identity.

Acknowledgment

Thanks Professor Xu Honggang for her encouragement during the process of my research and her valuable suggestions on the overall framework of the paper! Thank my tutor Professor BaoJigang for his enlightenment on my research and his help for laying the foundation for this study during the process of writing my doctoral thesis! Thank Doctor Lin Qingqig for her encouragement and support! Thank Doctor Zhou Ling and my classmate Wang Ke for their help in collecting foreign materials! Thank Liu Deng and Zheng Zetian, leaders of Zhongshan City, Ms Wu Juan, journalist of *Zhongshan Daily*, Mr RuanHanbo from Tertiary Industry Office of Shiqi District, Mr Zheng Jisi, former director of Zhongshan Bureau of Culture, Ms Liang Yuying, director of Zhongshan Overseas Chinese Office as well as Wang Xiaohua and Chen Weipeng, my friends for their great support in the research. Thank all interviewees for their cooperation in the interviews.

Disclosure statement

No potential conflict of interest was reported by the author.

References

Bai, Y., & Chen, Y. C. (2008). *A study of social cost of urban renewal*. Nanjing: Southeast University Publishing House.

Bernardo, F., & Palma, J. M. (2005). Place change and identity processes. *Medio Ambiente y Comportamieto Humano, 6*(1), 71–87. Retrieved from http://mach.webs.ull.es/PDFS/Vol6_1/VOL_6_1_f.pdf

Breakwell, G. M. (2015). Risk: Social psychological perspectives. In J. D. Wright (Ed.), *International encyclopedia of the social & behavioral sciences* (2nd Ed.). New York, NY: Elsevier.

Chen, L. (2007). *A study of business street renewal in Hangzhou under the background of "Experience Economy"*. Hangzhou: Zhejiang University.

Chen, Y. F. (2009). *Metropolitan development-political sociology of space production*. Shanghai: Shanghai Classics Publishing House.

Construction Committee of Zhongshan City. (1996). *Chronicles of urban and rural construction in Zhongshan*. Zhongshan: Author.

Creswell, T. (2006). *Place – memory, imagination and identity*. (Xu Tailing & Wang Zhihong, Trans.). Taipei: Socio Publishing.

Deng, K. Q. (2011). *Sustainability appraisal on different models of city renewal*. Wuhan: Huazhong University of Science and Technology.

Ding, S. L. (2008). *An exploration on the evolution of Sunwenxilu traditional commercial street in Zhongshan City*. Guangzhou: Sun-Yatsen University.

Guo, X. M. (2006). *Toward multi-element balance*. Beijing: China Construction Industry Publishing House.

Harvey, D. (1996). *Justice, nature and the geography of difference*. Cambridge: Blackwell.

Harvey, D. (2000). *Spaces of hope*. Berkeley, CA: University of California Press.

Hu, C. W. (2013). Research on the conservation of China historic areas in the process of urbanization – an analysis frame based on urban governance theory. *Modern Urban Research, 7*, 62–67. Retrieved from http://www.cnki.net/

Jacobs, J. (2005). *The death and life of American cities*. (Jin H., Trans.). Beijing: Yilin Press.

Knez, I. (2005). Attachment and identity as related to a place and its perceived climate. *Journal of Environmental Psychology, 25*(2), 207–218.

Lewicka, M. (2011). Place attachment: How far have we come in the last 40 years? *Journal of Environmental Psychology, 31*, 207–230. doi:10.1016/.jenvp.2010.10.001

Li, F., Zhu, H., & Huang, W. (2010). A geography study on the collective memory of urban historical cultural landscape. *Human Geography, 114*(4), 60–66. doi:10.13959/j.issn.1003-2398.2010.04.004

Liao, C. H., & Yang, K. W. (2014). Globalization and place identity: Research of the urban historic district in a new perspective. *Academic Journal of Yunnan Normal University (Natural Science), 46*(1), 49–56. Retrieved from http://www.cnki.net/

Local Compilation Committee of Zhongshan City. (2006). *National territory & housing administration chronicles*. Guangzhou: Guangdong People's Publishing House.

Mazanti, B., & Ploger, J. (2003). Community planning: From politicized places to lived spaces. *Journal of Housing and Built Environment, 18*, 309–327. Retrieved from: http://link.springer.com/

Proshansky, H. M. (1978). The city and self identity. *Environment and Behavior, 10*, 147–169. Retrieved from http://search.proquest.com/

Proshansky, H. M., Fabian, A. K., & Kaminoff, R. (1983). Place-identity: Physical world socialization of the self. *Journal of Environmental Psychology, 3*(1), 57–83. doi:10.1016/S0272-4944(83)80021-8

Sik, H. N., Ping, K. K., & Raymond, W. M. P. (2005). People living in ageing buildings: Their quality of life and sense of belonging. *Journal of Environmental Psychology, 25*, 347–360. doi:10.1016/j.jenvp.2005.08.005

Stedman, R. (2002). Toward a social psychology of place: Predicting behavior from place-based cognitions, attitude and identity. *Environment and Behavior, 34*, 561–581. doi:10.1177/0013916502034005001

Tan, W. (2006). *Dynamic protection and gradual renewal – transformation strategy of business street in old city*. Changsha: Central South University of Forestry and Technology.

Tang, W. Y. (2013). *Study of placeness in tourism*. Beijing: Social Science Academic Press.

Tuan Y. F. (1977). *Space and place: The perspective of experience*. Minneapolis: University of Minnesota Press.

Twigger-Ross, C. L., & Uzzell, D. L. (1996). Place and identity processes. *Journal of Environmental Psychology, 16*, 205–220. Retrieved from http://www.sciencedirect.com/

Wan, Y. (2006). *Harmonious old city renewal*. Beijing: China Architecture & Building Press.

Wang, Y., & Deng, F. (2009). Changes in social structure and production of space in historic district renewal – a case study of Shantang, Suzhou. *Modern Urban Research*, (11), 60–64. Retrieved from http://www.cnki.net/

Wang, Y. M. (2006). *Wind blows Lingdingyang Bay*. Guangzhou: Guangdong People's Publishing House.

Ye, D. J. (2003). *A study of social fair problem in old city renewal in China [D]*. Hangzhou: Zhejiang University.

Yin, K. (1995). Historical study of Zhongshan City. *Literature and History of Zhongshan, 37*, 8–9.

Zhang, Q. (1988). Introduction of development and utilization of underground space in West Germany. *Underground Space, 8*(2), 28–32. Retrieved from http://www.cnki.net/

Zhao, D. J. (Ed.). (1997). *Chronicles of Zhongshan City*. Guangzhou: Guangdong People's Publishing House.

Zhao, Y., Lu, W., & Qi, H. (2012). A study of historic cultural district protection factors – a comparative study of China, the USA and France. *Urban Studies*, (12), 140–144. Retrieved from http://www.cnki.net/

Zhu, H., & Liu, B. (2011). Concepts analysis and research implications: Sense of place, place attachment and place identity. *Journal of South China Normal University(Natural Science)*, (1), 1–8. Retrieved from http://www.cnki.net/

Zhu, H., Qian, J. X., & Chen, X. L. (2010). Place and identity: The rethinking of place of European-American human geography. *Human Geography, 25*(6), 1–6. Retrieved from http://www.cnki.net/

Index

adaptive reuse of industrial heritage 51
A-level National Tourist Attraction 57
The analects 10
ancient cultural heritage 10
Annales 12
apologetic stances 80
April tomb cleaning ceremony 24
archaeological records 18–19
artefacts: meanings giving value 35
arterial waterways: Suzhou 40–41
Ashworth, G.J.: apologetic stances 80; industrial heritage contradiction between economic and cultural attributed 64; symbolic value of cultural heritage 35; tourists *versus* local residents' views on urban spaces 44
attachment to supporting values: industrial history identification 72
authenticity 5; Jinjiang Prince's site 24
automotive industrial heritage tourism in Germany 81

Bai Juyi: *Deng Changmen Xianwang* 42
Banpo archaeological excavation 18
Barraclough: history 12
Beijing: development of hutong neighbourhoods 3; housing shortage 2–3; hutongs 2–4; Municipal Institute of City Planning and Design city plan for 2016–2035 3–4; siheyuans 2
Birds Nest National Stadium 3
blurring place boundaries 102
The book of changes 15
'Book of diverse crafts': applying feng shui to man-made constructions 16
branch canals: Suzhou 39–40
Braunfels, W.: pre-industrial cities independence from central government 10
Breakwell, G.M.: identity dimension model 95–96; place identity processes 99
Bres: place identity 96
bridges: Suzhou water canals 43
Buddhism: reincarnations 29
buildings: context of existence in shan-shui landscape 24

built heritage: Guilin 22; harmony 28; Jingjiang Prince's site 23–24; western and Chinese parallel existence 29; western markers 27–28; Yellow Crane Pagoda 24–25

calligraphy: reading and writing 13
capital impact on culture 70–72
carpenter's square: 'Three Sovereigns and Five Sage Emperors' 14
Chen, Y.: Shan-Shui-City 26
Chengyun Audience Hall restoration 29
Chinese common knowledge 13; jiu ding 19
Chinese puzzle balls 11
Chinese state: direct ancestor 11
Chinese State Council: Temporal Regulation on Conservation of Cultural Relics 1
Ching Ming Festival 24
cities: central government 10; feng shui application 16; first real 18
city dwellers identification 99–100
city image reconstruction: city marketing 50–53; economic structures impact on images reconstruction 57; industrial development levels relationship 57; industrial elements 54–56; industrial heritage tourism 50; industrial heritage tourism products on official tourism websites 56–58; industrial images *versus* modern city images 58; traditional industrial cities competition with other intra-national and international cities 59; web content analysis 53
city marketing: city image reconstruction 50; enhancing competitiveness 53; industrial cities 52–53; traditional industrial cities competition with other intra-national and international cities 59
civilized person: mastery of calligraphy 13
Clark: place identity 96
colonial industrial development 87
common knowledge 13; jiu ding 19
community participation: industrial heritage 65
compass: 'Three Sovereigns and Five Sage Emperors' 14

competitiveness: city marketing 53, 59
concentration camps 80–81
Confucius: *I Ching* 15; 'Study the past, if you would divine the future' 10
conservation: purposeful act to convey symbolic messages 35
consumerism: rise 59
consumption: delocalization 104–107
contact zones: industrial heritage 84
continuity: crisis 104; place identity 99–103; stable 101
Conzen, M.R.G.: plan units 34
Conzenian School of urban morphology 34
cosmology: 'Three Sovereigns and Five Sage Emperors' 13–14
Cui Hao: 'Yellow Crane Tower' 24
Cultural Revolution 1; destruction of feng shui shrines 21
Cultural Tourism Pedestrian Street of Sunwenxilu 97
culture: capital impact 70–72; heritage protection 65; heroes 13–14; relic protection 1
current industrial heritage valorizations and inventories 89

Daode Jing 11, 19
Daoism: founder 19; nothing is constant, all things change 29; origins 14; writings 11
dark industrial heritage: Germany's third Reich legacies 80–81; great leap forward period 88; preservation 89; Third Line relocation 88; war-time periods 86–87
dark tourism 82
Davis: place identity 96
death camps 80–81
de-industrialization: industrial heritage tourism 58
delocalization: consumption 107; urban renewal 104–105
Demonstration Prize for UN Global Best Livable Area Award: Tiexi old industrial district 67
Deng Changmen Xianwang 42
Deng Xiaoping: open door policy 88
design: Guilin 22
destination identities: communicating via Internet 52
deterritorialization: industrial heritage 65
development: industrial heritage 50–52
'Develop the tertiary sector instead of the secondary sector' 51
differentiation: self-efficacy 103
direct ancestor of Chinese state 11
Disneyfication: hutongs 4
distinctiveness: crisis 104; place identity 99, 103
diversity: heritage conservation 45
Duke of Zhou: emblematic numbers theory 20; *I Ching* 15; illegality counter-actions 18–19; urban planning of Zhengzhou 19
Du Xunhe: *Songren You Wu* 37

ecologically sustainable development (ESD) 17
economics: capital impact on culture 70–72; industrial heritage 51, 64–66; transition to socialist market economy 59–60
emblematic numbers theory 20
entangled history 82
entangled industrial geographies 89–90
environment deterioration: place identity 101
escapers (LAi) 98
ESD (ecologically sustainable development) 17
European Heritage Year 65
European transnational industrial heritage: past archipelago of transnational trauma and tragedy 80–81; transboundary processes of remembrance 82–84
everyday living heritage 74
exploratory stage of industrial heritage 50–51
external promotion: industrial heritage 75

factory of the world 88
Fan Chengda: *Treatises* 22
'Farewell to Yellow Crane Pagoda' 24
feng shui 15–17; applying to man-made constructions 16; banned by Mao Zedong 21; conservation and good land management 17; Guilin 22; Heaven and Earth harmony 15; Jingjiang royal family mausoleum 23–24; placement of Guilin 21; The Purple Cloud Temple 16–17; re-emergence in urban planning 26; xue 15
festivals: place identity 96
financial resources: economic growth over conservation 2
first real city 18
folk museums in renovated siheyuans 4
Foochow Arsenal 86
Forbidden Palace 2
form: urban 34
French School of urban morphology 34
front-facing canal-alley patterns 41–42
functions: heritage conservation 45
Fu Xi 13–14; carpenter's square 14

geographical scales: urban morphology 34
geographies of identities 83
geomancers 15–16
Germany: colonial industrial development 87; industrial heritage tourism of automotive brands 81; third Reich dark industrial legacies 80–81
globalization: identity crisis 107; public memory intersection 82–84; traditional industrial cities competition with other intra-national and international cities 59; Zhongshan City 97
global memoryscape of transnational heritage 82–84
government: city system 10; role in industrial heritage conservation 73

Graham, B.: heritage more about meanings than physical artefacts 35; industrial heritage contradiction between economic and cultural attributed 64
Grand Canal: Suzhou water gird 37
great leap forward period 88
Guangzhou: three olds transformation policy 51
Guilin: built heritage sites 22; history 22; Holy Field 21–23; imperial mausoleum 23–24; Jingjiang Palace complex 23; Jinjiang Prince's site 23–24; lake revitalization plan 26–27; location and layout 22–23; natural scenery 21; placement 21; Qing Dynasty 23; as Shan-Shui-City 26–27; Solitary Beauty Peak 21
Gusu Cheng Tu 43
Gusu Fanhua Tu 42, 43

Han Dynasty: national master plan 20; rebuilding urban infrastructure destroyed by Qin Dynasty 19–20; *Zhou li* appendix 19–20
Hanyang Ironworks 86
harmony: built heritage 28
Hartmann, R.: apologetic stances 80
Harvey, D.: fixedness of place and mobility of capital 94
Helu Dacheng *see* Suzhou
heritage: conservation 1, 44–45, 65; definition 35; everyday living 74; more about meanings than physical artefacts 35; value 35–36
heritage sites: Jingjiang Palace complex 23–24; Yellow Crane Pagoda 24–25
heritagization 82–84
hidden piers 43
hierarchy of political and economic cities: Han national master plan 20
high self-efficiency 100
historical cities: conservation legislation 1
historical methodology 11–12
historical water block: Suzhou 41–42
historiography 12
Holy Field 15; Guilin 21–23
housing relocation plan (weight) 3
housing shortage: Beijing 2–3
Huang-di 14; Holy Field 14–15; modified civilization with Yangshao 18; religious ceremonies and rituals 18
hutongs: conservation of Beijing's image 2; destruction and transformation 3; development of hutong neighbourhoods 3; historic tours 4; housing shortage 2–3; need for conservation 3; revitalization 4

I Ching: feng sui 15
ICOMOS: lack of hard ancient edifices in Guilin 24
ideal standard of urban planning: Zhengzhou 19
identifying: xue 15–16

identities: communicating via Internet 52; geography 83; industrial 72–73; tourists *versus* local residents 44; *see also* place identities
image reconstruction *see* reconstructing city images
imagining a homeland 102–103
imperial capitals 20
Imperial Decree of May 1370 22
imperial mausoleum 23–24
incompetent place identity 102
industrial elements in city images 54–56
industrial heritage 49; acceptance 50; adaptive reuse 51; city marketing 52–53; contact zones 84; development stage 50; economic restructuring 51; exploratory stage 50; geographic locations 49–50; heritagization 82–84; intersection of public memory and globalization processes 82–84; origins 50; preservation 88–89; promoting through industrial heritage tourism 60; shared sites 83; time-space paths 84; transnationalizing 82
industrial heritage protection: black side 73; capital impact on culture 70–72; combining with public space 68–69; community participation 65; cultural attributes 65; economic attributes 64–65; economic re-use 66; everyday living heritage 74; external promotion 75; inheritance 74; institutional factors 73; life cycle model 65; site selection 64; socio-cultural factors 72–73; spatial distribution 68–69; temporal distribution 68, 74
industrial heritage tourism: adaptive reuse of industrial heritage 51; city image reconstruction 50–52; city marketing 52–53; definition 49; de-industrialization 58; development 52; economic structures impact on images reconstruction 57; industrial elements in city images 54–56; industrial images *versus* modern city images 58; industrial museums 68–69, products on official tourism websites 56–58; promoting industrial heritage culture 60; traditional industrial cities competition with other intra-national and international cities 59
industrial identities 72–73
industrialization 6–7; dark legacies of Germany's third Reich 80–81; death camps and concentration camps 80–81; image reconstruction relationships 57; past archipelago of transnational trauma and tragedy 80–81; Western transfer to non-Western nations 78; Western *versus* Chinese 65
industrial museums 57, 68–69
inheritance: industrial heritage 74
inhuman conditions: death by work 81
inner-urban boat tours 45–46
inner-urban canals of Suzhou 36

institutional factors: industrial heritage 73
intangible heritage conservation 1
interconnectivity: Suzhou water canal system 43
international commodities and services *versus* local consumption 104–105
Internet: projecting city images 52
intrinsic heritage dissonances 84
Ironworks 83
ISUF (International Seminar on Urban Form): urban morphology definition 34

Jacobs, Jane: urban renewal 94
Japanese colonial industrial development 87
Jiangnan Machine Manufacturers 86
Jingjiang Mausoleum Museum 23–24
Jingjiang Palace complex 22–24
Jinling Machinery Bureau 86
jiu ding 15; Chinese common knowledge 19

Kailuan Coal Mining company 86
Kao Gong ji: addition to Zhou li 19–20
'Kao Gong Ji': applying feng shui to man-made constructions 16

LAi (escapers) 98
landscapes: feng shui 16
Laozi 19
layout: Guilin 22–23
LBi (left-behind persons) 98; cultural distinctiveness 103; place identities 102
Li Bai: 'Farewell to Yellow Crane Pagoda' 24
lieu(x) de mémoire 82
Li Hongzhang's Westernization Movement 85–86
local consumption *versus* international commodities and services 104–105
local residents: *versus* tourist views on urban spaces 44
Longshan culture 11: cosmology 14–15; evolution of beliefs into feng shui 15; modified civilization with Yangshao 18; religious ceremonies and rituals 18
luopan wheel 15–16

Machinery Bureau 86
Magic Square 15; emblematic numbers theory 20
man-made constructions: applying feng shui 16
Mao Zedong: banning feng shui 21
Mazanti, B.: place identity 96
metropolitan ties: importance 7
Micro Yuan'er children's library and art centre 4–5
Ming Dynasty: hutong-based urban development 2; Shibajian 101
Mittelbau-Dora concentration camp 80
Mittelwerk GmbH underground facilities 80
modern heritage: protecting 64

modern industrialization: colonial industrial development 87; entangled industrial geographies 89–90; great leap forward period 88; preservation 88–89; Self-Strengthening Movement 85–86; socialist industrialization 88; tourism products 56–58; transnationalism 85–86; war-time periods 86–87
modernization: destroying old structures to build new ones 1–2; developing and redeveloping urban areas 11
Municipal Institute of City Planning and Design city plan for 2016–2035 3–4
Muratorian School of urban morphology 34

Nara Document on Authenticity 5
national industrialization: Self-Strengthening Movement 85–86; socialist industrialization 88; war-time periods 86–87
national master plan: Han dynasty 20
natural landscapes: place identity 96
Nazi dark industrial legacies 80–81
Neolithic settlements of the Yellow River 18
nine-squares-in-one 15; emblematic numbers theory 20; Zhu Shouqian 23
nine symbolism 15
Nora: lieu(x) de mémoire 82
Northeast china industry clusters 87
nothing is constant, all things change 29
numerology *see* nine-squares-in-one
Nu-wa 13–14; compass 14

official tourism websites: industrial heritage tourism products 56–58
old replaced by new 29
Olympic Games in Beijing in 2008: destruction of hutong neighbourhoods 3
open door policy 88
organic renewal model 94
overcrowding: Beijing 2–3
overload: hereditary position 18

Park of blast furnace no. 4 industrial heritage site 83
'Passion for Heritage' trend 51
past archipelago of transnational trauma and tragedy 80–81
Pedestrian Street of Sunwenxilu 97
Peenemünde military test site 80
Peoples Republic of China (PRC): establishment 85
Pingjiang Road conservation 45
Pingjiang Tu 37–38
place-congruent continuity: place identity 101–102
place distinctiveness: elimination 102
place identities 95–96; blurring boundaries 102; continuity crisis 104; continuity of imagining a homeland 102–103; crisis of distinctiveness

104; crisis of self-esteem 104; delocalization 104–105; distinctiveness 103; elimination of place distinctiveness 102; environment deterioration effect 101; high self-efficiency 100; place-congruent continuity 101–102; processes 99; reconstruction 94–95, 105–106; reminiscent recreational area of escapers 103; self-efficacy differentiation 103; self-esteem duality of left-behind persons 102; stable continuity 101; strong self-esteem 100; tourists *versus* local residents 44; urban renewal 99–100
plan units 34
Ploger, J.: place identity 96
Polo, Marco: Venice of the East 33
population increases: urban landscape 63
PRC (People's Republic of China): establishment 85
proportions of built environment: Suzhou 43–44
Proshansky, H.M.: place identities 95
protecting: cultural relics 1; hutongs 3; industrial heritage 88–89; modern heritage 64
protection movement 65
public memory: intersection with globalization processes 82–84
public space: combining with industrial heritage 68–69
The Purple Cloud Temple 16–17

Qin dynasty: establishment 19; unification of China 10
Qing Dynasty: Guilin 23; hutong-based urban development 2; Shibajian 96

reading calligraphy 13
real estate economy: urban development 59
rear-facing canal-alley patterns 41–42
reconstructing: place identity 105–106
reconstructing city images: city marketing 52–53; economic structures impact on images reconstruction 57; industrial development levels relationship 57; industrial elements 54–56; industrial heritage tourism 50; industrial heritage tourism products on official tourism websites 56–58; industrial images *versus* modern city images 58; traditional industrial cities competition with other intra-national and international cities 59; urban rejuvenation 50
reconstruction of ancient towns and villages as tourism sites 25
redevelopment: hutong neighbourhoods 3–4; tabular rasa 4; siheyuans 4
re-emergence of feng shui in urban planning 26
reflecting whole range of living conditions: heritage conservation 45
Regulation of Historical Famous City, Town and Village Conservation 1

reincarnations 29
religious ceremonies and rituals: Longshan 18
renovated hutongs 3
resources: choosing economic growth or conservation 2
reterritorialization: industrial heritage 65
re-use of industrial heritage 51, 66
rise of consumerism 59
Rites 11
Rites of Zhou: 'Three Sovereigns and Five Sage Emperors' 14
ritual cauldrons 15
Roggenbuck: place identity 95
Russian colonial industrial development 87

scale: Suzhou 43–44; urban morphology 34
schools of urban morphology 34
Scripture of the way and its power 11
self-efficacy: decrease from environmental deterioration 101; delocalization 104–105; differentiation 103; place identity 99
self-efficiency: place identity 100
self-esteem: crisis 104; left-behind persons' duality 102; loss from physical environment decline 101; place identity 99; strong prior to decline 100
Self-Strengthening Movement 85–86
semi-renovated hutongs 3
shared heritage sites 83
Shibajian 96, 101
Shiqi Main Raod 101
siheyuans: conservation of Beijing's image 2; destruction 3; folk museums 4; revitalization 4
Sino-Japanese War 87
Sino-Russian Secret Treaty 87
sites: feng shui assessments 15–16
socialist industrialization 88
socialist market economy: transition 59–60
socio-cultural factors: industrial heritage 72–73
Solitary Beauty Peak 21
Songren You Wu 37
spatial distribution: capital impact on culture 70–72; industrial heritage 74; institutional factors 73; socio-cultural factors 72–73; Tiexi industrial heritage 68–69
specialized architecture: Great Hall in Banpo 18
'Specification on the Historical Cities Conservation Plan' regulation 1
Spring and Autumn period 19
stable continuity: place identity 101
Stein: place identity 96
stone stepped piers: Suzhou water canals 43
street names: Tiexi old industrial district 68
Sunwenxilu business center in Zhongshan City 96
Sunwenxilu urban renewal identity construction: actively leaving 102; city dwellers identification 99–100; cultural distinctiveness 103;

environment deterioration effect 101; helplessly staying behind 101; high self-efficiency 100; identity crisis in late stage of renewal 104–105; identity reconstruction 105–106; imagining a homeland 102–103; place distinctiveness elimination 102; reminiscent recreational area of escapers 103; self-esteem duality of left-behind persons 102; services and small shop disappearance 103; stable continuity 101; strong self-esteem 100

Suzhou 6; arterial waterways decline 40–41; branch waterways decline 39–40; canals as poetry themes depicting the city 37; first inner-urban canals 36; Grand Canal 37; heritage conservation 44–45; historical water block 41–42; interconnectivity of canal system 43; layout of canals 38; linking elements between grids 43; map 37–38; Northern Song period 37; Pingjiang Road conservation 45; reconnecting the waterways 43; scale and proportions 43–44; stone stepped piers 43; tourism development 45–46; urban form 35; urban morphology 41–44; water and street grids 2015 map 39; water and street grids in 1229 and canals added until 1639 map 38

Suzhou water system 6

symbolic messages: conservation 35

symbolism: figure nine 15

tabula rasa redevelopment 4

templates: calligraphy 13

temporal distribution: industrial heritage 68, 74

Temporal Regulation on Conservation of Cultural Relics 1

territorialization: industrial heritage 65

Third Line industries 88

three olds transformation policy 51

Three-plus-one trading-mix 100

'Three Sovereigns and Five Sage Emperors' 13–14; archaeological records 18–19; compass and carpenter's square 14; emperor to maintain harmony between Heaven and Earth 14; Holy Field 15

Tiexi old industrial district: background 67; Demonstration Prize for UN Global Best Livable Area Award 67; distribution chart of selected industrial heritage items 70; economic factors 70–72; external promotion of industrial heritage 75; heritage protection policies 67; inheritance 74; institutional factors 73; officially protected sites/entities 71; socio-cultural factors 72–73; spatial distribution 68–69; spatial distribution patterns 74; street names 68; temporal distribution 68, 74

time: urban morphology 34

time periods: emphasis in heritage conservation 44–45

time-space paths: industrial heritage 84

tourism: dark 82; Internet 52; versus local residents views on urban space 44; role in urban heritage 6; Suzhou 45–46

tourist gaze 46

Towner, J.: history 12

traditional culture spokesperson place identity 102

traditional industrial cities 50; adaptive reuse of industrial heritage 51; city marketing 52–53; competition with other intra-national and international cities 59; definition 50; economic restructuring 51; economic structures impact on images reconstruction 57; industrial elements in city images 54–56; industrial heritage tourism products on official tourism websites 56–58; industrial images versus modern city images 58; transition to urbanization 60; web content analysis 53

transition to socialist market economy 59–60

translation houses 86

transnational industrialization 89; China's modern industrialization 85; colonial industrial development 87; contact zones 84; entangled history 82; entangled industrial geographies 89–90; Germany's third Reich dark legacies 80–81; great leap forward period 88; intersection of public memory and globalization processes 82–84; preservation 89; Self-Strengthening Movement 85–86; socialist industrialization 88; war-time periods 86–87

transnationalizing heritage 82; entangled history 82; Germany's third Reich dark industrial legacies 80–81; themes 7

transnational trauma and tragedy 80–81

Treatises 22

Turnbridge, J.E.: industrial heritage contradiction between economic and cultural attributed 64

Twigger-Ross, C.L.: place identity 95–96

UNESCO: lack of hard ancient edifices in Guilin 24

unification of China: by Qin 10

urban form 34; Suzhou water canals 41–42

urbanization 2; city image reconstruction 50–52; city marketing competitiveness 53; delocalization 104–105; developing and redeveloping urban areas 11; emblematic numbers theory 20; entrepreunerurialism 59; feng shui revival 26; hutongs 2; influence 94; national planning 20; Neolithic settlements of the Yellow River 18; organic renewal model 94; place identities 94–96; population increases 63; real estate economy 59; rebuilding after Qin Dynasty destruction 19–20; tourism role in heritage 6; traditional industrial cities transition 60; weigai 3; Western experiences focus 94; Zhengzhou 19; Zhongshan City 97–98 urban morphology 34; application 35; components 34; definition 34; heritage conservation 44–45; scale and proportions 43–44; schools 34; Suzhou 41–44; tourism development 45–46; urban form 41–42

urban renewal place identity in Sunwenxilu: actively leaving 102; city dwellers identification 99–100; cultural distinctiveness 103; environment deterioration effect 101; helplessly staying behind 101; high self-efficiency 100; identity crisis in late state of renewal 104–105; identity reconstruction 105–106; imagining a homeland 102–103; place distinctiveness elimination 102; reminiscent recreational area of escapers 103; self-esteem duality of left-behind persons 102; services and small shop disappearance 103; stable continuity 101; strong self-esteem 100

urban spaces: tourists *versus* local resident views 44

urban tourism: competitive city marketing 53

Uzzell, D.L.: place identity 95–96

V2 (Vengeance weapon No. 2) 80

valorizing industrial heritage 89

value: artefacts 35; heritage 35–36; industrial heritage 72

Venice of the East *see* Suzhou

Verdun Memorial 83

Wall, G.: history 12

Warring States period 19

Water Cube National Aquatic Center 3

water systems 6

The way 19

weigai 3

Weizhou, Han: Zehngzhou 19

western authenticity: increasing conservation 29; Jingjiang Prince's site 24; Yellow Crane Pagoda 25

Western world development: built heritage markers 27–29; *versus* Chinese industrial

development 65; transfer to non-Western nation 78

Williams, M.: place identity 95

Wolong giant panda reserve 25

work camps 80–81

world heritage sites 6

writing calligraphy 13

Wu: hutong characteristics 2

Wu Kingdom: first inner-urban canals 36

Wu Lian-yong: Guilin as Shan-Shui-City 26–27

'Wuxi Advice' 51

Xibao, Vice Premier Wen: preservation of hutong neighbourhoods 3

Xie: industrial heritage life cycle model 65

xue 15; Guilin 22–23; identifying 15–16

Yan: feng shui 15

Yangshao 18

Yan Yanzhi 21

Yellow Crane Pagoda 24–25

'Yellow Crane Tower' 24

Yellow Emperor 14

Ying Zheng 19

Yuan Dynasty 2

Yu the Great 14

ZAP/standard architecture 4–5

Zhang traditional water wheel-driven flour grinding mill 25

Zhengzhou: ideal standard of urban planning 19

Zhongdong railway 87

zhonghua wenhua 13; Guilin 24; interpret built-heritage as place-making extending over centuries 30

Zhongshan City: globalization 97; history 96–97; old district transformation 97–98

Zhou Li 11; applying feng shui to man-made constructions 16; *Kao Gong ji* addition 19–20

Zhu Shouqian: nine-squares-in-one numorological template 23

For Product Safety Concerns and Information please contact our EU
representative GPSR@taylorandfrancis.com
Taylor & Francis Verlag GmbH, Kaufingerstraße 24, 80331 München, Germany